MW00364407

# Wisdom of the Elders

Printed in the United States of America

ISBN-13 #978-1-937884-03-1

# Table of Contents

# About the Author

Bohdi Sanders is a lifelong student of wisdom literature and the martial arts. He has dedicated his life to educating others, both in the classroom and the martial arts arena. During his 20 years as a school teacher and coach, he has always strived to teach his students, not only the core subjects, but also the character traits and virtues which he has discovered in his quest to discover the truth behind the ancient wisdom texts from around the world. He is the author of:

Warrior Wisdom: Ageless Wisdom for the Modern Warrior
Warrior Wisdom: The Heart and Soul of Bushido
The Warrior Lifestyle: Making Your Life Extraordinary
Secrets of the Soul
The Secrets of Worldly Wisdom
Modern Bushido: Living a life of Excellence
Wisdom of the Elders

Dr. Sanders' books have received high praise from the book industry and fellow authors alike. His books have won several awards including:

The USA Book News Best Books of 2010 1st Place Award
Indie Excellence Book Awards 1st Place Winner 2010
IIMAA Best Martial Arts Books of the Year 2011
USA Martial Arts Hall of Fame Literary Man of the Year 2011
USMAA Inspiration of the Year 2011
United States Martial Arts Hall of Fame Author of the Year 2011

For more information on Dr. Sanders or his books visit his website:

www.TheWisdomWarrior.com

# Preface

I have always enjoyed reading good quote books. Even as a youngster, I found that I enjoyed reading quote books that my parents or grandparents had in the house. As a teenager, I would read books such as *Apples of Gold* over and over again, meditating on the wisdom that they held for those who were willing to spend the time and effort to actually assimilate the wisdom that these books provided. Goethe put it this way, "It is delightful to transport one's self into the spirit of the past to see how a wise man has thought before us." In my opinion, this is what a good quote book does for the reader.

Over the years my interest in quote books remained just as strong as it had been as a teenager and my personal collection of quote books grew and grew. I literally bought every one that I ran across and quickly devoured each one that I brought home. Some of these books were good and some were filled with mostly quotes that could best be described as nothing but filler material – void of any real wisdom and only meant to entertain those who care little about true wisdom.

Of course there is a place for humorous quote books or quote books filled with quotes from celebrities or sports figures whose words are only included because of their name and not because of the actual content, but those were not the type of books that I found interesting. I was only interested in reading quotes which contained wisdom and something which could be of value in my life, not fluff. I have never really been as impressed by what the current celebrities thought about life, as I have been by what the sages believed and taught.

This attitude has led to many a disappointed hour reading what I had hoped would be a book full of wisdom and sage advise, only to find that it was a book full of celebrities and well known people trying to be witty, with a few morsels of wisdom scattered throughout like pieces of gold in a river bed of worthless pebbles. This was a bit frustrating to say the least. It seemed that most of the quote books that I ran across had a handful of great quotes which were useful in guiding people in ways to improve their lives and tons of quotes which were utterly useless for anything more than a quick moment of entertainment.

Although this was a bit wearisome, it led to a specific habit which has served me well over the years – highlighting. I began to highlight every book that I read, marking only those quotes or passages which I considered worthy of reading again or going back and meditating on at a later date. All of my books were highlighted and some even color coded with different colors for different categories so I could quickly go back and find exactly what I wanted to study.

My frustration in finding the wisdom that I wanted in quote books also led me to go straight to the source to find the wisdom that the sages had to offer instead of hoping to find the wisdom that I was looking for bundled up in a nice, neat package for quick and easy access. I began to study the religious texts from throughout the ages and across the world. I read the original works of men which time had proven to be men of great wisdom and insight. I began to study paremiology, the study of proverbs, and research the origins of many of the wise sayings that we all recognize.

In short, I searched the world of literature for all of the wisdom that I could find, and not simply wisdom, but universal wisdom – wisdom which holds true throughout time and in various locations. What I found through this exercise is that there is indeed such a thing as universal wisdom. There are values and principles which hold true for people throughout the world. I discovered that the same proverb that was found in America could also be found in Asia or Europe, although it may be phrased a little differently in each place. The same thing applied to the universal principles of wisdom.

The same wisdom that has been taught for centuries in our country can also be found in other countries and other time periods. Specific principles concerning specific actions have been taught throughout the centuries in all different cultures and locations. Human beings have certain traits that appear to be universal and because of this they can be counted on to behave in a certain predictable manner; this has held true throughout the ages. Therefore certain wisdom pertaining to human behavior generally holds true regardless of the time period or geographic location.

One example to illustrate my point is people's tendency to talk too much and say things that they may later regret. I have found proverbs and writings from virtually every culture which warn people of the danger of speaking too much or speaking without first thinking of what you should and should not say. This is a good example of a universal human trait, and it is also a good example of universal wisdom which is good advice for people throughout the world, regardless of their culture or other factors. True wisdom does not grow old or become outdated.

As you might imagine, my library quickly grew to require a sizable number of bookshelves to hold all of the books which I had purchased over years of researching wisdom (the library takes a dim view of highlighting their books). My collection of wisdom literature quickly grew to monstrous proportions, with each book being completely covered in a spectrum of colors from my highlighting what I considered to be the important parts. I had an open mind where wisdom was concerned. My philosophy was (and is) that you can learn wisdom from anyone or any source. You simply have to use what is useful and disregard what is not useful.

I found wisdom in the ancient texts of Egypt, China, and India, and I also found wisdom from the Vikings and the Native Americans. The source did not matter. What mattered was that the wisdom rang true in my spirit. I devoured text after text, highlighting each as I went for future reference, but found one small problem – when I wanted to refer back to the wisdom which I had highlighted, it was scattered throughout many, many different books. This was a bit of a inconvenience to say the least. I wanted all of this wisdom easily located in one central book for easy reference and study, so I began to put all of my highlighted wisdom into a single computer data base.

I wanted this wisdom to be convenient and to the point, spelled out in short anecdotes and maxims for easy reference in order to keep it fresh in my mind. What I wanted was the kind of quote book that I had spent years hoping to find in the bookstores – a quote book filled with wisdom, minus the fluff. This was where *Wisdom of the Elders* was conceived. I wanted to compile the best quote book on wisdom available. Notice that I said that I wanted *Wisdom of the Elders* to be the *best* quote book available, not the *most exhaustive* quote book available. As Christian Bovee stated, "A book should be luminous, not voluminous."

There are many reference books available which contain hundreds of pages of quotes from various sources and pertaining to various subjects. This is not what *Wisdom of the Elders* is, nor its goal. *Wisdom of the Elders* is not an exhaustive reference book or an encyclopedia-size book full of various quotes. It contains quotes specifically dedicated to wisdom and living a life of excellence. As Francis Bacon stated, "Some books are to be tasted, other to be swallowed, and some few to be chewed and digested." *Wisdom of the Elders* is to be chewed and digested, then applied to your life.

Goethe said that a collection of anecdotes and maxims is the greatest treasure for a man of the world. *Wisdom of the Elders* contains over 5,100 anecdotes, proverbs, maxims, and insights from the sages and some of the wisest men and women the world has known. It is divided into 59 different categories, each addressing either specific character traits or subjects designed to give the reader insight and help the reader improve his or her life in order to live a life of excellence. As with anything that you read, you should meditate on how these wise sayings apply to your life, take what you find useful, and disregard what doesn't "feel" right to you.

None of the wise words included in this book will be of any use in your life if you don't take the time to meditate on them and actively apply them.

You can have all the money in the world at your disposal, but it will not do you any good until you actually put that money to use. *Wisdom of the Elders* gives you access to an abundance of wisdom, how it affects your life is completely up to you. Elizabeth Drew stated that the test of literature is whether we ourselves live more intensely for the reading of it. Hopefully *Wisdom of the Elders* will pass the test and you will live more intensely after reading it and applying it to your own life.

Bohdi Sanders, Ph.D.

# WISDOM
# of the
# ELDERS

The wisdom of the wise and the experience of ages may be preserved by quotation.
*Benjamin Disraeli*

Hold fast to the words of your ancestors.
*Maori Proverb*

Study the teachings of the great sages as impartially as you can.
*Gongs and Drums of Gampopa Precepts*

Proverbs are short sentences drawn from long experience.
*Cervantes*

A proverb is much matter distilled into a few words.
*R. Buckminster Fuller*

A proverb is a child of experience.
*English Proverb*

Books are preserved minds.
*Japanese Proverb*

Through old things, we learn new things.
*Korean Proverb*

Teach him what has been said in the past...Speak to him, for there is none born wise.
*Ptah-Hotep*

The ancients tell us what is best.
*Franklin*

The mental disease of the present generation is impatience of study, contempt of the great masters of ancient wisdom.
*Samuel Johnson*

To be ignorant of the lives of the most celebrated men of antiquity is to continue in a state of childhood all our days.
*Plutarch*

There is more profit in understanding the classics than there is in amassing gold.
*Chinese Proverb*

Truly good books are more than mines to those who can understand them. They are breathings of the great souls of past times. Genius is not embalmed in them, but lives in them perpetually.
*William Ellery Channing*

The wisdom herein...has been tried and tested century after century.
*Tiruvalluvar*

The great thing about the Ancients, especially the Socratic school, is that they set before us the sources and guidelines of all life and action, not for the purpose of idle speculation, but as a call to life and deeds.
*Goethe*

A collection of anecdotes and maxims is the greatest treasure for a man of the world – as long as he knows how to weave the former into suitable points of the course of conversation, and to recall the latter on fitting occasions.
*Goethe*

All we can do is show the way to the traveler; we cannot walk it for him. We can write the prescription, but we cannot drink the medicine for him. All teachings are like medicine which is given to the sick according to the disease they have.
*Lao Tzu*

Past events shed light on the future. For the world has always been the same, and everything that is and will be, once was; and the same things recur, but with different names and colors.
*Francesco Guicciardini*

Sages are the mirrors of God's Eternal Wisdom...Generation after generation have gone into the dark, but the Divine Attributes are changeless and eternal.
*Rumi*

Believe those who are seeking the truth; doubt those who find it.
*Andre Gide*

A short saying often contains much wisdom.
*Sophocles*

We must believe what is good and true about the prophets, that they were sages, that they did understand what proceeded from their mouths, and that they bore prudence on their lips.
*Origen*

The wise ones fashioned speech with their thought, sifting it as grain is sifted through a sieve.
*Buddha*

All this worldly wisdom was once the unamiable heresy of some wise man.
*Henry David Thoreau*

The young man knows the rules, but the old man knows the exceptions.
*Oliver Wendell Holmes*

Human beings, who are almost unique in having the ability to learn from the experience of others, are also remarkable for their apparent disinclination to do so.
*Douglas Adams*

No man was ever wise by chance.
*Lucius Annaeus Seneca*

2

# Wisdom of Books

The books we read should be chosen with great care, that they may be, as an Egyptian king wrote over his library, "The medicines of the soul." Be careful of the books you read, as of the company you keep: for your habits and character will be as much influenced by the former as by the latter.
*Edwin Paxton Hood*

Excellent men live in a kind of despair because they consider as useless and harmful what their office and rules oblige them to teach and pass on to posterity.
*Goethe*

A life being very short, and quiet hours of it few, we ought to waste none of them in reading valueless books.
*John Ruskin*

Among the many curious stupidities of the schools, none seems to me so ridiculous as the strife about the authenticity of old writings or old works. For I ask you, is it the author or the works we are admiring or censuring? Our sole concern is always and only the author before us; why should we bother about the names when we are interpreting a work of the spirit.
*Goethe*

It is delightful to transport one's self into the spirit of the past to see how a wise man has thought before us.
*Goethe*

Consider what you have in the smallest chosen library. A company of the wisest and wittiest men that could be picked out of all civil countries, in a thousand years, have set in best order the results of their learning and wisdom.
*Emerson*

A library may be regarded as the solemn chamber in which a man may take counsel with all who have been wise, and great, and good, and glorious among the men that have gone before him.
*George Dawson*

All books are divisible into two classes, the books of the hour, and the books of all time.
*John Rushin*

Live always in the best company when you read.
*Sydney Smith*

To produce a mighty book you must choose a mighty theme.
*Herman Melville*

It signifies nothing to read a thing once, if one does not mind and remember it...One should always think of what one is about...if you do not mind your book while you are at it, it will be a double trouble to you for you must learn it all over again.
*Lord Chesterfield*

We are too civil to books. For a few golden sentences we will turn over and actually read a volume of four or five hundred pages.
*Emerson*

When a book raises your spirit, and inspires you with noble and manly thoughts, seek for no other test of its excellence. It is good, and made by a good workman.
*Jean de la Bruyere*

Happy are those who heed the words of the dead. Read good works and be guided by them.

*Leonardo da Vinci*

A book should be luminous, not voluminous.

*Christian Nevell Bovee*

The wisdom of the wise, and the experience of ages, may be preserved by quotations.

*Isaac D'Israeli*

Some books are to be tasted, others to be swallowed, and some few to be chewed and digested.

*Francis Bacon*

The oldest books are only just out to those who have not read them.

*Samuel Butler*

It is chiefly through books that we enjoy the intercourse with superior minds... In the best books, great men talk to us, give us their most previous thought, and pour their souls into ours. God be thanked for books.

*William Ellery Channing*

A room without books is like a body without a soul.

*Cicero*

The test of literature is, I suppose, whether we ourselves live more intensely for the reading of it.

*Elizabeth Drew*

If you never ask yourself any questions about the meaning of a passage, you cannot expect the book to give you any insight you do not already possess.

*Mortimer Adler*

Some books leave us free and some books make us free.

*Emerson*

Readers are plentiful, thinkers are rare.

*Harriet Martineau*

The books that help you most are those which make you think the most. The hardest way of learning is that of easy reading; but a great book that comes from a great thinker is a ship of thought, deep freighted with truth and beauty.

*Theodore Parker*

For books are more than books, they are the life The very heart and core of ages past, The reason why men lived and worked and died, The essence and quintessence of their lives.

*Amy Lowell*

Life-transforming ideas have always come to me through books.

*Bell Hooks*

4

# WISDOM

生

Wisdom is to the soul what health is to the body.
*La Rochefoucauld*

Knowledge comes but wisdom lingers.
*Alfred Lord Tennyson*

Get wisdom, get understanding; do not forget my words or swerve from them. Do not forsake wisdom, and she will protect you; love her, and she will watch over you. Wisdom is supreme; therefore get wisdom.
*The Book of Proverbs*

The riches that are in the heart cannot be stolen.
*Russian Proverb*

Wisdom thoroughly learned will never be forgotten.
*Pythagoras*

The wisdom of elders is better than the learning of youth.
*Slovakian Proverbs*

Where wisdom doesn't go in it doesn't come out.
*Swedish Proverb*

Wisdom is easy to carry but difficult to load.
*Czech Proverb*

Wisdom is in the head and not in the beard.
*Swedish Proverb*

To have wisdom is worth more than pearls.
*The Book of Job*

Wisdom is a thing of which one can never have enough.
*Minokhired*

Never a friend more faithful, nor greater wealth, than wisdom.
*The Havamal*

Of all our possessions, wisdom alone is immortal.
*Socrates*

Great is wisdom; infinite is the value of wisdom. It cannot be exaggerated; it is the highest achievement of man.
*Thomas Carlyle*

Wisdom is not wisdom when it is derived from books alone.
*Horace*

Wisdom is the right use of knowledge.
*Charles H. Spurgeon*

Wisdom outweighs any wealth.
*Sophocles*

Make wisdom your provision for the journey from youth to old age, for it is a more certain support than all other possessions.
*Bias*

Those who possess wisdom possess everything. Whatever others possess, without wisdom they have nothing.
*Tiruvalluvar*

When your wisdom is profound, pure, one-pointed, and restrained, the Master will show you the inner secrets. You will recognize the Truth.
*Swami Muktananda*

Desires are brought to life depending upon one's wisdom. Wisdom gives direction to desires.
*Takuan Soho*

5

Perfect wisdom has four parts:
1. Wisdom, the principle of doing things aright.
2. Justice, the principle of doing things equally in public and private.
3. Fortitude, the principle of not fleeing danger, but meeting it.
4. Temperance, the principle of subduing desires and living moderately.
*Plato*

Wisdom reveals what is righteous and what is not. It indicates which actions are proper and which are not.
*Swami Muktananda*

Wisdom does not show itself so much in precept as in life – in a firmness of mind and mastery of appetite. It teaches us to do as well as talk; and to make our actions and words all of a color.
*Seneca*

The plainest sign of wisdom is continual cheerfulness; her state is like that of things in the regions above the moon, always clear and serene.
*Montaigne*

There is no purifier in this world equal to wisdom.
*The Bhagavad Gita*

The invariable mark of wisdom is to see the miraculous in the common.
*Emerson*

Wisdom makes a weak man strong, a poor man king, a good generation of a bad one, and a foolish man reasonable.
*Irish Proverb*

The function of wisdom is to discriminate between good and evil.
*Cicero*

Wisdom never lies.
*Homer*

To know how to grow old is the master work of wisdom, and one of the most difficult chapters in the great art of living.
*Henri Frederic Amiel*

It is a characteristic of wisdom not to do desperate things.
*Thoreau*

The only thing that we can know is that we know nothing and that is the highest flight of human wisdom.
*Leo Tolstoy*

Knowledge shrinks as wisdom grows.
*Alfred North Whitehead*

With wisdom doubt grows.
*Goethe*

Wisdom is like a beacon set on high which radiates its light even in the darkest light.
*Japanese Buddhist Meditations*

As the light of a torch illuminates the objects in a dark room, even so the light of wisdom illuminates all men, whosoever they be, if they turn towards it.
*Fo-shu-hing-tsan-king*

The possession of wisdom leads to true happiness.
*Porphyry*

A happy life is the fruit of wisdom achieved; life bearable, of wisdom commenced.
*Seneca*

It is far better for us to possess only a few maxims of philosophy that are nevertheless always at our command and in use than to acquire vast knowledge that notwithstanding serves no useful purpose.
*Demetrius the Cynic*

6

Boasting begins where wisdom stops.
*Japanese Proverb*

The wisdom that does not increase by the day diminishes by the day.
*Chinese Proverb*

Arrogance diminishes wisdom.
*Arabian Proverb*

Make no parade of your wisdom; it is a vanity which cost dear to many. Let wisdom correct your vices, but not attack those of others.
*Seneca*

Wisdom enters not into a malicious mind.
*Francois Rabelais*

One cannot teach wisdom to a fool.
*African Proverb*

There are many who know many things, yet are lacking in wisdom.
*Democritus*

In seeking wisdom, thou art wise; in imagining that thou hast found it, thou art a fool.
*Ben Sira*

It is unwise to be too sure of one's own wisdom.
*Gandhi*

To say witty things is not always a sign of wisdom.
*Greek Proverb*

He whose wisdom cannot help him, gets no good from being wise.
*Ennius*

The height of human wisdom is to bring our tempers down to our circumstances – and to make a calm within, under the weight of the greatest storm without.
*Daniel Defoe*

Learn the words of wisdom uttered by the wise and apply them in your own life. Live them – but do not make a show of reciting them, for he who repeats what he does not understand is no better than an ass that is loaded with books.
*Kahlil Gibran*

Moonlight floods the whole sky from horizon to horizon; how much it can fill your room depends on its windows.
*Rumi*

By three methods we may learn wisdom: first, by reflection, which is noblest; second, by imitation, which is the easiest; and third, by experience, which is the bitterest.
*Confucius*

Be humble, if thou would'st attain to wisdom. Be humbler still, when wisdom thou hast mastered.
*Helena Petronova Blavatsky*

From Wankan Tanka comes wisdom and power to heal.
*Flat Iron*

All true wisdom that mankind have, they have received from God, whether they know it or not… There is only One Source, whether he knows or believes it or not. There is only one source from whence men obtain wisdom, and that is God, the fountain of wisdom...
*Brigham Young*

It requires wisdom to understand wisdom; the music is nothing if the audience is deaf.
*Walter Lippmann*

All of the far-reaching, unfaded teachings of the ancient sages come from the same source: the subtle truth of great oneness. Different expressions are merely the result of different times and places.
*Lao Tzu*

Self-reflection is the school of wisdom.
*Baltasar Gracian*

We do not receive wisdom; we have to discover it for ourselves by a voyage that no one can take for us.
*Marcel Proust*

Wisdom is acquired by meditation.
*Syrus*

Youth is the time to study wisdom; old age is the time to practice it.
*Jean Jacques Rousseau*

You must dive deep into the sea to get the pearls. What good does it do to dabble among the waves near the shore and assert that the sea has no pearls?
*Sai Baba*

Mistakes are lessons of wisdom.
*Hugh White*

If a man does not go after wisdom, wisdom will not come to him.
*The Talmud*

Good sense, not age, brings wisdom.
*Syrus*

Wisdom must be sought.
*Edward Young*

A man of understanding delights in wisdom.
*The Book of Proverbs*

Not to speak is the flower of wisdom.
*Japanese Proverb*

The only medicine for suffering, crime, and all other woes of mankind, is wisdom.
*Thomas Huxley*

Not engaging in ignorance is wisdom.
*Bodhidharma*

Wisdom is not acquired save as the result of investigation.
*Sankara Acharya*

He who rises early will gather wisdom.
*Danish Proverb*

A man may learn wisdom even from a foe.
*Aristophanes*

Not by age but by capacity is wisdom acquired.
*Titus Maccius Plautus*

Wisdom is found only in truth.
*Goethe*

Cleverness is not wisdom.
*Euripides*

We must not pretend to study philosophy, but really study it; for it is not seeming healthy that we need, but true health.
*Epicurus*

The beginning of wisdom is the sincere desire for instruction.
*The Book of Wisdom*

All wisdom is one: to understand the spirit that rules all by all.
*Heraclitus*

The things that were written in the past, were written for your benefit.
*The Book of Romans*

True knowledge does not grow old, so have declared the sages of all times.
*The Pali Canon*

Great doubts deep wisdom. Small doubts little wisdom.
*Chinese Proverb*

Wisdom is knowing when to stop speaking, because language is inadequate.
*Chuang Tzu*

8

Wisdom is the most precious of riches.
*Buddha*

Caution is the eldest child of wisdom.
*Victor Hugo*

Knowledge without wisdom is a load of books on the back of an ass.
*Japanese Proverb*

Wisdom will harness the mind, diverting it from wrong and directing it toward right.
*Tiruvalluvar*

The wisdom of life consists in the elimination of nonessentials.
*Lin Yutang*

Of all our possessions wisdom alone is immortal.
*Isocrates*

Knowledge is proud that he has learned so much; Wisdom is humble that he knows no more.
*William Cowper*

Wisdom is not in words; it is in understanding.
*Rumi*

Better weight than wisdom a traveler cannot carry.
*The Havamal*

Applicants for wisdom, do what I have done: Inquire within.
*Heraclitus*

We can be knowledgeable with other men's knowledge but we cannot be wise with other men's wisdom.
*Montaigne*

The more sand that has escaped from the hourglass of our life, the clearer we should see through it.
*Jean Paul*

The first point of wisdom is to discern that which is false; the second to know that which is true.
*Lactanius*

It is not white hair that engenders wisdom.
*Menander*

Where fear is present, wisdom cannot be.
*Lactantius*

With men of understanding, wisdom counts for everything…
*Baltasar Gracian*

I, wisdom, dwell together with prudence; I possess knowledge and discretion.
*The Book of Proverbs*

A short saying often contains much wisdom.
*Sophocles*

Life is the only real counselor; wisdom unfiltered through personal experience does not become a part of the moral tissue.
*Edith Wharton*

Besides the noble art of getting things done, there is the noble art of leaving things undone. The wisdom of life consists in the elimination of non-essentials.
*Lin Yutang*

We learn wisdom from failure much more than from success.
*Samuel Smiles*

Learn wisdom from the ways of a seedling. A seedling which is never hardened off through stressful situations will never become a strong productive plant.
*Stephen Sigmund*

These days people seek knowledge, not wisdom. Knowledge is of the past, wisdom is of the future.
*Vernon Cooper*

# CHARACTER TRAITS of the WISE MAN

From the errors of others, a wise man corrects his own.
*Syrus*

Shallow men believe in luck, wise and strong men in cause and effect.
*Emerson*

Those who aren't affected by impurities are sages.
*Bodhidharma*

Wise men who see reality will give you knowledge.
*The Bhagavad Gita*

A word to the wise is sufficient.
*Terence*

If you are wise, your wisdom will reward you.
*The Book of Proverbs*

The wise wake up. They choose reason over custom.
*Bodhidharma*

Wise men store up knowledge...
*The Book of Proverbs*

He who knows others is wise; he who knows himself is enlightened.
*Lao Tzu*

The wise man acts toward all beings even as towards himself.
*The Mahabharata*

The heart of the discerning acquires knowledge; the ears of the wise seek it out.
*The Book of Proverbs*

The sage increases his wisdom by all that he can gather from others.
*Fenelon*

A wise person becomes full of goodness even if one gathers it little by little.
*The Dhammapada*

Who is a wise man? He who learns of all men.
*The Talmud*

The wise learn many things from their foes.
*Aristophanes*

A single conversation with a wise man is worth a month's study of books.
*Chinese Proverb*

A wise man should have money in his head, not in his heart.
*Jonathan Swift*

A wise man though possessed of immense perfections, will learn from others.
*Sakya Pandit*

He is wise who learns at another's expense.
*Norwegian Proverb*

The wise are joyful in the truth revealed by the noble ones.
*The Dhammapada*

The wise person possesses humility.
*Harold C. Chase*

The wise and the brave dares own that he was wrong.
*Franklin*

The good and wise lead quiet lives.
*Euripides*

The wise man will want to be ever with him who is better than himself.
*Plato*

The wise person possesses humility.
*Harold C. Chase*

The man who questions opinion is wise; the man who quarrels with fact is a fool.
*Frank A. Garbutt*

The wise man does not expose himself needlessly to danger.
*Aristotle*

The wise man thinks about his troubles only when there is some purpose in doing so...
*Bertrand Russell*

The wise man forgets insults as the ungrateful forget benefits.
*Chinese Proverb*

A wise man, to accomplish his end, may even carry his foe on his shoulders.
*Panchatantra*

No man was ever wise by chance.
*Seneca*

Even as a solid rock is unshaken by the wind, so are the wise unshaken by praise or blame.
*The Dhammapada*

That man alone is wise who remains master of himself.
*Confucius*

The wise enter with great care...scout out the hidden...Go slowly...Let foresight feel the way, and let caution determine the ground.
*Baltasar Gracian*

The wise live among people, but are indifferent to their praise or blame.
*Chuang Tzu*

Ordinary people are friendly with those who are outwardly similar to them. The wise are friendly with those who are inwardly similar to them.
*Lieh Tzu*

The wise stand out, because they see themselves as part of the Whole. They shine, because they don't want to impress. They achieve great things, because they don't look for recognition. Their wisdom is contained in what they are, not their opinions. They refuse to argue, so no one argues with them.
*Lao Tzu*

A man of wisdom is independent, with a free, enriched mind, who gives and shares happiness with others. He has a sense of solidarity, fulfills social duties, and leads people along a right path cheerfully and gently. A man of wisdom is the one who always has an attitude of appreciation and tries to express his kindness and gratitude to everybody.
*Kazumi Tabata*

The wise man knows nothing if he cannot benefit from his wisdom.
*Cicero*

You are a wise person if you can easily direct your attention to whatever needs it.
*Terence*

In the whole of history there has never existed a single person whose conduct was always perfect. Understanding this, the wise don't try to be perfect.
*Lao Tzu*

The wise man reads both books and life itself.
*Lin Yutang*

The wise don't abandon Tao just because no one notices how wise they are. It is their nature to be the way they are.
*Lao Tzu*

For never, never, wicked man was wise.
*Homer*

Wise people, even though all laws were abolished, would still lead the same life.
*Aristophanes*

The wise establish virtue firmly within themselves, and are honored for generations to come.
*Lao Tzu*

A person of wisdom should be truthful, without arrogance, without deceit, not slanderous and not hateful. The wise person should go beyond the evil of greed and miserliness.
*Buddha*

The wise utterly devote themselves to everything in which they partake, every situation which contains them and within which they evolve.
*Chuang Tzu*

The art of being wise is the art of knowing what to overlook.
*William James*

The wiser the man, the more careful should he be of his conduct.
*The Talmud*

The superior man is watchful over himself even when alone.
*The Chung Yung*

Superior men avoid the intoxicated.
*Chinese Proverb*

A wise man neither suffers himself to be governed, nor attempts to govern others.
*Jean De La Bruyere*

Though by wicked acts one may reach one's aim, a wise man never resorts to such means. The wise are not ashamed if they do not reach their goal, provided they have rightly endeavored for it.
*Sakya Pandit*

…the wise mold themselves.
*The Dhammapada*

A wise man, whenever he acts, must consider the moral effects.
*Sakya Pandit*

The wise chooses the good in preference to the pleasant.
*The Katha Upanishad*

The wise man weighs his words on the goldsmith's scale.
*German Proverb*

Wise men do not argue with idiots.
*Japanese Proverb*

A wise man, in great or small matters, must act with due consideration.
*Sakya Pandit*

The wise man has long ears, big eyes and a short tongue.
*Russian Proverb*

A wise head keeps a shut mouth.
*Irish Proverb*

A wise man cannot be recognized by what he says in the public square…quick as he may be in judgment, so slow is he in making it public… let the wise man take refuge in his silence...
*Baltasar Gracian*

A wise man conceals his intelligence.
*Yiddish Proverb*

A wise man will not reprove a fool.
*Chinese Proverb*

A wise and reasonable person is unassuming and hides rather than flaunts his talents and wisdom.

*Taisou*

The steadfastness of the wise is but the art of keeping their agitation locked in their hearts.

*La Rochefoucauld*

Like a piece of water that is deep, calm and limpid...the wise live in a complete serenity.

*The Dhammapada*

The wise in joy and in sorrow depart not from equality of their souls.

*Buddha*

Even as the high mountain-chains remain immobile in the midst of the tempest, so the true sage remains unshaken amidst praise and blame.

*The Dhammapada*

A wise man makes straight his trembling and unsteady thought...

*Buddha*

He is wise who tries everything before arms.

*Terence*

A change in fortune hurts a wise man no more than a change of the moon.

*Franklin*

Let a wise man blow off the impurities of himself, as a smith blows off the impurities of silver, one by one, little by little, and from time to time.

*Buddha*

Good men indeed walk warily under all circumstances...whether touched by happiness or sorrow wise people never appear elated or depressed.

*Buddha*

The wise man is satisfied and composed; the mean man is always full of distress.

*Confucius*

He is wise who never consorts with fools.

*Baltasar Gracian*

The wise man avoids evil by anticipating it.

*Syrus*

The wise man does not set his mind either for anything or against anything; what is right, he will follow.

*Confucius*

The wise calmly considers what is right and what is wrong.

*The Dhammapada*

A wise man does at once, what a fool does at last.

*Baltasar Gracian*

The stupid speak of the past, the wise of the present, and fools of the future.

*Napoleon*

The wise man is always good, but a good man is not always wise.

*Chinese Proverb*

A foolish man proclaims his qualifications; a wise man keeps them secret within.

*Sakya Pandit*

The brave and the wise can both pity and excuse; when cowards and fools show no mercy.

*Franklin*

Wise men learn more from fools than fools from the wise.

*Cato the Elder*

A wise man begins in the end; a fool ends in the beginning.

*English Proverb*

A wise man turns chance into good fortune.
*Thomas Fuller*

Opportunity is rare and a wise man will never let it go by him.
*Bayard Taylor*

Those who wish to appear wise among fools, among the wise seem foolish.
*Quintilian*

Wise people have a lot in common.
*Aeschylus*

A wise man never refuses anything to necessity.
*Syrus*

The wisest of the wise may err.
*Aeschylus*

The wise man is great in small things.
*Chinese Proverb*

A wise man stumbles once over a peg.
*Pashto*

He is not wise who will not be instructed.
*Irish Proverb*

He is wise that follows the wise.
*English Proverb*

The way of a wise man is knowledge.
*Nagarjuna*

A wise man, though in decline, affords pleasure to others by his elegant sayings.
*Sakya Pandit*

The wise man doubts often, and changes his mind when needed.
*Akhenton*

When nothing can be done about the way things are, the wise stop worrying about the situation.
*Lao Tzu*

The man of wisdom sees everything as the Divine Substance.
*Sai Baba*

Time ripens all things: no man is born wise.
*Cervantes*

Without exertion, it is impossible to become wise.
*Sakya Pandit*

More is demanded to produce one wise man today than seven formerly...
*Baltasar Gracian*

The wise transform the inner to make the outer enjoyable, they don't try and transform the outer to make the inner enjoyable. They experience spontaneous enjoyment within themselves.
*Lao Tzu*

The sign of a person of wisdom is infinite love.
*Sai Baba*

A wise man's country is the world.
*Aristippus*

The wise man never trusts in appearances.
*Confucius*

The wise pursue understanding; fools follow the reports of others.
*Tibetan Proverb*

A wise man will make more opportunities than he finds.
*Francis Bacon*

A wise man is superior to any insults which can be put upon him, and the best reply to unseemly behavior is patience and moderation
*Moliere*

The wise man never trusts in appearances.
*Confucius*

The wise pursue understanding; fools follow the reports of others.
*Tibetan Proverb*

The wise focus their attention inside.
*Lao Tzu*

The views of men of wise counsel are much the same.
*Liu Bei*

The wise man does not set his mind either for anything or against anything; what is right, he will follow.
*Confucius*

A wise man guides his own course of action.
*Sakya Pandit*

The wise man doesn't tell what he does, and never does what cannot be told.
*Chinese Proverb*

Those with little learning have great pride; grown wise, they are quiet.
*Sakya Pandit*

It is part of a wise man to keep himself today for tomorrow, and not to venture all his eggs in one basket.
*Cervantes*

Travel makes a wise man better, but a fool worse.
*English Proverb*

The wise witness events evolve, yet keep to the Source.
*Lao Tzu*

Wise men may not be learned, learned men may not be wise.
*Chinese Proverb*

The heart of a wise man lies quiet like clear water.
*Cameroon Proverb*

If you buy worthless anxiety, how can you be called wise?
*Swami Muktananda*

The wise practice spiritual wisdom.
*The Sri Guru Granth Sahib*

A wise man makes his own decisions; an ignorant man follows public opinion.
*Chinese Proverb*

A wise man changes his mind; a fool, never.
*Spanish Proverb*

The wise don't obey useless laws.
*Lao Tzu*

To be idle is a short road to death and to be diligent is a way of life; foolish people are idle, wise people are diligent.
*Buddha*

# CHARACTER

生

A thousand men have been ruined for the pleasure of a little time short as a dream.
*Ptah-Hotep*

We should not transgress moral codes.
*Nagarjuna*

Every action we take, everything we do, is either a victory or defeat in the struggle to become what we want to be.
*Anne Byrhhe*

I have discovered that we may be in some degree whatever character we choose. Besides, practice forms a man to anything.
*James Boswell*

We gain the strength of the temptation we resist.
*Ralph Waldo Emerson*

There is one thing alone that stands the brunt of life throughout its length: a quiet conscience.
*Euripides*

What does it profit a man if he gains the whole world and loses his own soul?
*Jesus*

Because a human being is so malleable, whatever one cultivates is what one becomes.
*Lao Tzu*

A hundred lifetimes may not be enough to rectify the mistake made in one short morning.
*Chinese Proverb*

We are what we repeatedly do.
*Aristotle*

If you refuse to be made straight when you are green, you will not be made straight when you are dry.
*African Proverb*

Never regard something as doing you good if it makes you betray a trust, or lose your sense of shame, or makes you show hatred, suspicion, ill will, or hypocrisy; or a desire for things best done behind closed doors.
*Marcus Aurelius*

Never do anything against conscience even if the state demands it.
*Einstein*

If you compromise with your own conscience, you will weaken your conscience. Soon your conscience will fail to guide you and you never will have real wealth based on peace of mind.
*Napoleon Hill*

Never exchange a good conscience for the good will of others, or to avoid their ill-will.
*Charles Simmons*

We are spinning our own fates, good or evil, and never to be undone. Every smallest stroke of virtue or of vice leaves its never so little scar...Nothing we ever do is, in strict scientific literalness, wiped out.
*William James*

The reputation of a thousand years may be determined by the conduct of a single hour.
*Japanese Proverb*

As human beings, we are endowed with freedom of choice, and we cannot shuffle off our responsibility upon the shoulders of God or nature. We must shoulder it ourselves. It is up to us.
*Arnold J. Toynbee*

Choose well; your choice is brief, and yet endless.
*Goethe*

What is it to you if a man is such and such, if another does or says this or that? You will not have to answer for others, but you will have to give an account of yourself.
*Thomas a'Kempis*

Sometimes when I consider what tremendous consequences come from little things...I am tempted to think...there are no little things.
*Bruce Barton*

The worst punishment of all is that in the court of his own conscience no guilty man is acquitted.
*Juvenal*

Our character is but the stamp on our souls of the free choices of good and evil we have made.
*John Cunningham Geikie*

One's own faults are one's mortal enemies. It follows that to guard against them is life's gravest concern.
*Tiruvalluvar*

There is nothing so delicate as your moral character, and nothing which it is your interest so much to preserve pure... I will recommend to you a most scrupulous tenderness for your moral character, and the utmost care not to say or do the least thing that may, ever so slightly, taint it.
*Lord Chesterfield*

A man's character is his fate.
*Heraclitus*

There is no more important lesson to be learned or habit to be formed than that of right judgment and of delighting in good characters and noble actions.
*Aristotle*

Thoughts lead on to purposes; purposes go forth in action; action forms habits; habits decide character; and character fixes our destiny.
*Tryon Edwards*

A good character is more valuable than gold.
*Philippine Proverb*

It matters not how a man dies, but how he lives.
*Samuel Johnson*

Character is higher than intellect.
*Emerson*

Dignity does not consist in possessing honors, but in deserving them.
*Aristotle*

The strong calm man is always loved and revered. He is like a shade-giving tree in a thirsty land, or a sheltering rock in a storm.
*James Allen*

Character is better than wealth.
*Irish Proverb*

A clear conscience is the greatest armor.
*Chinese Proverb*

Character is destiny.
*Heraclitus*

It is not the oath that makes us believe the man, but the man the oath.
*Aeschylus*

If you conduct yourself properly, fear no one.
*Arabic Proverb*

The superior man lives in peace with all men without acting absolutely like them. The vulgar man acts absolutely like them without being in accord with them.
*Confucius*

The quality of a person's life is in direct proportion to their commitment to excellence, regardless of their chosen field of endeavor.
*Vince Lombardi*

Cattle die, and kinsmen die,
And so one dies one's self;
But a noble name will never die,
If good renown one gets.
*The Havamal*

When strict with oneself, one rarely fails.
*Confucius*

A clear conscience is more valuable than wealth.
*Filipino Proverb*

A firm tree does not fear the storm.
*Indonesian Proverb*

If I keep my character, I'll be rich enough.
*Plutonius*

His own character is the arbiter of every one's fortune.
*Syrus*

Never esteem anything as of advantage to you that will make you break your word or lose your self-respect.
*Marcus Aurelius*

A good reputation is more valuable than money.
*Publius Syrus*

The path of duty lies in what lies near at hand; and men seek for it in what is remote.
*Japanese Proverb*

It is not only what we do, but what we do not do, for which we are accountable.
*Moliere*

A promise is a debt.
*Irish Proverb*

Willing is not enough, we must do.
*Goethe*

Endeavor always to be gracious, that your own conduct be without defects.
*Ptah-Hotep*

Arrogance is not gentlemanly.
*Swahili Proverb*

God has given principles to live by, but only you yourself can follow them.
*African Proverb*

Avoid gaining your livelihood by means of deceit and theft.
Avoid acts of levity and thoughtlessness as lower you in another's esteem.
Avoid useless conduct and actions.
*Gongs & Drums of Gampopa Precepts*

Stand firm.
Motto of Queen Lili Uokalani

Observe good conduct and action. Never fall victim to anger, lust, or greed. Banish bad thoughts from your mind.
*Swami Muktananda*

Let us respect men, and not only men of worth, but the public in general.
*Cicero*

In matters of style, swim with the current; in matters of principle, stand like a rock.
*Thomas Jefferson*

Hold yourself responsible for a higher standard than anyone else expects of you. Never excuse yourself.
*Henry Ward Beecher*

He then remains equally calm when the majority is on his side as when he finds himself in a minority; for he has done his part: he has expressed his convictions; he is not lord over minds and attitudes.
*Goethe*

18

It is the duty of every human being to look carefully within and see himself as he is, and spare no pains to improve himself in body, mind and soul.
*Gandhi*

What it boils down to-do the right thing.
*Yurok*

Each day look into your conscience and amend your faults; if you fail in this duty you will be untrue to the Knowledge and Reason that are within you.
*Kahlil Gibran*

Look for benefits that last.
*Ten Bears*

Engage always in good deeds and beneficial activities. Speak the truth, do not inflict pain by word or deed - or even by thought.
*Sai Baba*

Keep a watchful eye over yourself as if you were your own enemy; for you cannot learn to govern yourself, unless you first learn to govern your own passions and obey the dictates of your conscience.
*Kahlil Gibran*

We should pursue the path we believe to be right.
*Black Hawk*

Show respect for all men, but grovel to none.
*Tecumseh*

Pardon the other man's faults but deal strictly with your own.
*Sai Baba*

Be not too moral. You may cheat yourself out of much of life. Aim above morality. Be not simply good; be good for something.
*Thoreau*

The only thing necessary for the triumph of evil is for good men to do nothing.
*Edmond Burke*

Cherish good conduct. Become established on the path of morality. Earn virtue; shun defects.
*Swami Muktananda*

Whatever others may say about your faults (that you know you do not have), do not respond emotionally.
*Sai Baba*

Walk the good road...Be dutiful, respectful, gentle and modest... Be strong with the warm, strong heart of the earth.
*Sioux Proverb*

Remember to preserve a calm soul amid difficulties.
*Horace*

Neither display your own qualities nor look for others' faults. Do not see dirt at others' doors; keep your own porch swept. Only if your mirror is clean can it reflect clearly.
*Swami Muktananda*

Whatever gives you healthy joy, welcome it, but do not lower yourself by indulging in vulgar pastimes.
*Sai Baba*

One should not pry into the faults of others but into one's own deeds.
*The Dhammapada*

Why do you look at the splinter that is in your brother's eye but you don't see the beam that is in your own eye?
*Jesus*

Never yield to indolence or despair. Suffer loss and grief with an even minded attitude - this will strengthen your character.
*Sai Baba*

Withdraw into yourself and look. And if you do not find yourself beautiful yet, act as does the creator of a statue that is to be made beautiful: he cuts away here, he smoothes there, he makes this line lighter, this other purer, until a lovely face has grown upon his work. So do you also: cut away all that is excessive, straighten all that is crooked, bring light to all that is overcast, labor to make all one glow of beauty and never cease chiseling your statue, until there shall shine out on you from it the godlike splendor of virtue, until you see the perfect goodness surely established in the stainless shrine.

*Plotinus*

One ought to examine himself for a very long time before thinking of condemning others.

*Moliere*

A true person is more calm and deliberate.

*Rumi*

Change the skin, wash the heart.

*Chinese Proverb*

Listen to your conscience, and talk with reason. Behave correctly even when you are by yourself.

*Ibn Arabi*

Keep conscience clear, and then never fear.

*Franklin*

The superior man seeks what is right; the inferior one, what is profitable.

*Confucius*

It is the duty of every human being to look carefully within and see himself as he is and spare no pains to improve himself in body, mind and soul. He should realize the mischief wrought by injustice, wickedness, vanity, and the like and do his best to fight them.

*Gandhi*

He who trusts in God is able to remove his attention from worldly anxieties and devote it entirely to doing what is right.

*Bakhya Ibn Pakuda*

To compose our character is our duty.

*Montaigne*

Worry not that no one knows of you; seek to be worth knowing.

*Confucius*

Resolve to perform what you ought; perform without fail what you resolve.

*Franklin*

In pursuit, even of the best things, we ought to be calm and tranquil.

*Cicero*

Do not seek to follow in the footsteps of the men of old, seek what they sought.

*Matsuo Basho*

However troubled the times, men of imperturbable perception never commit shameful or sordid deeds.

*Tiruvalluvar*

Would you live with ease,
Do what you ought,
And not what you please.

*Franklin*

The man who in the view of gain thinks of righteousness, who in the view of danger is prepared to give up his life, and who does not forget an old agreement however far back it extends, such a man may be reckoned a complete man.

*Confucius*

If we were humble, nothing would change us – neither praise nor discouragement. If someone were to criticize us, we would not feel discouraged. If someone were to praise us, we also would not feel proud.

*Mother Teresa*

When away from home act as respectfully as you would toward an important guest; handle the people as respectfully as you would the grand sacrifice.
*Confucius*

Whatever the world may say or do, my part is to remain an emerald and to keep my color true.
*Marcus Aurelius*

The superior man does not give up good conduct because the inferior man rails against him.
*Hsun-Tzu*

The superior man, although giving his respect to men of the highest caliber, maintains a proper regard for all.
*Confucius*

It would be wrong for anything to stand between you and attaining goodness...So make your choice straightforwardly, once and for all, and stick to it. Choose what is best.
*Marcus Aurelius*

Whenever you are to do a thing, though it can never be known but to yourself, ask yourself how you would act were all the world looking at you, and act accordingly.
*Thomas Jefferson*

Do nothing base with others or alone, And, above all, thine own self respect.
*Pythagoras*

Do your duties faithfully...Surrender the fruits of your actions to God... Above all; acquire an eager thirst for righteousness, truth and freedom.
*Srimad Bhagavatam*

He that understands well the difference between an excellent man and low man knows how to act.
*Sakya Pandit*

Perfection of character: to live your last day, every day, without frenzy, or sloth, or pretense.
*Marcus Aurelius*

Let us endeavor to live so that when we come to die even the undertaker will be sorry.
*Mark Twain*

The superior man demands it of himself; the inferior man, of others.
*Confucius*

Stop talking about what the good man is like, and just be one.
*Marcus Aurelius*

Every man who is truly a man must learn to be alone in the mist of all others, and if need be against all others.
*Romain Rolland*

The responsibility is all yours; no one can stop you from being honest or straightforward.
*Marcus Aurelius*

In your secret chamber are you judged;
See you do nothing to blush for,
Though but the ceiling looks down on you.
*Tse-sze*

Rule your desires lest your desires rule you.
*Publilius Syrus*

Avoid three qualities: jealousy, greed, and arrogance... do not borrow anything from anyone; and do not make yourself a judge between two people.
*Hadith*

If you would convince a man that he does wrong, do right. But do not care to convince him. Men will believe what they see. Let them.
*Thoreau*

It's important to let people know what you stand for. It's equally important that they know what you won't stand for.
*B. Bader*

Leisure with dignity.
*Cicero*

The great man does not think beforehand of his words that they be sincere, nor his actions that they may be resolute - he simply speaks and does what is right.
*Mencius*

Harmony in discord.
*Horace*

If you know that a thing is unrighteous, then use all dispatch in putting an end to it.
*Mencius*

Live among men as if God beheld you; speak to God as if men were listening.
*Seneca*

First keep the peace within yourself, then you can also bring peace to others.
*Thomas a'Kempis*

To do a great right, do a little wrong.
*Shakespeare*

Do your duty and leave the rest to heaven.
*Pierre Corneille*

Whoso would be a man must be a nonconformist.
*Emerson*

Disciplining himself, his mind controlled, a man of discipline finds peace, the pure calm that exists in me.
*The Bhagavad Gita*

Do noble things, do not dream them all day long.
*Charles Kingsley*

In adversity, remember to keep an even mind.
*Horace*

Do not lose your inward peace for anything whatsoever, even if your whole world seems upset.
*Saint Francis de Sales*

Do not weep; do not wax indignant. Understand.
*Baruch Spinoza*

Be sure never to depart from uprightness of intention...act upon just grounds, for heaven always favors good desires.
*Cervantes*

Treat your playmates... "according to your own dignity rather than their deserts."
*Shakespeare*

The ideal man bears the accidents of life with dignity and grace, making the best of circumstances.
*Aristotle*

Do not let your peace depend on the hearts of men; whatever they say about you, good or bad, you are not because of it another man, for as you are, you are.
*Thomas a'Kempis*

Be always sure you're right, then go ahead.
*Davy Crockett*

Simplicity of character is the natural result of profound thought.
*William Hazlitt*

It is no easy thing for a principle to become a man's own unless each day he maintains it and works it out in his life.
*Epictetus*

Choose always the way that seems best, however rough it may be...
*Pythagoras*

Do not repay anyone evil for evil. Be careful to do what is right in the eyes of everybody.
*The Apostle Paul*

Never "for the sake of peace and quiet" deny your convictions.
*Dag Hammarskjold*

Suggest what is right, oppose what is wrong; what you think, speak; try to satisfy yourself, and not others; and if your are not popular, you will at least be respected; popularity last but a day, respect will descend as a heritage to your children.
*T. C. Halliburton*

Better break your word than do worse in keeping it.
*Thomas Fuller*

Important principles may and must be inflexible.
*Lincoln*

Grace under pressure.
*Ernest Hemingway*

The higher self of a tranquil man whose self is mastered is perfectly poised in cold or heat, joy or suffering, honor or contempt.
*The Bhagavad Gita*

Test everything. Hold on to the good. Avoid every kind of evil.
*The Apostle Paul*

The way to gain a good reputation is to endeavor to be what you desire to appear.
*Socrates*

Don't be humble with fools. Don't take pride into the presence of a master.
*Rumi*

Quality is not an act. It is a habit.
*Aristotle*

Don't leave the high road for a shortcut.
*Portuguese Proverb*

If you are standing upright, do not fear a crooked shadow.
*Chinese Proverb*

...an upright man gives thought to his ways.
*The Book of Proverbs*

Little by little one walks far.
*Peruvian Proverb*

...never tire of doing what is right.
*The Apostle Paul*

Make every effort to add to your faith goodness; and to your goodness, knowledge; and to your knowledge, self-control; and to self-control, perseverance; and to perseverance, godliness; and to godliness, brotherly kindness; and to brotherly kindness, love.
*Simon Peter*

If you want to be strong, know your weaknesses.
*German Proverb*

When you are losing, wear a winning face.
*French Proverb*

Little by little does the trick.
*Aesop*

The fall of dropping water wears away the stone.
*Lucretius*

Do what you ought, and come what will.
*Scottish Proverb*

Let a wise man blow off the impurities of himself, as a smith blows off the impurities of silver, one by one, little by little, and from time to time.
*Buddha*

A just man. He stands on the side of right with such conviction, that neither the passion of the mob, nor the violence of a despot can make him overstep the bounds of reason.
*Baltasar Gracian*

The superior man is governed by decorum; the inferior man is ruled by law.
*Chinese Proverb*

Do nothing to make you lose respect for yourself, or to cheapen yourself in your own eyes; let your own integrity be the standard of rectitude, and let your own dictates be stricter than the precepts of any law. Forego the unseemly, more because of this fear of yourself, than for fear of the sternness of outer authority.
*Baltasar Gracian*

Apply yourself to think what is good, speak what is good, do what is good.
*Zend-Avesta*

The man of principle never forgets what he is, because of what others are.
*Baltasar Gracian*

Let men decide firmly what they will not do; then they will be free vigorously to do what they ought to do.
*Mencius*

If we are ever in doubt what to do, it is a good rule to ask ourselves what we shall wish on the morrow that we had done.
*Sir John Lubbock*

The right way is not always the popular and easy way. Standing for right when it is unpopular is a true test of moral character.
*Margaret Chase Smith*

Character is like a tree and reputation like its shadow. The shadow is what we think of it, the tree is the real thing.
*Lincoln*

The greatest man is he who chooses the right with invincible resolution; who resists the sorest temptations from within and without; who bears the heaviest burdens cheerfully; who is calmest in storms and most fearless under menace and frowns; and whose reliance on truth, on virtue, and on God, is most unfaltering.
*William Ellery Channing*

One should be careful to improve himself continually.
*Shu Ching*

What I must do is all that concerns me, not what the people think.
*Emerson*

Character builds slowly, but it can be torn down within incredible swiftness.
*Faith Baldwin*

A man of substance…There ought to always be more on the inside than on the outside…
*Baltasar Gracian*

Let nothing be done in your life, which will cause you fear if it becomes known to your neighbor.
*Epicurus*

Let us take care above all not to walk like a flock of sheep each in the other's traces; let us inform ourselves rather of the place where we ought to go than of that where others are going.
*Seneca*

The superior man enacts equity, and justice is the foundation of all his deeds.
*Confucius*

A wise man, whenever he acts, must consider the moral effects. Among a hundred persons, it is rare to find even one of accomplished moral merits.
*Sakya Pandit*

The superior man watches attentively over the secret inspirations of his conscience.
*Tsu Tse*

Watch diligently over yourselves, let not negligence be born in you.
*Fo-shu-hing-tsan-king*

No compromises; to live resolutely in integrity, plentitude and beauty.
*Goethe*

Be steadfast and immovable.
*The Apostle Paul*

The just man is not one who does harm to none, but one who having the power to harm represses the will.
*Pythagoras*

All you have to do then is to command yourselves.
*Cicero*

We have the choice; it depends on us to choose the good or the evil by our own will.
*Hermes*

Banish injustice even from your thought. It is not the actions alone, but the will that distinguishes the good from the wicked.
*Democritus*

Think before you act.
*Pythagoras*

The true seeker must, before anything else, cleanse his heart.
*Baha-ullah*

Live your daily life in a way that you never lose yourself.
*Thich Nhat Hanh*

In all things to do what depends on oneself and for the rest to remain firm and calm.
*Epictetus*

Attentive in the midst of the heedless, awake amidst sleepers, the intelligent man walks on leaving the others far behind.
*The Dhammapada*

Be as you wish to seem.
*Socrates*

For when moral value is considered, the concern is not the actions, which are seen, but rather with their inner principles, which are not seen.
*Kant*

Be at war with your vices, at peace with your neighbors, and let every New-Year find you a better man.
*Franklin*

The superior man in dealing with the world is not for anything or against anything. He follows righteousness as the standard.
*Confucius*

If a person has built a sound character, it makes but little difference what people say about him, because he will win in the end.
*Napoleon Hill*

The supreme excellence is not in being better than others, but in being better than your former self.
*Indian Proverb*

What matters to an active man is to do the right thing; whether the right things come to pass should not bother him.
*Goethe*

Discriminate between the right and the wrong and do only the right. Strive every moment to be aware of the presence of God.
*Sai Baba*

He that understands well the difference between an excellent man and low man knows how to act.
*Sakya Pandit*

It is not enough to have great qualities; one must know how to manage them.
*La Rochefoucauld*

Thou shalt be everywhere and always the champion of the Right and Good against Injustice and Evil.
*Leon Gautier*

The appellation of Gentleman is never to be affixed to a man's circumstances, but to his behavior in them.
*Richard Steele*

Indeed, the man who has fully educated and developed himself in a higher sense can always reckon to have the majority against him.
*Goethe*

If you conduct yourself properly, then fear no one.
*Iraq Proverb*

He who fears the opinion of the world more than his own conscience has but little self-respect.
*The Talmud*

It is impossible to arrive at the summit of the mountain without passing through rough and difficult paths.
*Confucius*

Great spirits have always encountered violent opposition from mediocre minds.
*Einstein*

Defeat in doing right is nevertheless victory.
*Frederick W. Robertson*

Circumstances reveal us to others and still more to ourselves.
*La Rochefoucauld*

It is needful to watch over oneself.
*Shu Ching*

The character of every act depends on the circumstances in which it is done.
*Oliver Wendell Holmes*

Often man is preoccupied with human rules and forgets the inner law.
*Antoine the Healer*

The superior man is in all the circumstances of his life exempt from prejudices and obstinacy; he regulates himself by justice alone.
*Confucius*

Wish not so much to live long as to live well.
*Franklin*

A man's heart shows him what he should do...
*Ecclesiasticus*

Do what you know to be good without expecting from it any glory. Forget not that the vulgar are a bad judge of good actions.
*Demophilus*

A gem is not polished without friction, nor a person perfected without trials.
*Chinese Proverb*

Reputation is what men and women think of us; character is what God and angels know of us.
*Thomas Paine*

Our characters are the result of our conduct.
*Aristotle*

Talent is nurtured in solitude; character is formed in the stormy billows of the world.
*Goethe*

The wise man will always reflect concerning the quality, not the quantity of life.
*Seneca*

Difficulties are the things that show what men are.

*Epectetus*

It is circumstances and proper timing that give an action its character and make it either good or bad.

*Agesilaus*

A man has no more character than he can command in a time of crisis.

*Ralph W. Sockman*

The true test of character is...how we behave when we don't know what to do.

*John Holt*

Just trust yourself, then you will know how to live.

*Goethe*

When the character of a man is not clear to you, look at his friends.

*Japanese Proverb*

We are all ready to be savage in some cause. The difference between a good man and a bad one is the choice of the cause.

*William James*

Never take a course of action on the sole grounds that reprehensible people are urging the opposite course.

*D. Sutten*

...decent behavior is the best adornment of inner wisdom.

*Akhenaton*

To become a person of value, one needs to understand and be able to completely transform oneself.

*Takuan Soho*

Two roads diverged in a wood, and I – I took the one less traveled by and that has made all the difference.

*Robert Frost*

Adversity is a mirror that reveals one's true self.

*Chinese Proverb*

A real individual is self-substantial, a man who builds on his own genes for better or for worse, a man who would hate to be anybody but himself, a man who likes the flesh that sticks to his own ribs, a man who shows his natural face and does not care too much how others like it. A real individual consults himself. Waits for the inner lift or fall of feeling...

*Henry A. Murray*

As long as we make the best effort we are capable of, we cannot feel discouraged by our failures.

*Mother Teresa*

It is cowardice to fail to do what is right.

*Confucius*

It is by living a life in common with a person that we learn of that person's moral character.

*Buddha*

A person experiences the events of life, and the experiences of life in turn reveal something about the person.

*Lao Tzu*

Convince the world by your character...

*Chief John Ross*

Character is formed in the stormy billows of the world.

*Goethe*

I do not consider the tongue and its words;
I look at the spirit and character.
I look into the heart to see if it's evil;
The heart's the essence, words only the accident:
The accident's accessory, the essence is what matters.

*Rumi*

If you do not know what to do in some particular case or in your general conduct, think of what sense of duty, what kindness, independent of public opinion, some holy men of your neighborhood, whether of an order or not, would show in like circumstance; if you do not know what to think about a man, think what some such holy man would think about him.

*The Upanishads*

Reason is not measured by size or height, but by principle.

*Epictetus*

When men are pure, laws are useless; when men are corrupt laws are broken.

*Disraeli*

Character is perfectly educated will.

*Novalis*

Morality is always the same. However, immorality varies from generation to generation.

*Dagobert D. Runes*

Anyone can sail a ship when the sea is calm.

*Chinese Proverb*

If the desire to have God within us is there, progress, however slow, is bound to be. Man cannot be transformed from bad to good overnight.

*Gandhi*

Water does not lose its purity because of a bit of weed floating in it.

*Rumi*

I never come back home with the same moral character I went out with; something or other becomes unsettled where I had achieved internal peace; some one or other of the things I had put to flight reappears on the scene.

*Seneca*

A precious stone will not lose its shine just because someone drops it in a cesspool.

*Malay Proverb*

No great thing is created suddenly, any more than a bunch of grapes or a fig. If you tell me that you desire a fig, I answer that there must be time. Let it first blossom, then bear fruit, then ripen.

*Epictetus*

Perfection is attained by slow degrees; she requires the hand of time.

*Voltaire*

It is to be lamented that great characters are seldom without a blot.

*George Washington*

Man is the creature of the era he lives in; very few can raise themselves above the ideas of the time.

*Voltaire*

The creation of a thousand forests is in one acorn.

*Emerson*

The only obligation which I have a right to assume is to do any time what I think right.

*Thoreau*

There have been as great souls unknown to fame as any of the most famous.

*Franklin*

Great minds have purposes others have wishes.

*Washington Irving*

When no wind blows, even the weathervane has character.

*Stanislaw J. Lec*

The superior man must always remain himself in all situations of life.

*Chung Yung*

You learn to know a pilot in a storm.
*Seneca*

Anyone can hold the helm when the sea is calm.
*Syrus*

The first duty of men is, to take none of the principles of conduct upon trust; to do nothing without a clear and individual conviction that it is right to be done.
*William Godwin*

A man's action is a picture book of his creed.
*Emerson*

There is very little difference between one man and another; but what little difference there is, is very important. This distinction seems to me to go to the root of the matter.
*William James*

Great winds are powerless to disturb the water of a deep well.
*Chinese Proverb*

The measure of a man is the way he bears up under misfortune.
*Plutarch*

Any man may play the part in the mummery, and act the honest man on the scaffolding; but to be right within, in his own bosom, where all is allowed, where all is concealed – there's the point! The next step is to be so in our own home, in our ordinary actions, of which we need render no account to any man, where there is no study, no make believe.
*Montaigne*

The just man is himself his own law.
*Catacombs Inscription*

Character is based on virtuous action, and virtuous action is grounded on truth.
*Gandhi*

Never hope to conceal any shameful thing which you have done; for even if you do conceal it from others, your own heart will know.
*Isocrates*

We ought to do everything both cautiously and confidently at the same time.
*Epictetus*

Character is much easier kept than recovered.
*Thomas Paine*

Everything one has a right to do is not best to be done.
*Franklin*

A man carries his success or his failure with him...it does not depend on outside conditions.
*Emerson*

One bad example destroys more than twenty good ones built up.
*Hungarian Proverb*

Deprived of all else, one remains undisgraced if still endowed with strength of character.
*Tiruvalluvar*

It is necessary to the happiness of man that he be mentally faithful to himself.
*Thomas Paine*

It is the heart that makes a man rich. He is rich according to what he is, not according to what he has.
*Henry Ward Beecher*

Wealth stays with us a little moment if at all; only our characters are steadfast, not our gold.
*Euripides*

Character is power.
*Sai Baba*

Our true character silently underlies all our words and actions, as the granite underlies the other strata.
*Thoreau*

It is circumstance and proper measure that give an action its character, and make it either good or bad.
*Plutarch*

What does not destroy me makes me stronger.
*Nietzsche*

...all men make mistakes, but a good man yields when he knows his course is wrong, and repairs the evil.
*Sophocles*

He who plants a forest in the morning cannot expect to saw planks the same evening.
*Chinese Proverb*

If an urn lacks the characteristics of an urn, how can we call it an urn?
*Confucius*

It is needful to watch over oneself.
*Shu Ching*

Character makes life immortal; character survives even death... character is power...Qualities that make up a flawless character are love, patience, forbearance, steadfastness and charity. These are the highest qualities and have to be respected.
*Sai Baba*

Every garden may have some weeds.
*English Proverb*

Cultivate vigor, forgiveness, and firmness; become a storehouse of good qualities. Perform all your tasks with right understanding. Never act mindlessly. Practice self-control and contentment.
*Swami Muktananda*

It is for you to make something of yourselves...
*Sitting Bull*

Enumerate your weaknesses, both great and small, and eliminate them. Don't just prune back their branches, uproot them.
*Swami Muktananda*

We must always follow the directions of the Great Spirit, and we must listen to him, as it was he that made us: determine to listen to nothing that is bad.
*Tenkswataya*

Cleanse your mind and intellect. Awake from the dream of the world.
*Swami Muktananda*

Never let anybody be in a position to puzzle you in regard to what is right.
*Winnebago*

Instead of searching for the faults of others, examine yourself for personal faults that need to be corrected.
*Sai Baba*

Lay down for yourself, at the outset, a certain stamp and type of character for yourself, which you are to maintain whether you are by yourself or are meeting with people. And be silent for the most part, or else make only the most necessary remarks, and express these in few words.
*Epictetus*

Show yourself in all respects a model of good deeds.
*The Book of Titus*

Under all circumstances be vigilant.
*Baha-ullah*

The right way is not always the popular and easy way. Standing for right when it is unpopular is a true test of moral character.
*Margaret Chase Smith*

30

Follow the good and learn their ways.
*Chinese Proverb*

The mature person accepts his situation... He makes sure that his own conduct is correct and seeks nothing from others; thus he is never disappointed... therefore the mature person lives in perfect serenity.
*Tzu-Ssu*

A superior man first practices what he preaches and then preaches what he practices.
*Confucius*

The superior man is watchful over himself even when alone.
*Chung Yung*

No matter what anyone says or does, my task is to be good. Like gold or emerald or purple repeating to itself, "No matter what anyone says or does, my task is to be emerald, my color undiminished."
*Marcus Aurelius*

You should always question yourself so hard that it may seem excessive; self-growth will never happen without it. If you reflect well upon your past conduct, this will help you grow. When you help someone, you should not allow this act to linger in your mind and expect any return from him. When you trouble someone, you should always remember it, and never repeat the same mistake. While it is desirable to completely discard a grudge against others, you should never forget favors from others.
*Kou Ji Sei*

Prefer a noble life before a long life.
*Shakespeare*

You should not live one way in private, another in public.
*Syrus*

Love all, trust few. Do wrong to none.
*Shakespeare*

Let them know a real man, who lives as he was meant to live.
*Marcus Aurelius*

It is easy in the world to live after the world's opinion; it is easy in solitude to live after our own; but the great man is he who in the midst of the crowd keeps with perfect sweetness the independence of solitude.
*Emerson*

Knowing is not enough, we must apply. Willing is not enough, we must do.
*Goethe*

If you think it right to differ from the times, and to make a stand for any valuable point of morals, do it, however rustic, however antiquated, however pedantic it may appear; do it, not for insolence, but seriously, and grandly, as a man who wears a soul of his own in his bosom, and does not wait till it shall be breathed into him by the breath of fashion.
*Sydney Smith*

All know the way, few actually walk it.
*Bodhidharma*

I am the master of my fate:
I am the master of my soul.
*William Henley*

He that does good for good's sake seeks neither praise nor reward, though sure of both at last.
*William Penn*

The superior man will watch over himself when he is alone. He examines his heart that there may be nothing wrong there, and that he may have no cause of dissatisfaction with himself.
*Confucius*

A change in scenery does not change one's character.
*Aesop*

Though the wind blows, the mountain does not move.
*Japanese Proverb*

We are not trying to please men but God, who tests our hearts.
*The Apostle Paul*

Thatch your roof before rainy weather; dig your well before you become parched with thirst.
*Chinese Proverb*

If you are standing upright, don't worry if your shadow is crooked.
*Chinese Proverb*

If it is not right, do not do it; if it is not true, do not say it.
*Marcus Aurelius*

Be indifferent to the praise and blame of men; consider it as if the croakings of frogs.
*Ramakrishna*

It is not enough to make something look good. The underlying principle must be good.
*Joyce Sequichie Hifler*

A good man...whatever may befall him, will behave gracefully; approving his conduct exact, square, and blameless. Slight misfortunes are unable to shake his well-balanced happiness... Of the circumstances in which he is placed, he will always make the best and most honorable use...
*Aristotle*

Wish not so much to live long as to live well.
*Franklin*

Fear not the reproach of men, nor be afraid of their revilings.
*The Book of Isaiah*

It is shameful to confuse a lowly mind.
*Ptah-Hotep*

Lowly men are never high, even when elevated. High souls are never low, even when downtrodden.
*Tiruvalluvar*

Respect for women is a sign of real culture.
*Sai Baba*

Take care that no one hates you justly.
*Syrus*

Submit to the rule you laid down.
*English Proverb*

Courtesy is the mark of a civilized person.
*Chinese Proverb*

The best index to a person's character is (a) how he treats people who can't do him any good, and (b) how he treats people who can't fight back.
*Abigail Van Buren*

The integrity of the upright guides them.
*The Book of Proverbs*

# IF

If you can keep your head when all about you
Are losing theirs and blaming it on you;
If you can trust yourself when all men doubt you,
But make allowance for their doubting too;
If you can wait and not be tired by waiting,
Or, being lied about, don't deal in lies,
Or, being hated, don't give way to hating,
And yet don't look too good, nor talk too wise;

If you can dream - and not make dreams your master;
If you can think - and not make thoughts your aim;
If you can meet with triumph and disaster
And treat those two impostors just the same;
If you can bear to hear the truth you've spoken
Twisted by knaves to make a trap for fools,
Or watch the things you gave your life to broken,
And stoop and build 'em up with worn-out tools;

If you can make one heap of all your winnings
And risk it on one turn of pitch-and-toss,
And lose, and start again at your beginnings
And never breathe a word about your loss;
If you can force your heart and nerve and sinew
To serve your turn long after they are gone,
And so hold on when there is nothing in you
Except the Will which says to them: "Hold on!"

If you can talk with crowds and keep your virtue,
Or walk with kings - nor lose the common touch;
If neither foes nor loving friends can hurt you;
If all men count with you, but none too much;
If you can fill the unforgiving minute
With sixty seconds' worth of distance run -
Yours is the Earth and everything that's in it,
And - which is more - you'll be a Man, my son!
*Rudyard Kipling*

# VIRTUE

The happiest man is not the one who has lived the longest, but the one who has made the most of his life. The span of life should be measured not by years but by our deeds well performed... Surely virtue is its own reward.

*Desiderius Erasmus*

If you follow virtue for your mean, and strive to do virtuous deeds, you need not envy those that are born of Princes and great men, for blood is inherited, but virtue is achieved.

*Cervantes*

A noble spirit will seek the reward of virtue in the consciousness of it, rather than in popular opinion.

*Pliny the Younger*

Find the reward in doing right, in right... Scorn those who follow virtue for her gifts.

*The Bhagavad Gita*

Now 'tis the spring, and weeds are shallow-rooted; suffer them now and they'll o'ergrow the garden.

*Shakespeare*

The great virtue of man lies in his ability to correct his mistakes and to continually make a new man of himself.

*Wang Yang-Ming*

Hate what is evil; cling to what is good... Do not be overcome by evil, but overcome evil with good.

*The Apostle Paul*

Men of superior virtue practice it without thinking of it; those of inferior virtue go about it with intention.

*Lao Tzu*

The best people honor their virtuous nature and apply themselves to study and inquiry.

*Zi-si*

Follow the path of virtue. The virtuous rest in bliss in this world and in the next.

*The Dhammapada*

The superior man thinks of virtue; the small man thinks of comfort...

*Confucius*

Nature does not bestow virtue; to be good is an art.

*Seneca*

No man has a right to be respected for any other possessions but those of virtue and talents. Titles are tinsel, power a corrupter, glory a bubble, and excessive wealth a libel on its possessor.

*Percy Bysshe Shelley*

Act only on that maxim through which you can at the same time will that it should become a universal law!

*Immanuel Kant*

Seek not goodness from without; seek it within yourselves, or you will never find it.

*Epictetus*

The growth of moral virtues depends upon one's self.

*Nagarjuna*

One should live one's life based on correct, moral thoughts.

*Kok Yim Ci Yuen*

Even after death, our virtue is not lost.

*Euripides*

Better than the one who knows what is right is he who loves what is right.
*Confucius*

We must continue throughout our lives to do what we conceive to be good.
*Black Hawk*

As virtue is its own reward; so is vice its own punishment: for he who lives too fast is quickly through, and in a double sense: while he who rests in virtue, never dies.
*Baltasar Gracian*

It's quite possible to be a good man without anyone realizing it. Remember that.
*Marcus Aurelius*

What is well planted cannot be pulled up. What is closely embraced cannot slip away. The wise establish virtue firmly within themselves, and are honored for generations ever after.
*Lao Tzu*

Does it make any difference to you if other people blame you for doing what's right? It makes no difference.
*Marcus Aurelius*

Like a statue that is fixed steadily on its base, the virtuous man ought to be stable in character.
*Socrates*

Ten years on the path of virtue are not enough; one day of wickedness is too much.
*Chinese Proverb*

You are mistaken my friend, if you think that a man who is worth anything ought to spend his time weighing up the prospects of life and death. He has only one thing to consider in performing any action, that is, whether he is acting justly or unjustly, like a good man or a bad man.
*Socrates*

The most unholy and savage animal is a human being without virtue.
*Aristotle*

There are nine hundred and ninety-nine patrons of virtue to one virtuous man.
*Thoreau*

Certain good qualities are like the senses: people entirely lacking in them can neither perceive nor comprehend them.
*La Rochefoucauld*

A man's faults all conform to his type of mind. Observe his faults and you may know his virtues.
*Confucius*

Though there may be many learned men who know and proclaim what virtuous action is, there are very few in this world who would practice it, having thus understood.
*Sakya Pandit*

You may try many times before finding a good man.
*Syrus*

We do not despise all those with vices, but we do despise all those without a single virtue.
*La Rochefoucauld*

Few men have virtue to withstand the highest bidder.
*George Washington*

Disaster is virtue's opportunity.
*Seneca*

Weakness, even more than vice, is the enemy of virtue.
*La Rochefoucauld*

As threshing separates the wheat from the chaff, so does affliction purify virtue.
*Robert Burton*

Wickedness is weakness.
*John Milton*

To flee vice is the beginning of virtue, and to have got rid of folly is the beginning of wisdom.
*Horace*

Virtue itself turns vice, being misapplied; and vice sometime's by action dignified.
*Shakespeare*

Virtue is harder to be got than a knowledge of the world; and, if lost in a young man, is seldom recovered.
*John Locke*

In law a man is guilty when he violates the rights of others. In ethics he is guilty if he only thinks of doing so.
*Immanuel Kant*

Vice is ignorance. Virtue is knowledge.
*Plato*

When men grow virtuous in their old age they are merely making a sacrifice to God of the devil's leavings.
*Jonathan Swift*

Maintain clarity and purity, and be a model of deep virtue for all people.
*Lao Tzu*

After one vice a greater follows.
*Spanish Proverb*

One who knows what virtue is but does not practice it – of what use is his religion?
*Sakya Pandit*

Pleasures are temporary but virtues immortal.
*Periander*

Neglect mending a small fault, and it will soon be a great one.
*Franklin*

Put no new names or notions upon authentic virtues and vices. Think not that morality is ambulatory; that vices in one age are not vices in another; or that virtues, which are under the everlasting seal of right reason, may be stamped by opinion.
*Sir Thomas Browne*

He that is good will infallibly become better, and he that is bad will as certainly become worse, for vice, virtue, and time are three things that never stand still.
*Charles Caleb Colton*

Watch with care over your heart and give not way to heedlessness; practice conscientiously every virtue and let not there be born in you any evil inclination.
*Buddha*

Above all things avoid heedlessness; it is the enemy of all virtue.
*Fo-shu-hing-tsan-king*

There is only one Ethics, as there is only one geometry. But the majority of men, it will be said, are ignorant of geometry.
*Voltaire*

He who wants to keep his garden tidy doesn't reserve a plot for weeds.
*Dag Hammerskjold*

There is nothing more rewarding than virtue, nor anything more ruinous than its neglect.
*Tiruvalluvar*

Even little things that you think no one will ever know about will ultimately become widely known. If you, yourself, know something, then all the gods (kami) of heaven and earth are also aware of it.
*Takuan Soho*

Do not abandon everlasting values in pursuit of short-lived values.
*Sai-Kon Tan*

36

Wisdom, love, and courage are the three universal virtues.

Zi-si

Be tough, be courageous, and have a strong sense of justice

Gichou

Fearlessness, purity, determination in the discipline of knowledge, charity self-control, sacrifice, study of sacred lore, penance, honesty; Nonviolence, truth, absence of anger, disengagement, peace, loyalty, compassion for creatures, lack of greed, gentleness, modesty, reliability; Brilliance, patience, resolve, clarity, absence of envy and of pride; these characterize a man born with divine traits.

The Bhagavad Gita

Do good at all times for you can never call back a day to perform a good deed that was neglected.

The Jain Scriptures

While living I want to live well. I know I have to die sometime, but even if the heavens were to fall on me, I want to do what is right.

Geronimo

Although the Tao holds no favoritism or partiality, it always supports those who are naturally virtuous.

Lao Tzu

You must start with the first step: the cleansing of the mind and the cultivation of virtue.

Sai Baba

Add to your virtues and root out your faults.

Swami Muktananda

Virtue consists, not in abstaining from vice, but in not desiring it.

George Bernard Shaw

A person's value does not depend on his qualities but on the way he uses them.

Aristotle

The more you practice virtue the easier to practice it becomes.

Euripides

The greatest good, compared, to which all others are trifling, is to harm no one and to help everyone as much as you can.

Francesco Guicciardini

Consider well the seed from which you grew; You were not formed to live like animals but rather to pursue virtue and knowledge.

Dante

Do not let the artificial obliterate the natural...do not let virtue be sacrificed for fame.

Chuang Tse

No vice is so small that it can be practiced without harm, nor any virtue so trivial that it should be neglected.

Chinese Proverb

The one thing worth living for is to keep one's soul pure.

Marcus Aurelius

There can be no greater virtue than to hold honor dear. Men who do will fear no danger nor commit any unseemly act.

Francesco Guicciardini

The superior man is he whose virtues exceed his talents.

Chinese Proverb

True goodness springs from a man's own heart.

Confucius

The only reward of virtue is virtue.

Emerson

For virtue is the bond of all the perfections, and the heart of all life's satisfactions. It makes a man sensible, alert, far-seeing, understanding, wise, courageous, considerate, upright, joyous, welcomed, truthful, and a universal idol... Virtue is the sun of our lesser world, the sky over which is a good conscience. It is so beautiful, that it finds favor of God, and of man. There is nothing lovely without virtue... for virtue is the essence of wisdom, and all else is folly: capacity and greatness must be measured in terms of virtue...Virtue alone is sufficient unto itself, and it, only, makes a man worth loving in life and in death, worth remembering.

*Baltasar Gracian*

The virtue of good people never ages.

*Buddha*

Virtue is merely that which should be done in life, and vice is merely that which should be avoided.

*Tiruvalluvar*

Virtue shows itself in the lowest as well as in the sublimest things.

*Confucius*

A kindly countenance and sweet words spoken from the heart are virtue's way.

*Tiruvalluvar*

The perfection of virtue consists in a certain equality of soul and of conduct which should remain unalterable.

*Seneca*

The power of man's virtue should not be measured by his special efforts, but by his ordinary doing.

*Blaise Pascal*

Unless virtue guide us our choice must be wrong.

*William Penn*

Keep the mind free from impurity. That alone is the practice of virtue.

*Tiruvalluvar*

Virtue is more valuable than life.

*Heber J. Grant*

Virtuous conduct leads a man to eminent greatness. Therefore, it should be guarded as more precious than life itself.

*Tiruvalluvar*

Life, like every other blessing, derives its value from its use alone. Not for itself, but for a nobler end the Eternal gave it; and that end is virtue.

*Samuel Johnson*

Virtue finds no friends.

*Shakespeare*

Perfection of moral virtue does not wholly take away the passion, but regulates them.

*Saint Thomas Aquinas*

Virtue is more clearly shown in the performance of fine actions than in the nonperformance of base ones.

*Aristotle*

The greatest source of virtue, both visible and invisible, is right knowledge. Therefore, if you strive for virtue, take hold of wisdom in its entirety.

*Nagarjuna*

Virtue is a state of war, and to live in it we have always to combat with ourselves.

*Jean-Jacques Rousseau*

Virtue and happiness are Mother and Daughter.

*Franklin*

To walk safely through the maze of human life, one needs the light of wisdom and the guidance of virtue.

*Buddha*

38

The fact is that a man who wants to act virtuously in every way necessary comes to grief among so many who are not virtuous.
*Niccolo Machiavelli*

Not doing harm to others,
Not bowing down to low people,
Not abandoning the path of virtue,
These are small things, but of great importance.
*Nagarjuna*

It is virtuous activities that determine our happiness, and the opposite kind that produce the opposite effect.
*Aristotle*

He who has knowledge is firm. The holy, even when destitute, do not discard moral virtues, Although scorched by the sun's natural heat. The natural cold of snow is not taken away.
*Nagarjuna*

Above all - begin the cultivation of virtues.
*Sai Baba*

Because of the diverse conditions of humans, it happens that some acts are virtuous to some people, as appropriate and suitable to them, while the same acts are immoral for others, as inappropriate to them.
*Saint Thomas Aquinas*

Let virtue garnish your thoughts unceasingly...
*Doctrine & Covenants*

Conviction is worthless unless it is converted into conduct.
*Thomas Carlyle*

I do what is mine to do; the rest doesn't disturb me.
*Marcus Aurelius*

The most valuable things in the world are moral principle and virtue.
*Chou Tzu Ch'iian-shu*

Virtue, then, is a state of character concerned with choice...
*Aristotle*

There is no attribute of the superior man greater than his helping men to practice virtue.
*Mencius*

A noble spirit will seek the reward of virtue in the consciousness of it, rather than in popular opinion.
*Pliny the Younger*

Men of principle are always bold, but those who are bold are not always men of principle.
*Confucius*

A truly virtuous person cannot be indifferent to the troubled world in which he lives...
*Lao Tzu*

What is the product of virtue? Tranquillity.
*Epictetus*

The only path to a tranquil life is through virtue.
*Juvenal*

Virtue does not always demand a heavy sacrifice – only the willingness to make it when necessary.
*Frederick Dunn*

One of natural whole virtue respects his own life...he does what is right and gives up what is not right.
*Lao Tzu*

Virtue itself is not enough; there must also be the power to translate it into action.
*Aristotle*

Every smallest stroke of virtue or of vice leaves its ever so little scar.
*William James*

Virtue may not always make a face handsome, but vice will certainly make it ugly.
*Franklin*

Our whole life is startlingly moral. There is never an instant's truce between virtue and vice.
*Thoreau*

Immorality in the house is like a worm in the vegetables.
*The Talmud*

Virtue is the health of the soul.
*Joseph Joubert*

Do not count as riches anything that can be lost. Virtue is the true wealth and reward of its owner.
*Leonardo da Vinci*

One should practice steadfast and indiscriminative virtue without demanding others to do the same in return.
*Lao Tzu*

The virtuous man has a steadfast character and opinion...
*Theognis*

The end of knowledge should be in virtuous action.
*Sir Philip Sidney*

Virtue extends our days: he lives two lives who relives his past with pleasure.
Martial

Sell not virtue to purchase wealth...
*Franklin*

No man ever becomes wicked all at once.
*Juvenal*

To think one is sufficiently virtuous is to lose hold of virtue.
*Shu Ching*

No compromises; to live resolutely in integrity, plentitude and beauty.
*Goethe*

Circumstances, though they attack obstinately the man who is firm, cannot destroy his proper virtue, firmness.
*Bhartrihari*

Virtues are acquired through endeavor, which rests wholly upon yourself.
*Nagarjuna*

A virtuous man concentrates on his own work, not that of others.
*Zengzi*

With a pure mind and an attitude that takes delight in the truth, one will naturally come to be a person of virtue. No treasure is more worthy of our desire than virtue.
*Kok Yim Ci Yuen*

Do right always. It will give you satisfaction in life.
*Wovoka*

There is a primary law, eternal, invariable, engraved in the hearts of all; it is Right Reason. Never does it speak in vain to the virtuous man, whether it ordains or prohibits. The wicked alone are untouched by its voice. It is easy to be understood and is not different in one country and in another; it is today what it will be tomorrow and for all time.
*Cicero*

All of the earth's gold is not worth virtue.
*Plato*

It is not enough to merely possess virtue, as if it were an art; it should be practiced.
*Cicero*

Test everything. Hold on to the good. Avoid every kind of evil.
*The Apostle Paul*

The virtuous control themselves.
*Buddha*

We are to practice virtue, not possess it.
*Meister Eckhart*

There is a natural aristocracy among men. The grounds of this are virtue and talents.
*Thomas Jefferson*

Wisdom is knowing what to do next; virtue is doing it.
*David Starr Jordan*

What most persons consider as virtue, after the age of 40 is simply a loss of energy.
*Voltaire*

All virtue is summed up in dealing justly.
*Aristotle*

Who sows virtue reaps honor.
*Leonardo da Vinci*

The strength of a man's virtue should not be measured by his special exertions, but by his habitual acts.
*Blaise Pascal*

Happiness is secured through virtue; it is a good attained by man's own will.
*Saint Thomas Aquinas*

Silver and gold are not the only coin; virtue too passes current all over the world.
*Euripides*

Recommend virtue to your children; it alone, not money, can make them happy. I speak from experience.
*Ludwig van Beethoven*

Reputation is rarely proportioned to virtue.
*Saint Francis de Sales*

Virtue is the truest nobility.
*Cervantes*

Hypocrisy is a tribute vice pays to virtue.
*La Rochefoucauld*

# TRUTH

If you add to the truth, you subtract from it.

*The Talmud*

Do not veil the truth with falsehood, nor conceal the truth knowingly.

*Muhammad*

He who does not bellow the truth when he knows the truth makes himself the accomplice of liars and forgers.

*Charles Peguy*

In the war between falsehood and truth, falsehood wins the first battle and truth the last.

*Sheikh Mujibur Rahman*

Things are not always what they seem; the first appearance deceives many: the intelligence of a few perceives what has been carefully hidden.

*Phaedrus*

Swerve not from truth.

*Srimad Bhagavatam*

There should be truth in thought, truth in speech, and truth in action.

*Gandhi*

Throughout your life choose truth and your words will be more believable than other people's oaths.

*Isocrates*

Beware that you do not lose the substance by grasping at the shadow.

*Aesop*

Look beneath. For ordinary things are far other than they seem...The false is forever the lead in everything, continually dragging along the fools: the truth brings up the rear, is late, and limps along upon the arm of time.

*Baltasar Gracian*

As a rule, I always look for what others ignore.

*Marshall McLuhan*

Look within things.

*Marcus Aurelius*

Weigh the meaning and look not at the words.

*Ben Johnson*

Understand the spirit of those with whom you deal... the man of passion always speaks of matters far differently from what they are...thus does everyone babble according to his feelings or his mood, and all, very far from the truth.

*Baltasar Gracian*

Do not become archivists of facts. Try to penetrate to the secret of their occurrence, persistently search for the laws which govern them.

*Ivan Pavlov*

There is always a way to be honest without being brutal.

*Arthur Dobrin*

When you shoot an arrow of truth, dip its point in honey.

*Arab Proverb*

One must receive the Truth from wheresoever it may come.

*Maimonides*

The sky is not less blue because the blind man does not see it.

*Danish Proverb*

Truth alone conquers, not falsehood.
*Mundaka Upanishad*

Those who know the truth are not equal to those who love it, and those who love it are not equal to those who live it.
*Confucius*

I have seldom known any one who deserted truth in trifles that could be trusted in matters of importance.
*William Paley*

A thing does not therefore cease to be true because it is not accepted by many.
*Benedict Spinoza*

All truth passes through three stages. First, it is ridiculed. Second, it is violently opposed. Third, it is accepted as being self-evident.
*Arthur Schopenhauer*

Truth is perfect and complete in itself. It is not something newly discovered; it has always existed.
*Dogen*

Facts do not cease to exist because they are ignored.
*Aldous Huxley*

Should one say that something does not exist, merely because we have never seen or heard of it?
*Ge Hung*

The truth is for the few, the false is for the populace, because popular.
*Baltasar Gracian*

The fact that an opinion has been widely held is no evidence that it is not utterly absurd; indeed in view of the silliness of the majority of mankind, a widespread belief is more often likely to be foolish than sensible.
*Bertrand Russell*

"Learn what is true in order to do what is right" is the summing up of the whole duty of man.
*Thomas Huxley*

Truth doesn't change because it is, or is not, believed by a majority of the people.
*Giordano Bruno*

Truth cannot change or cease to be; untruth can never survive for long.
*Sai Baba*

Knowing the truth one is not afraid no matter what happens.
*Lao Tzu*

There are certain old truths which will be true as long as this world endures.
*Theodore Roosevelt*

It is much easier to recognize error than to find truth; the former lies on the surface, this is quite manageable; the latter resides in depth, and this quest is not everyone's business.
*Goethe*

We never fully grasp the importance of any true statement until we have a clear notion of what the opposite untrue statement would be.
*William James*

A light is still a light, even though the blind man cannot see it.
*Austrian Proverb*

Appearances are deceptive.
*Aesop*

Is not the truth the truth?
*Shakespeare*

He who knows nothing is closer to the truth than he whose mind is filled with falsehoods and errors.
*Thomas Jefferson*

Do not consider a thing as proof because you find it written in books; for just as a liar will deceive with his tongue, he will not be deterred from doing the same thing with his pen. They are utter fools who accept a thing as convincing proof simply because it is in writing.

*Moses Maimonides*

There is no advantage in deceiving yourself.

*Bodhidharma*

Most men...love better to deceive themselves and fight obstinately for an opinion which is to their taste than to seek without obduracy the truth.

*Cicero*

He who discerns the truth as truth and the illusion as an illusion, attains to the truth and is walking on the right road.

*The Dhammapada*

Instead of thinking how things may be, see them as they are.

*Samuel Johnson.*

Don't rely on the label on the bag.

*French Proverb*

The great majority of mankind are satisfied with appearances, as though they were realities and are often more influenced by the things that seem than by those that are.

*Niccolo Machiavelli*

No oath has ever yet made any criminal speak the truth.

*Cesare Bonesana di Beccaria*

What is true by lamplight is not always true by sunlight.

*Joseph Joubert*

Be not deceived with the first appearance of things, for show is not substance.

*English Proverb*

The ear is the side door of truth, but the front door of falsehood. The truth is sometimes seen, but rarely heard: on the fewest of occasions does it arrive in its elemental purity, especially if it has traveled far, for then it is always soiled by what has happened on the road.

*Baltasar Gracian*

Things do not pass for what they are, but for what they seem...things are judged by what they look, even though most things are far different from what they appear.

*Baltasar Gracian*

A man ought to desire that which is genuine instead of that which is artificial.

*Okute*

To return to the root is to find the meaning, but to pursue appearances is to miss the source.

*Seng Ts'an*

Begin with an error of an inch, and end by being a thousand miles off the mark.

*Chinese Proverb*

Nobody can write the life of a man, but those who have eat and drunk and lived in social intercourse with him.

*Samuel Johnson*

At all times, look at the thing itself – the thing behind the appearance.

*Marcus Aurelius*

When the moon's light is reflected on the surface of the ocean, the waves make the moon appear restless, but in reality the moon is calm and serene. It is the water that is restless.

*Maitreya*

You don't have to travel all around the world in order to understand that the sky is blue everywhere.

*Goethe*

44

No statement should be believed because it is made by an authority.
*Hans Reichenbach*

In quarreling the truth is always lost.
*Syrus*

When the fox preaches, look to your geese.
*German Proverb*

I renounce the honors to which the world aspires and desire only to know the Truth.
*Socrates*

God has made many doors opening into truth which He opens to all who knock upon them with hands of faith.
*Kahlil Gibran*

Truth is exact correspondence with reality.
*Paramahansa Yogananda*

The truth simply is that's all. It doesn't need reasons: it doesn't have to be right: it's just the truth. Period.
*Carl Frederick*

All truths are easy to understand once they are discovered; the point is to discover them.
*Galileo*

Truth will always be truth, regardless of lack of understanding, disbelief or ignorance.
*W. Clement Stone*

What kind of truth is it which is true on one side of the mountain and false on the other?
*Montaigne*

Impartiality is either a delusion of the simple-minded, a banner of the opportunist, or the boast of the dishonest. Nobody is entitled to be unbiased toward truth or falsehood.
*Gaetano Salvemini*

Truth is power.
*Lakota Maxim*

Truth triumphs over untruth.
*Gandhi*

Truth is not a matter of personal viewpoint.
*Vernon Howard*

How many legs does a dog have if you call the tail a leg? Four; calling a tail a leg doesn't make it a leg.
*Lincoln*

Nothing is easier than self-deceit. For what each man wishes, that he also believes to be true.
*Demosthenes*

As scarce as truth is, the supply has always been in excess of the demand.
*Josh Billings*

There's a world of difference between truth and facts. Facts can obscure the truth.
*Maya Angelou*

Even if you are a minority of one, the truth is the truth.
*Mohandas Gandhi*

Opinions are made to be changed - or how is truth to be got at?
*Lord Byron*

Strive to get clear notions about all.
*Seneca*

# SINCERITY

生

We are so accustomed to wearing a disguise before others that eventually we are unable to recognize ourselves.
*La Rochefoucauld*

The most exhausting thing in life, I have discovered, is being insincere.
*Anne Morrow Lindbergh*

Sincerity is an openness of heart that is found in very few people. What we usually see is only an artful disguise people put on to win the confidence of others.
*La Rochefoucauld*

Earnestness is the path of immortality.
*Buddha*

With sincerity, there is virtue.
*Shinto teaching*

The mature person values sincerity above all things.
*Tzu-ssu*

The first duty is to behave with purity of intention... Actions performed with complete sincerity and for God's sake are accepted and approved.
*Sheikh Muzaffer*

Those who pretend to be what they are not, sooner or later, find themselves in deep water.
*Aesop*

Sincerity is the single virtue that binds the divine and man in one.
*Shinto teaching*

We forfeit three-fourths of ourselves in order to be like other people.
*Arthur Schopenhauer*

Insist on yourself; never imitate.
*Emerson*

Just act sincerely, in accordance with your true nature.
*Tzu-ssu*

What I am, I am.
*Sitting Bull*

Appear as you are; be as you appear.
*Rumi*

Everything is based on mind, is led by mind, is fashioned by mind. If you speak and act with a polluted mind, suffering will follow you, as the wheels of the oxcart follow the footsteps of the ox. Everything is based on mind, is led by mind, is fashioned by mind. If you speak and act with a pure mind, happiness will follow you, as a shadow clings to a form.
*Buddha*

When you are content to be simply yourself and don't compare or compete, everybody will respect you.
*Lao Tzu*

Insincerity is always weakness; sincerity even in error is strength.
*George Henry Lewes*

Sincerity is impossible, unless it pervades the whole being, and the pretence of it saps the very foundation of character.
*James Russell Lowell*

Sincerity is moral truth.
*George Henry Lewes*

The weak cannot be sincere.
*La Rochefoucauld*

# HONOR

Our own heart, and not other men's opinion, form our true honor.
*Samuel Coleridge*

Deal solely with men of honor…they who do not cherish honor do not cherish virtue, and honor is the throne of virtue.
*Baltasar Gracian*

Be honorable yourself if you wish to associate with honorable people.
*Welsh Proverb*

Rather fail with honor than succeed by fraud.
*Sophocles*

He who falls with honor soon gets to his feet again.
*German Proverb*

Men of good will were ever men of peace, and men of honor, men of good will.
*Baltasar Gracian*

He who lives without discipline dies without honor.
*Icelandic Proverb*

A sense of honor pervades all aspects of Indian life.
*Ohiyesa*

By honest conduct one achieves honorable eminence.
*Tiruvalluvar*

Honor is a harder master than the law.
*Mark Twain*

He has honor if he holds himself to an ideal of conduct though it is inconvenient, unprofitable, or dangerous to do so.
*Walter Lippmann*

An honorable man esteems his moral health too much to lower himself willingly by any act that may seem base. He is true to himself and values honor for its highest meaning…There can be no real success in life unless it is accompanied by this high sense of honor.
*Robert Wood*

The glory of great men must always be measured against the means they have used to acquire it.
*La Rochefoucauld*

The most honorable among you are those who carry themselves with the most outstanding conduct.
*Hadith*

Pursue the enjoyments which are of good repute; for pleasure attended by honor is the best thing in the world, but pleasure without honor is the worst.
*Isocrates*

The shortest and surest way to live with honor in the world is to be in reality what we would appear to be; all human virtues increase and strengthen themselves by the practice and experience of them.
*Socrates*

There is a difference between a brave man and one who faces danger out of regard for honor. Both recognize danger; but the former believes he can defend himself against it, and if he did not, he would not face it. The latter may even fear the danger more than he should, but he stands firm – not because he is unafraid but because he has decided he would rather suffer harm than shame.
*Francesco Guicciardini*

47

You are a man; do not dishonor mankind.
*Jean Jacques Rousseau*

Shun any actions that will diminish honor.
*Tiruvalluvar*

It is not necessary that while I live I live happily; but it is necessary that so long as I live I should live honorably.
*Immanuel Kant*

Consider your honor, as a gentleman, of more weight than an oath. Never tell a lie. Pay attention to matters of importance.
*Solon*

Show me a man of honor, and I will show you what kind of a man you are.
*Thomas Carlyle*

Honor is something that must not be lost.
*Arthur Schopenhauer*

For a man of honor shame is worse than death.
*The Bhagavad Gita*

Better die in honor than live in disgrace.
*Vietnamese Proverb*

Honor cannot be bought.
*Philippine Proverb*

People of superior refinement and of active disposition identify happiness with honor...
*Aristotle*

You are permitted in time of great danger to walk with the devil until you have crossed the bridge.
*Bulgarian Proverb*

Do not lose honor through fear.
*Spanish Proverb*

Where there is no shame, there is no honor.
*African Proverb*

Life is light when compared to honor.
*Japanese Proverb*

My honor is dearer to me than my life.
*Cervantes*

Mine honor is my life; both grow in one; Take honor from me and my life is done.
*Shakespeare*

Either live or die with honor.
*Scottish Proverb*

Never trust your honor to another.
*Baltasar Gracian*

Better poor with honor than rich with shame.
*Dutch Proverb*

Honor is better than honors.
*Belgian Proverb*

Dishonor is worse than death.
*Russian Proverb*

What is left when honor is lost?
*Syrus*

To be without money is better than to be without honor.
*Norwegian Proverb*

Honor is self-esteem made visible in action.
*Ayn Rand*

Honor is the reward of virtue.
*Cicero*

All virtues spring from honor.
*Albanian Proverb*

He who wants to sell his honor will always find a buyer.
*Arabian Proverb*

# COURAGE

生

The world has no room for cowards. We must all be ready somehow to toil, to suffer, to die. And yours is not the less noble because no drum beats before you when you go out into your daily battlefields, and no crowds shout about your coming when you return from your daily victory or defeat.
*Robert Louis Stevenson*

The coward is ignoble, shameful, and foreign to the ways of heaven.
*The Bhagavad Gita*

Cowards die many times before their deaths, the valiant never taste of death but once.
*Shakespeare*

It is cowardice that makes you conceal the truth…Be bold, and there will be no need for subterfuge.
*Sai Baba*

To evade danger is not cowardice.
*Philippine Proverb*

He who sees righteousness and does not do it is not brave.
*Japanese Proverb*

Whenever conscience commands anything, there is only one thing to fear, and that is fear.
*Saint Theresa of Jesus*

To see what is right and not to do it is cowardice.
*Confucius*

Be brave and courageous, for adversity is the proving ground of virtue.
*Battista Alberti*

Courage is the most important of all virtues, because without it we can't practice any other virtue with consistency.
*Maya Angelou*

Courage is not simply one of the virtues, but the form of every virtue at the testing point.
*C. S. Lewis*

Morality may consist solely in the courage of making a choice.
*Leon Blum*

True courage is…the firm resolve of virtue and reason.
*Paul Whitehead*

Without courage, wisdom bears no fruit.
*Baltasar Gracian*

People with courage distinguish what is right from what is wrong, and what is fact from what is not.
*Kok Yim Ci Yuen*

Courage is to take hard knocks like a man when occasion calls.
*Plautus*

This is courage…to bear unflinchingly what heaven sends.
*Euripides*

The test of courage comes when we are in the minority.
*Emerson*

The better part of valor is discretion.
*Shakespeare*

No man loses honor who had any in the first place.
*Syrus*

Courage is grace under pressure.
*Ernest Hemingway*

The gods look with favor on superior courage.
*Tacitus*

He who recognizes dangers but does not fear more than necessary, is brave.
*Francesco Guicciardini*

The bravest are surely those who have the clearest vision of what is before them, glory and danger alike, and, notwithstanding, go out to face it.
*Thucydides*

Brave hearts do not back down.
*Euripides*

He is the best man who, when making his plans, fears and reflects on everything that can happen to him, but in the moment of action is bold.
*Herodotus*

The brave man, we contend, yields neither to fear nor anger, desire nor agony. He is at all times master of himself; His courage rises to the heights of chivalry...
*Ohiyesa*

The true test of a man's spirit comes when he is visited by an unexpected danger. Those who hold out – and they are few – may truly be called brave and dauntless.
*Francesco Guicciardini*

Fortune fears the brave soul; she crushes the coward.
*Seneca*

Let us be brave in the face of adversity.
*Marcus Aurelius*

Happy the man who ventures boldly to defend what he holds dear.
*Ovid*

Bravery never goes out of fashion.
*William Thackeray*

The courage we desire and prize, is not the courage to die decently but to live manfully.
*Thomas Carlyle*

The man of true valor lies between the extremes of cowardice and rashness.
*Cervantes*

Fate assists the courageous.
*Japanese Proverb*

Be men of courage; be strong.
*The Apostle Paul*

Men of principle have courage.
*Chinese Proverb*

Victory is obtained through courage.
*Philippine Proverb*

Be strong and of a good courage; fear not.
*The Book of Deuteronomy*

Be strong; fear not.
*The Book of Isaiah*

The pressure of adversity does not affect the mind of the brave man... It is more powerful than external circumstances.
*Seneca*

The brave and generous have the best lives. They're seldom sorry.
*The Havamal*

There will be darkness, disappointment and even worse; but we must have courage enough to battle against all these and not succumb to cowardice.
*Gandhi*

Yield not to cowardice; do not give up inward bliss and confidence.
*Sai Baba*

Fate often saves an undoomed warrior when his courage endures.
*Beowulf*

The man, then, who faces and who fears the right things and from the right motive, in the right way and at the right time, and who feels confidence under the corresponding conditions, is brave.
*Aristotle*

Some have been thought brave, because they were afraid to run away.
*English Proverb*

When good is in danger, only a coward would not defend it.
*Confucius*

It is sheer mental weakness and cowardice that allows hypocrisy to develop. If you have the courage to face the consequences you will never utter a falsehood.
*Sai Baba*

Courage is resistance to fear, mastery of fear – not absence of fear.
*Mark Twain*

Courage is a special kind of knowledge: the knowledge of how to fear what ought to be feared and how not to fear what ought not to be feared.
*David Ben-Gurion*

The essence of courage is not that your heart should not quake, but that nobody else knows that it does.
*E. B. Benson*

Only the wise are brave. Others are either temerarious or foolhardy. Thus, we can say that every brave man is wise but not that every wise man is brave.
*Francesco Guicciardini*

Fortune favors the brave.
*Virgil*

The superior man has neither anxiety nor fear.
*Confucius*

Let us train our minds to desire what the situation demands.
*Seneca*

To have courage for whatever comes in life – everything lies in that.
*Saint Teresa of Avila*

In times of stress, be bold and valiant.
*Horace*

Often the test of courage is not to die but to live.
*Vittorio Alfieri*

Life shrinks or expands in proportion to one's courage.
*Anais Nin*

Compromise does not mean cowardice.
*John F. Kennedy*

Courage is what it takes to stand up and speak; courage is also what it takes to sit down and listen.
*Winston Churchill*

Courage is rightly esteemed the first of human qualities... because it is the quality which guarantees all others.
*Winston Churchill*

Every man has his own courage, and is betrayed because he seeks in himself the courage of other persons.
*Emerson*

Courage without discretion is useless.
*Philippine Proverb*

# JUSTICE

生

The voice of the majority is no proof of justice.
*Friedrich von Schiller*

There is a point at which even justice does injury.
*Sophocles*

He that is unjust in the least is unjust also in much.
*The Gospel of Luke*

Banish injustice even from your thought. It is not the actions alone, but the will that distinguishes the good from the wicked.
*Democritus*

Never tolerate injustice and corruption...never be afraid to attack wrong...
*Joseph Pulitzer*

As long as justice and injustice have not terminated their ever renewing fight for ascendancy in the affairs of mankind, human beings must be willing, when need is, to do battle for the one against the other.
*John Stuart Mill*

To avoid action when justice is at stake demonstrates a lack of courage.
*Gichin Funakoshi*

You can also commit injustice by doing nothing.
*Marcus Aurelius*

Who does not punish wrong condones it.
*Leonardo da Vinci*

The more laws, the less justice.
*Cicero*

Laws like cobwebs catch small flies, great ones break through before your eyes.
*Franklin*

Justice delayed, is justice denied.
*William E. Gladstone*

Justice is that which is right.
*Gichin Funakoshi*

An unjust deed doesn't escape the god's attention.
*Plato*

The just path is always the right one.
*Yiddish Proverb*

Let justice be done, though the sky falls.
*William Murray*

To do injustice is the greatest of all evils.
*Plato*

Be just - the unjust never prosper.
*Abu Bakr*

Only the just man enjoys peace of mind.
*Epicurus*

Often man is preoccupied with human rules and forgets the inner law.
*Antoine the Healer*

The superior type of man is in all the circumstances of his life exempt from prejudices and obstinacy; he regulates himself by justice alone.
*Confucius*

The just man is himself his own law.
*Catacombs Inscription*

The superior man enacts equity, and justice is the foundation of all his deeds.
*Confucius*

52

Just as a stick must be either straight or crooked, so a man must be either just or unjust. Nor again are there degrees between just and unjust.
*Zeno the Stoic*

A just man. He stands on the side of the right with such conviction, that neither the passion of a mob, nor the violence of a despot can make him overstep the bounds of reason.
*Baltasar Gracian*

When you are just you use your character as law.
*Menander*

To do injustice is to do yourself an injustice – it degrades you.
*Marcus Aurelius*

In critical times, one must be devoted utterly to the cause of justice.
*Gichin Funakoshi*

Time alone reveals the just man; but you might discern a bad man in a single day.
*Sophocles*

The strictest justice is sometimes the greatest injustice.
*Terence*

Who does not punish evil, invites it.
*German Proverb*

The just man is not one who does hurt to none, but one who having the power to hurt represses the will.
*Pythagoras*

To do justice is what God demands of every man: it is the supreme commandment...
*Rabbi Herschel*

Shun injustice. Observe right conduct in mind and speech.
*Swami Muktananda*

Don't appear just; be just.
*Aeschylus*

Pardoning the bad, is injuring the good.
*Franklin*

Always be just.
*Swami Muktananda*

Extreme law is often injustice.
*Terence*

The virtue of justice consists in moderation, as regulated by wisdom.
*Aristotle*

In the matter of justice, all should be equal in your eyes.
*Abu Bakr*

Justice prevails over transgression when she comes to the end of the race.
*Hesiod*

Be brave, justice always prevails!
*Euripides*

# SELF-CONTROL

生

What lies in our power to do, it lies in our power not to do.
*Aristotle*

Let us not be like others, who are asleep, but let us be alert and self-controlled.
*The Apostle Paul*

Make the body obey your will. Never give in to it and follow its whims. Be prepared to put it aside; resolve to control it and keep it under strict control.
*Sai Baba*

Be self-controlled and alert.
*Simon Peter*

All you have to do then is to command yourselves.
*Cicero*

Keep over your actions an absolute empire; be not their slave, but their master.
*Thomas a' Kempis*

He who conquers others is strong; he who conquers himself is mighty.
*Lao Tzu*

The mind has to be controlled...
*Sai Baba*

Prepare your minds for action; be self-controlled.
*Simon Peter*

Be a man of self-control, for it evidences prudence.
*Baltasar Gracian*

He who does not control his impulse classes himself with beasts.
*Leonardo da Vinci*

What we do upon some great occasion will probably depend on what we already are; and what we are will be the result of previous years of self-discipline.
*Percy Bysshe Shelley*

Ask for advice from those who evidence good self-discipline.
*Leonardo da Vinci*

Tis easier to suppress the first desire than to satisfy all that follow it.
*Franklin*

Self control will place one among the gods, while lack of it will lead to deepest darkness.
*Tiruvalluvar*

Self-reverence, self-knowledge, self-control, these three alone lead life to sovereign power.
*Lord Alfred Tennyson*

Self-control brings calm to the mind, without it the seed of all the virtues perishes.
*Fo-shu-hing-tsan-king*

Difficult is union with God when the self is not under governance.
*The Bhagavad Gita*

Comprehending and acquiring self-control confers upon one the esteem of wise men.
*Tiruvalluvar*

A leader who is not captain of his body is not one to be honored...
*Rumi*

Most powerful is he who has himself in his own power.
*Seneca*

54

No man is free who is not master of himself.
*Epictetus*

The hardest victory is victory over self.
*Aristotle*

Self-conquest is the most glorious of victories; it shall better serve a man to conquer himself than to be master of the whole world.
*The Dhammapada*

True strength is to have power over oneself.
*Tolstoy*

Better is he that rules his spirit than he that conquers a city.
*The Book of Proverbs*

Guard your self-control as a precious treasure.
*Tiruvalluvar*

Make self-control a habit.
*Pythagoras*

The soul must master the inner world first and become impervious to temptations.
*Sai Baba*

It is one thing to be tempted, another thing to fall.
*Shakespeare*

A really self-restrained person grows every day from strength to strength and from peace to more peace. The very first step in self-restraint is the restraint of thoughts.
*Gandhi*

The man who conquers his own soul will forever be called conqueror of conquerors.
*Plautus*

Not being able to govern events, I govern myself.
*Montaigne*

He who reigns within himself and rules his passions, desires, and fears is more than a king.
*John Milton*

Who is strong? He who subdues his passion.
*The Talmud*

The greatest strength and wealth is self-control.
*Pythagoras*

By constant self-discipline and self-control you can develop greatness of character.
*Grenville Kleiser*

Use self restraint.
*Baltasar Gracian*

# MODERATION

生

Be moderate in all things.
*The Talmud*

Observe moderation.
*Hesiod*

Drink nothing to the dregs, either of the bad, or of the good, for to moderation in everything has one sage reduced all wisdom.
*Baltasar Gracian*

Moderation is the key to lasting enjoyment.
*Hosea Ballou*

Ask the gods nothing excessive.
*Aeschylus*

The heart is great which shows moderation in the midst of prosperity.
*Marcus Aurelius*

Moderation in all things.
*Terence*

Keep to moderation, keep the end in view, follow nature.
*Lucan*

Tis not drinking that is to be blamed, but the excess.
*John Seldon*

When the well's dry, we know the worth of water.
*Franklin*

Let us not give ourselves up to excess.
*Shih Ching*

To learn moderation is the essence of sound sense and real wisdom.
*Jacques Benigne Bossuet*

Drink wine by all means, but do not get drunk.
*Confucius*

All extremes...are unnatural and to be avoided.
*Chuang Tzu*

I hold this as a rule of life: Too much of anything is bad.
*Terence*

Never go to excess, but let moderation be your guide.
*Cicero*

The mean is the best in every case.
*Pythagoras*

To live long and well, employ moderation.
*Chinese Proverb*

The secret of life is balance, and the absence of balance is life's destruction.
*Hazrat Inayat Khan*

I believe that...greater things can be accomplished by patience and moderation than by impetuosity and boldness.
*Francesco Guicciardini*

Frogs don't drink up all the water in the ponds they live in.
*Sioux Proverb*

A thing moderately good is not so good as it ought to be. Moderation in temper is always a virtue; but moderation in principle is always a vice.
*Thomas Paine*

Moderation is the silken string running through the pearl-chain of all virtues.
*Thomas Fuller*

Everything carried to excess becomes a vice.
*Baltasar Gracian*

Anything in excess is unhealthy.
*Yiddish Proverb*

Be moderate in everything, including moderation.
*Horace Porter*

Candor and generosity, unless tempered by due moderation, leads to ruin.
*Tacitus*

Excess on occasion is exhilarating. It prevents moderation from acquiring the deadening effect of a habit.
*W. Somerset Maugham*

If one oversteps the bounds of moderation, the greatest pleasures cease to please.
*Epictetus*

Moderation is a virtue only in those who are thought to have an alternative.
*Henry A. Kissinger*

Moderation is the center wherein all philosophies, both human and divine, meet.
*Benjamin Disraeli*

Nothing in excess.
*Thales*

Only actions give life strength; only moderation gives it charm.
*Jean Paul*

Throw moderation to the winds, and the greatest pleasures bring the greatest pains.
*Democritus*

Moderation is the inseparable companion of wisdom, but with it genius has not even a nodding acquaintance.
*Charles Caleb Colton*

# SELF-RELIANCE

生

Those who live by the plow live in self-sufficiency. All others lean on them to simply subsist.
*Tiruvalluvar*

It is thrifty to prepare today for the wants of tomorrow.
*Aesop*

One should seek the truth himself while profiting by the directions which have reached us from ancient sages and saints.
*Tolstoy*

The gods help them who help themselves.
*Aesop*

It never ceases to amaze me: we all love ourselves more than other people, but care more about their opinions than our own.
*Marcus Aurelius*

You may always be victorious if you will never enter into any contest where the issue does not wholly depend upon yourself.
*Epitetus*

Recognize that if it's humanly possible, you can do it too.
*Marcus Aurelius*

The best things in life must come by effort from within...
*Fred Corson*

Look well into yourself; there is a source which will always spring up if you will search there.
*Marcus Aurelius*

It is vain to beg from the gods what one is competent to supply for oneself.
*Epicurus*

Individually free is he who is responsible to no man.
*Max Stirner*

The greatest fruit of self-sufficiency is freedom.
*Epicurus*

Remember this: whoever lives a life of chance will in the end find himself a victim of chance. The right way is to think, to examine, and to consider every detail carefully, even the most minute.
*Francesco Guicciardini*

Never trouble another for what you can do for yourself.
*Thomas Jefferson*

If you want something done well, do it yourself.
*Napoleon*

Do not rely completely on any other human being, however dear. We meet all life's greatest tests alone.
*Agnes Macphail*

It is extravagance to ask of others what can be procured by oneself.
*Seneca*

More satisfying far, that many depend upon you, than that you depend upon anybody.
*Baltasar Gracian*

The superior soul asks nothing from any but itself.
*Confucius*

Be your own torch and your own refuge...Seek refuge in no others but only in yourself.
*The Mahaparinibbana Sutta*

I have no faith in their paths, but believe that every man must make his own path!
*Black Hawk*

Depend on others and you will go hungry.
*Nepalese Proverb*

Depend on your walking stick; not on other people.
*Japanese Proverb*

Each individual is responsible for his own evolution...
*Lao Tzu*

I am master of my condition; I am master of my own body.
*Adario*

I am the maker of my own fortune.
*Tecumseh*

Trust God, but tie up your camel.
*Hadith*

Prepare yourself for you must travel alone.
*Book of the Golden Precepts*

Let the wise man be sufficient unto himself... Learn to rely upon yourself.
*Baltasar Gracian*

The self-sufficient is most wealthy of all.
*Epicurus*

Be a lamp to yourself. Be your own confidence.
*Buddha*

The reason Wankan Tanka does not make two birds...or two human beings exactly alike is because each is placed here...to be an independent individual to rely on himself.
*Okute*

Develop self-reliance; that is the best tonic.
*Sai Baba*

Everyone suffers who doesn't act for himself.
*Goethe*

Rise by your own efforts.
*The Bhagavad Gita*

Freedom comes from strength and self-reliance.
*Lisa Murkowski*

Do we not realize that self respect comes with self reliance?
*Abdul Kalam*

You cannot build character and courage by taking away a man's initiative and independence.
*Lincoln*

If money is your hope for independence you will never have it. The only real security that a man will have in this world is a reserve of knowledge, experience, and ability.
*Henry Ford*

Dependence begets subservience and venality, suffocates the germ of virtue, and prepares fit tools for the designs of ambition.
*Thomas Jefferson*

You are your only master.
*Buddha*

# SELF-KNOWLEDGE

生

If a man does not keep pace with his companions, perhaps it is because he hears a different drummer. Let him step to the music which he hears, however measured or far away.
*Thoreau*

This above all: to thine own self be true.
*Shakespeare*

We should know what our convictions are, and stand for them...Therefore it is wise to be as clear as possible about one's subjective principles.
*Carl Jung*

Consciousness of God is self-consciousness. Knowledge of God is self-knowledge.
*Ludwig Feuerbach*

Whoever knows himself knows God.
*Muhammad*

He who knows himself, knows his Lord.
*Mohyuddin ibn Arabi*

The greatest science is the knowledge of oneself. He, who knows himself, knows God.
*Saint Clement of Alexandria*

Your own treasure house already contains everything you need. Why don't you use it freely, instead of chasing after something outside yourself.
*Ma-tzu*

If we go down into ourselves we find that we possess exactly what we desire.
*Simone Weil*

We must find out what we really are and what we really want.
*Nelson Boswell*

Knowing others is wisdom, knowing yourself is Enlightenment.
*Lao Tzu*

Learn what you are and be such.
*Pindar*

Know thyself.
*Socrates*

Ninety percent of the world's woe comes from people not knowing themselves... Most of us go almost all the way through life as complete strangers to ourselves.
*Sydney J. Harris*

The most difficult thing in life is to know yourself.
*Thales*

Examine yourselves.
*The Apostle Paul*

The sage knows himself.
*Lao Tzu*

One of the most important precepts of wisdom is to know oneself.
*Socrates*

Know yourself and you shall know the Non-ego and the Lord of all.
*Ramakrishna*

One must know oneself.
*Blaise Pascal*

Learn to know yourself.
*Muhammad*

The more a man explores himself, the more power he finds within.
*Rumi*

Make it your business to know yourself – which is the most difficult lesson in the world.
*Cervantes*

The wise and intelligent practice attaining self-knowledge.
*Viveka Chudamani*

The unexamined life is not worth living.
*Socrates*

One may conquer in battle a thousand times a thousand men, yet he is the best of conquerors who conquers himself.
*The Dhammapada*

Only those who continually re-examine themselves and correct their faults will grow.
*The Hagakure*

Know yourself and you shall know the universe and the gods.
*Inscription of the Temple of Delphi*

A humble knowledge of oneself is a surer road to God than a deep searching of the sciences.
*Thomas a' Kempis*

The longest journey is the journey inward.
*Dag Hammarskjold*

Let each contemplate himself.
*Cicero*

He who has studied himself is his own master.
*Indian Proverb*

No man can be master of himself, who does not first understand himself.
*Baltasar Gracian*

It is a first principle that in order to improve yourself, you must first know yourself.
*Baltasar Gracian*

The life which is unexamined is not worth living.
*Plato*

Self-knowledge is the beginning of self-improvement.
*Spanish Proverb*

Let the man in whom there is intelligence... know himself.
*Hermes*

Whoever knows himself, has light.
*Lao Tzu*

One is reduced below a beast if one ceases to know oneself; for to other animals it is natural to be ignorant of oneself; with humans it comes by vice.
*Boethius*

There are three things extremely hard: steel, a diamond, and to know one's self.
*Franklin*

Knowing yourself is the beginning of all wisdom.
*Aristotle*

# ACTIONS

生

The Noble Eightfold Path:
1) Right Understanding
2) Right Thought
3) Right Speech
4) Right Action
5) Right Livelihood
6) Right Effort
7) Right Mindfulness
8) Right Concentration
                    *Buddha*

A man's action is only a picture book of his creed.
                    *Emerson*

Behavior is the perpetual revealing of us. What a man does, tells us what he is.
                    *F. D. Huntington*

The actions of men are the best interpreters of their thoughts.
                    *John Locke*

You will know them by their fruits.
                    *Jesus*

A man bears beliefs, as a tree bears apples.
                    *Emerson*

By the work one knows the workman.
                    *Jean De La Fontaine*

Behavior is a mirror in which everyone shows his image.
                    *Goethe*

Many can speak words of wisdom; few can practice it themselves.
                    *The Hitodadesa*

First say to yourself what you would be; and then do what you have to do.
                    *Epictetus*

Every man teaches as he acts.
                    *Ptah-Hotep*

The brave man carves out his fortune, and every man is the sum of his own works.
                    Cervantes

The only measure of what you believe is what you do. If you want to know what people believe, don't read what they write, don't ask what they believe, just observe what they do.
                    *Ashley Montagu*

A life spent worthily should be measured by deeds, not years.
                    *Richard B. Sheridan*

What you do speaks so loud I cannot hear what you say.
                    *Emerson*

To talk good is not to be good; to do good, that is being good.
                    *Chinese Proverb*

If the heart is right the deeds will be right.
                    *Japanese Proverb*

Let your words correspond with your actions and your actions with your words.
                    *Confucius*

Act as you speak.
                    *Lalita Vistara*

Improve others not by reasoning but by example. Let your existence, not your words, be your preaching.
                    *Amiel*

Words may show a man's wit, but actions his meaning.
                    *Franklin*

They make the greatest show of what they have done, who have done least... Rest in accomplishment, and leave talk to others. Do, and do not brag...Aspire to be heroic, not only to seem it.
*Baltasar Gracian*

All men who live are alike at birth. Diverse actions define their distinction and distinctiveness.
*Tiruvalluvar*

Every action we take, everything we do, is either a victory or defeat in the struggle to become what we want to be.
*Anne Byrhhe*

You cannot have a proud and chivalrous spirit if your conduct is mean and paltry; for whatever a man's actions are, such must be his spirit.
*Demosthenes*

By nature, men are nearly alike; by practice, they get to be wide apart.
*Confucius*

Our deeds still travel with us from afar, and what we have been makes us what we are.
*George Eliot*

To know and to act are one and the same.
*Samurai Maxim*

The Universal Way is not just a matter of speaking wisdom, but one of continual practice...
*Lao Tzu*

You carry your deeds with you wherever you go.
*Guru Nanak*

Whatever people do...let them put their whole heart into their task; let them be diligent and energetic.
*Buddha*

Each man is capable of doing one thing well. If he attempts several, he will fail to achieve distinction in any.
*Plato*

While the work or play is on...don't constantly feel you ought to be doing the other.
*Franklin P. Adams*

When walking, walk. When eating, eat.
*Zen Maxim*

Do whatever you do intensely.
*Robert Henri*

Each one achieves success by focusing on his own action.
*The Bhagavad Gita*

It is not enough to be busy; so are the ants. The question is: What are we busy about?
*Thoreau*

He who begins much finishes little.
*German Proverb*

If anything is to be done, let one do it vigorously.
*The Dhammapada*

Cultivate one-pointed steadfastness in whatever you do.
*Sai Baba*

Put your heart, mind, intellect and soul even to your smallest acts. This is the secret of success.
*Swami Sivananda*

The way of the sage is to act but not to compete.
*Lao Tzu*

Delight in your actions; enjoy your world. Act with utter absorption of mind and body, and without expectation.
*Swami Muktananda*

Trifles make perfection…
*Michelangelo*

There is always a best way of doing everything.
*Emerson*

It is just the little difference between the good and the best that makes the difference between the artist and the artisan. It is just the little touches after the average man would quit that make the master's fame.
*Orison Swett Marden*

Hold yourself responsible for a higher standard than anybody else expects of you. Never excuse yourself.
*Henry Ward Beecher*

If a man has done his best, what else is there?
*George S. Patton*

The talent of success is nothing more than doing what you can do well, and doing well whatever you do.
*Henry Wadsworth Longfellow*

Your only duty is to do the best you can.
*David Seabury*

A little knowledge that acts is worth infinitely more than much knowledge that is idle.
*Kahlil Gibran*

All who set themselves up against an ingenious cause are just striking at coals; sparks fly and kindle where they would otherwise have had no effect.
*Goethe*

The success of very important matters often depends on doing or not doing something that seems trivial. Even in little things, therefore, you must be cautious and thoughtful.
*Francesco Guicciardini*

Approach the easy as though it were difficult, and the difficult, as though it were easy.
*Baltasar Gracian*

What you are doing do thoroughly.
*French Proverb*

There is no one else who can ever fill your role in the same way, so it's a good idea to perform it as well as possible.
*Humphry Osmond*

Let not the fruit of action be your motive to action. Your business is with action alone, not with the fruit of action.
*The Bhagavad Gita*

Do every act of your life as if it were your last.
*Marcus Aurelius*

Perform all your work for God.
*Swami Muktananda*

Be persistent in good actions.
*Muhammad*

The greatest of all mistakes is to do nothing because you can only do a little. Do what you can.
*Sydney Smith*

Nothing will ever be attempted if all possible objections must first be overcome.
*Samuel Johnson*

A journey of a thousand miles begins with one step.
*Lao Tzu*

Our grand business is not to see what lies dimly at a distance, but to do what lies clearly at hand.
*Thomas Carlyle*

No one knows what he can do till he tries.
*Syrus*

Never refuse or hesitate to take steps against impending dangers...because you think they are too late. Since things often take much longer than expected, because of their very nature and because of the various obstacles they encounter, it very often happens that the steps you have omitted to take, thinking they would have been too late, would have been in time.
*Francesco Guicciardini*

There is nothing impossible to him who will try.
*Alexander the Great*

Doing nothing is sometimes a good remedy.
*Hippocrates*

Knowing is not enough; we must apply. Willing is not enough; we must do.
*Goethe*

Heaven does not help the man who will not act.
*Sophocles*

Your own duty done imperfectly is better than another man's duty done well.
*The Bhagavad Gita*

You, yourself must make the effort.
*Buddha*

Do what you ought, and let what will come of it.
*Italian Proverb*

If and When were planted and Nothing grew.
*Turkish Proverb*

Embark upon an action after careful thought.
*Tiruvalluvar*

Postpone not a good action.
*Irish Proverb*

For us, there is only the trying. The rest is not our business.
*T. S. Eliot*

Satisfaction lies in the effort, not in the attainment. Full effort is full victory.
*Gandhi*

Whatever failures I have known, whatever errors I have committed, whatever follies I have witnessed in private and public life have been the consequence of action without thought.
*Bernhard M. Baruch*

Consult and deliberate before you act, that you may not commit foolish actions.
*Pythagoras*

Let no act be done haphazardly...
*Marcus Aurelius*

In every enterprise consider where you would come out.
*Syrus*

Say and do everything according to soundest reason.
*Marcus Aurelius*

If you're not sure, don't act.
*Bodhidharma*

Our actions are like rhymes: anyone can fit them in to mean what he likes.
*La Rochefoucauld*

To be wise before an action is wisdom. To be wise during the course of an action is cautiousness. To be wise after an action is folly.
*Swami Shivananda*

Take care of the small things.
*Xun Zi*

Action is the proper fruit of knowledge.
*Thomas Fuller*

Prudent men lock up their motives; letting familiars have a key to their heart as to their garden.
*William Shenstone*

It will not do to act recklessly to no purpose and cause trouble for others.
*Gichin Funakoshi*

We should often blush at our noblest deeds if the world were to see all their underlying motives.
*La Rochefoucauld*

In the works of man as in those of nature, what most deserves notice is his intention.
*Goethe*

Each one should test his own actions.
*The Apostle Paul*

A countless number of acts that appear foolish have secret motives that are very wise and weighty.
*La Rochefoucauld*

All actions are judged by the motives that cause them.
*Hadith*

Noble deeds that are concealed are most esteemed.
*Blaise Pascal*

God considered not action, but the spirit of the action. It is the intention, not the deed, wherein the merit or praise of the doer consists.
*Peter Abelard*

I expect to pass through this world but once; any good thing therefore that I can do, or any kindness that I can show to any fellow-creature, let me do it now.
*Stephen Grellet*

Let us do or die.
*Robert Burns*

You must never be inattentive or slacken in your efforts. You must constantly come back to yourself and look seriously within.
*Takuan Soho*

For opportunity knocks at your door just once, and in many cases you have to decide and to act quickly.
*Francesco Guicciardini*

Tackle difficulties when they are easy. Accomplish great things when they are small. Handle what is going to be rough when it is still smooth. Control what has not yet formed its force. Deal with a dangerous situation while it is safe. Manage what is hard while it is soft. Eliminate what is vicious before it becomes destructive.
*Lao Tzu*

Each is responsible for his own actions.
*H. L. Hunt*

If you attempt certain things at the right time, they are easy to accomplish – in fact, they almost get done by themselves. If you undertake them before the time is right, not only will they fail, but they will often become impossible to accomplish even when the time would have been right. Therefore, do not rush things madly, do not precipitate them; wait for them to mature, wait for the right season.
*Francesco Guicciardini*

Perform without fail what you resolve.
*Franklin*

Whatever is worth doing at all, is worth doing well.
*Philip Dormer Stanhope*

You cannot make yourself feel something you do not feel, but you can make yourself do right in spite of your feelings.
*Pearl S. Buck*

66

Bad actions and actions harmful to ourselves are easy to do; what is beneficial and good, that is very difficult to do.

*The Dhammapada*

Do not persist in folly. Some make a duty of failure and having started down the wrong road, think it a badge of character to continue…

*Baltasar Gracian*

Do good deeds with a sense of urgency, before death's approaching rattle strangles the tongue.

*Tiruvalluvar*

Each action is performed from a place of fundamental wisdom…it is completely different from the ordinary behavior of a fool. Even if it looks the same, it is different on the inside.

*Takuan Soho*

How far that little candle throws his beams! So shines a good deed in a naughty world.

*Shakespeare*

Doing what should not be done will bring ruin, and not doing what should be done will also bring ruin.

*Tiruvalluvar*

Do that which will not afflict you afterwards, nor oblige you to repent.

*Pythagoras*

What one has, one ought to use; and whatever he does, he should do with all his might.

*Cicero*

Sins committed in the dark are seen in Heaven like sheets of fire.

*Chinese Proverb*

Do only the things that cannot hurt you, and deliberate before you do them.

*Pythagoras*

It is not only what we do, but also what we do not do, for which we are accountable.

*Moliere*

If we are ever in doubt what to do, it is a good rule to ask ourselves what we shall wish on the morrow that we had done.

*Sir John Lubbock*

There is no act, however trivial, but has its train of consequences.

*Samuel Smiles*

Heed how thou livest. Do not act by day which from the night shall drive thy peace away.

*John Greenleaf Whittier*

Let nothing be done in your life which will cause you fear if it becomes known to your neighbor.

*Epicurus*

Few there are who go to the Further Shore, the rest only run about on the bank.

*The Dhammapada*

Never cut what can be untied.

*Portuguese Proverb*

Only perform such acts as you will not regret later.

*Pythagoras*

A person may cause evil to others not only by his actions but by his inaction, and in either case he is justly accountable to them for the injury.

*John Stuart Mill*

Every wicked act clings to the soul.

*Japanese Proverb*

Shun any actions that will diminish honor.

*Tiruvalluvar*

Carpe diem. (Seize the day)

*Latin Maxim*

In whatever position you find yourself determine first your objective.
*Marshall Ferdinand Foch*

A man without purpose is like a ship without a rudder.
*Thomas Carlyle*

A little neglect may breed great mischief: for want of a nail the shoe is lost; for want of a shoe the horse is lost; for want of a horse the rider is lost.
*Franklin*

Do what you should do when you should do it; don't do what you shouldn't do; and when it is unclear, wait until you are more sure.
*Hadith*

First do it, then say it.
*Russian Proverb*

What we have to learn, we learn by doing.
*Aristotle*

Do ordinary things extraordinarily well.
*John W. Gardner*

It is quality rather than quantity that matters.
*Seneca*

You are your only master.
*Buddha*

When you have to make a choice and don't make it, that in itself is a choice.
*William James*

Evil deeds result in hardships and good deeds result in blessings.
*Bodhidharma*

The wrongdoer is often the person who has left something undone rather than the person who has done something.
*Marcus Aurelius*

Do not slide back two paces when you go one step forward.
*Sai Baba*

When you have a chance to get something you want, take it without hesitation. For things change so often in this world that you cannot be said to have something until you have it in your hand. For the same reason, when something is proposed that displeases you, try to put it off as long as you can. For, as you can see at every hour of the day, time brings accidents that get you out of your troubles.
*Francesco Guicciardini*

Act, and God will act.
*Joan of Arc*

Think before you act.
*Pythagoras*

The secret of success is before attempting anything, be very clear about why you are doing it.
*Guan Yin Tzu*

Actions will be judged according to intentions.
*Muhammad*

The first duty is to behave with purity of intention. It should never be forgotten that every deed and every action is judged according to the intention behind it.
*Sheikh Muzaffer*

Holy Mother Earth, the trees and all nature, are witnesses of your thoughts and deeds.
*Winnebago Saying*

The deed is everything, the glory is naught.
*Goethe*

If one method fails, try another, and suit your methods to the characters you have to deal with.
*Lord Chesterfield*

So whether you eat or drink or whatever you do, do it all for the glory of God.
*The Apostle Paul*

You must carefully consider the merits of any action...
*Takuan Soho*

A person is justified by what he does and not by faith alone.
*The Book of James*

Heaven takes account of a man's actions more quickly than his shadow.
*Chinese Proverb*

If you would rather no one know it don't do it.
*Chinese Proverb*

Even Time, the father of all, cannot undo what has been done, whether right or wrong.
*Pindar*

Not even the gods can undo what has been done.
*Plutarch*

What's done cannot be undone.
*Shakespeare*

Do not turn back when you are just at the goal.
*Syrus*

It will not always be summer: build barns.
*Hesiod*

Even if the stream is shallow, wade it as if it were deep.
*Korean Proverb*

Judge not before you have examined.
*Sakya Pandit*

Always do more than is required of you.
*George S. Patton*

The truly learned are those who apply what they know.
*Hadith*

Do nothing evil, neither in the presence of others, nor privately.
*Pythagoras*

He preaches well that lives well.
*Cervantes*

Keep over your actions an absolute empire; be not their slave, but their master.
*Thomas a' Kempis*

Their words correspond to their actions, and their actions correspond to their words. Are not the best people genuine?
*Confucius*

Devote your entire will power to mastering one thing at a time; do not scatter your energies.
*Paramahansa Yogananda*

To do two things at once is to do neither.
*Syrus*

Do one thing at a time extremely well, then move on to the next.
*Peter Nivio Zarlenga*

Perform all your work with discipline.
*Swami Muktananda*

Never mistake motion for action.
*Ernest Hemingway*

Each step should be as a prayer.
*Plains Indian Maxim*

Each little act is an offering to God.
*Sai Baba*

Thinking is easy, acting is difficult, and to put one's thoughts into action is the most difficult thing in the world.
*Goethe*

Whatever you do, do it to the purpose; do it thoroughly, not superficially. Go to the bottom of things. Any thing half done, or half known, is, in my mind, neither done nor known at all. Nay, worse, for it often misleads.
*Lord Chesterfield*

Do what you can, with what you have, where you are.
*Theodore Roosevelt*

The world is a dangerous place, not because of those who do evil, but because of those who look on and do nothing.
*Einstein*

Trust only movement. Life happens at the level of events, not of words. Trust movement.
*Alfred Adler*

To accomplish great things, we must not only act, but also dream; not only plan, but also believe.
*Anatole France*

One act of beneficence, one act of real usefulness, is worth all the abstract sentiment in the world.
*Ann Radcliffe*

How we spend our days is, of course, how we spend our lives.
*Annie Dillard*

You cannot change anything in your life with intention alone, which can become a watered-down, occasional hope that you'll get to tomorrow. Intention without action is useless.
*Caroline Myss*

In a word, neither death, nor exile, nor pain, nor anything of this kind is the real cause of our doing or not doing any action, but our inward opinions and principles.
*Epictetus*

It's important to know that words don't move mountains. Work, exacting work moves mountains.
*Danilo Dolci*

I prayed for twenty years but received no answer until I prayed with my legs.
*Frederick Douglas*

We are all inclined to judge ourselves by our ideals; others, by their acts.
*Harold Nicolson*

Action indeed is the sole medium of expression for ethics.
*Jane Addams*

Thinking is easy, acting is difficult, and to put one's thoughts into action is the most difficult thing in the world.
*Goethe*

I have always thought the actions of men the best interpreters of their thoughts.
*John Locke*

The superior man is modest in his speech, but excels in his actions.
*Confucius*

It is best to leave alone the things that do not concern you.
*Hadith*

Life is not a matter of holding good cards, but of playing a poor hand well.
*Robert Louis Stevenson*

# HABITS

生

Whatever you would make habitual, practice it; and if you would not make a thing habitual, do not practice it, but habituate yourself to something else.
*Epictetus*

The soul like the body accepts by practice whatever habit one wishes it to contract.
*Socrates*

Men acquire a particular quality by constantly acting in a particular way.
*Aristotle*

We must make automatic and habitual, as early as possible, as many useful actions as we can...in the acquisition of a new habit, we must take care to launch ourselves with as strong and decided initiative as possible...Never suffer an exception to occur till the new habit is securely rooted in your life.
*William James*

It is easier to prevent bad habits than to break them.
*Franklin*

With men as with silk, it is most difficult to change colors once the dye has set.
*Mo Zi*

It is harder to deal with the weeds once they have spread.
*Chinese Proverb*

Ill habits gather by unseen degrees, as brooks become rivers, rivers run to seas.
*John Dryden*

Powerful indeed is the empire of habit.
*Syrus*

The chains of habit are generally too small to be felt until they are too strong to be broken.
*Samuel Johnson*

Habit, if not resisted, soon becomes necessity.
*Saint Augustine*

Habits are at first cobwebs; at last, chains.
*English Proverb*

Trickling water, if not stopped, will become a mighty river.
*Confucius*

Habit becomes one's nature.
*Japanese Proverb*

Habit is a cable; we weave a thread of it each day, and at last we cannot break it.
*Horace Mann*

Old habits have deep roots.
*Norwegian Proverb*

The habits of early life will never be forgotten.
*Indian Proverb*

We are what we repeatedly do.
*Aristotle*

Character is simply habit long continued.
*Plutarch*

The strength of a man's virtue should not be measured by his special exertions, but by his habitual acts.
*Pascal*

Because a human being is so malleable, whatever one cultivates is what one becomes.
*Lao Tzu*

It is easier today to triumph over evil habits than it will be tomorrow.
*Confucius*

Habits change into character.
*Ovid*

Most of the time we are only partially alive. Most of our faculties go on sleeping because they rely on habit which can function without them.
*Marcel Proust*

Habits put us further and further apart.
*Confucius*

Any man who reads too much and uses his own brain too little falls into lazy habits of thinking.
*Einstein*

Right discipline consists, not in external compulsion, but in the habits of mind which lead spontaneously to desirable rather than undesirable activities.
*Bertrand Russell*

The habits of life form the soul, and the soul forms the countenance.
*Honore De Balzac*

The only proper way to eliminate bad habits is to replace them with good ones.
*Jerome Hines*

There are no good or bad habits. All habits are, by definition, bad.
*Jose Bergamin*

Two quite opposite qualities equally bias our minds - habits and novelty.
*Jean de la Bruyere*

Where evil habits are once settled, they are more easily broken than mended.
*Marcus Fabius Quintilian*

Your net worth to the world is usually determined by what remains after your bad habits are subtracted from your good ones.
*Franklin*

# SPEECH

生

Be slow of tongue and quick of eye.
*Cervantes*

Keep the golden mean between saying too much and saying too little.
*Syrus*

You always win by not saying the things you don't need to say.
*Chinese Proverb*

Spend words as efficiently as money.
*Okinawa Proverb*

Your words should be few.
*The Book of Ecclesiastes*

Lower your voice and strengthen your argument.
*Lebanon Proverb*

If you speak too much, you will learn too little.
*Armenian Proverb*

It does not require many words to speak the truth.
*Chief Joseph*

Say but little, and say it well.
*Irish Proverb*

Don't talk too much – your ignorance exceeds your knowledge.
*Spanish Proverb*

Communicate more with yourself than you do with others.
*Danish Proverb*

He knows not when to be silent who knows not when to speak.
*Syrus*

If the bird hadn't sung, it wouldn't have been shot.
*Japanese Proverb*

Silence can be more profitable to you than abundant speech.
*Ptah-Hotep*

A witless man, when he meets with men, had best in silence abide; For no one shall find that nothing he knows, if his mouth is not open too much.
*The Havamal*

Never say more than is necessary.
*Richard Brinsley Sheridan*

When you have nothing to say, say nothing.
*Charles Caleb Colton*

A superior man is modest in his speech, but exceeds in his actions.
*Confucius*

A chattering fool comes to ruin.
*The Book of Proverbs*

Everyone should be quick to listen, slow to speak…
*The Book of James*

Give every man thine ear, but few thy voice.
*Shakespeare*

When words are many, sin is not absent, but he who holds his tongue is wise.
*The Book of Proverbs*

Of what does not concern you say nothing good or bad.
*Italian Proverb*

A master speaks but few words.
*Greek Proverb*

Much talking is the cause of danger. Silence is the means of avoiding misfortune.
*Sakya Pandit*

In dangerous times wise men say nothing.
*Aesop*

We have two ears, but only one mouth, so that we may listen more and talk less.
*Zeno*

Misery is the end of those with unbridled mouths.
*Euripides*

A man who takes pleasure in speaking continuously fools himself in thinking he is not unpleasant to those around him.
*Sophocles*

Speak little; protect your own peace.
*Swami Muktananda*

The words of a man's mouth are as deep waters, and the wellspring of wisdom as a flowing brook.
*The Book of Proverbs*

As the stamp of great minds is to suggest much in few words, so, contrariwise, little minds have the gift of talking a great deal and saying nothing.
*La Rochefoucauld*

Speech is a mirror of the soul: as a man speaks, so is he.
*Syrus*

From a little spark may burst a mighty flame.
*Latin Proverb*

As a vessel is known by the sound, whether it is cracked or not, so men are proved by their speech whether they are wise or foolish.
*Demosthenes*

Brevity charms…it is common knowledge, that the man longwinded is rarely wise, either in what he has at disposal, or in the form of the disposal.
*Baltasar Gracian*

Pleasant words, full of tenderness and devoid of deceit, fall from the lips of virtuous men.
*Tiruvalluvar*

Men of few words are the best men.
*Shakespeare*

If one word is useless so will a thousand be.
*Chinese Proverb*

Everyone speaks as he is.
*Portuguese Proverb*

Those who speak with discretion are respected by mankind.
*Nagarjuna*

Wisdom is knowing when to stop speaking because language is inadequate.
*Chuang Tzu*

Speaking good of something bad is the same as speaking bad of something good.
Leonardo da Vinci

A man of few words will rarely be thoughtless in his speech. He will measure every word.
*Gandhi*

Good words do not last long unless they amount to something.
*Chief Joseph*

Let that which you speak implant true and just things in the life of your children.
*Ptah-Hotep*

Speak to the point or be still.
*The Havamal*

74

With a worse man speak not three words in dispute.

*The Havamal*

The empty vessel makes the greatest sound.

*Shakespeare*

In due season I will speak, not out of season. In truth will I speak, not in falsehood. Gently will I speak, not harshly. To one's profit will I speak, not to one's loss. With kindly intent will I speak, not in anger.

*Buddha*

Speak rightly or be silent.

*Hadith*

No carelessness in your actions. No confusion in your words.

*Marcus Aurelius*

Speak or act with an impure mind and trouble will follow you as the wheel follows the ox that draws the cart.

*Buddha*

Eloquence resides no less in a person's tone of voice, expression, and general bearing than in his choice of words.

*La Rochefoucauld*

One avoids harsh language and abstains from it. One speaks such words as are gentle, soothing to the ear, loving, such words as go to the heart, and are courteous, friendly, and agreeable to many.

*Buddha*

One avoids vain talk and abstains from it. One speaks at the right time, in accordance with facts, speaks what is useful, speaks of the law and the discipline; one's speech is like a treasure, uttered at the right moment, accompanied by understanding, moderate, and full of sense. This is called right speech.

*Buddha*

Never promise more than you can perform.

*Syrus*

If it is not true, don't say it.

*Marcus Aurelius*

It is always better for us to say straight out what we think without wanting to prove much; for all the proofs we put forward are really just variations on our own opinions, and people who are otherwise minded listen neither to one or to the other.

*Goethe*

A gentle response allays wrath; A harsh word provokes anger.

*The Book of Proverbs*

It is not language in itself that is correct, effective, graceful; it is the spirit embodied within language.

*Goethe*

Think before you speak but do not speak all that you think.

*Chinese Proverb*

Whoever wants to enter into an argument must be careful not to say things which no one is arguing about anyway.

*Goethe*

Talking and eloquence are not the same: to speak, and to speak well, are two different things. A fool may talk, but a wise man speaks.

*Ben Johnson*

A gentle word opens the iron gate.

*Bulgarian Proverb*

Man by his speech is known to men.

*The Havamal*

Speech is priceless if you speak with knowledge. Weigh it in your heart before it comes from the mouth.

*Kabir*

The secret of being tiresome is in telling everything.
*Voltaire*

Put away perversity from your mouth; keep corrupt talk far from your lips.
*The Book of Proverbs*

Refrain from speaking evilly.
*Ptah-Hotep*

Study the congregation before preaching your sermon.
*Japanese Proverb*

Do not say things which hurt the feelings of others. Do not speak in a very injurious way.
*Nagarjuna*

The steadfast who speak in few words and politely are very much respected by mankind.
*Nagarjuna*

Do not let any unwholesome talk come out of your mouths, but only what is helpful for building others up according to their needs, that it may benefit those who listen.
*The Apostle Paul*

Would you persuade, speak of interest, not of reason.
*Franklin*

Your mouth should produce nothing but good.
*The Kabbalah*

An injurious truth has no merit over an injurious lie. Neither should ever be uttered.
*Mark Twain*

In your speaking, say only that which is purposeful. Never utter words that lack purpose.
*Tiruvalluvar*

Both speech and silence transgress.
*Zen Maxim*

Speak little, and keep your words truthful and sweet. Say only what benefits others.
*Swami Muktananda*

It is to our good that we keep our words on a high level.
*Little Raven*

Never speak of yourself to others; make them talk about themselves instead; therein lies the whole art of pleasing. Everybody knows it, and everyone forgets it.
*Jules de Goncourt*

Talkers are no good doers.
*Shakespeare*

They think too little who talk too much.
*John Dryden*

People who know little are usually great talkers, while men who know much say little.
*Jean Jacques Rousseau*

If those who do not know were to be silent, discord would collapse.
*Socrates*

Hens that cackle much lay few eggs.
*Estonian Proverb*

People demand freedom of speech to make up for the freedom of thought which they avoid.
*Soren Kierkegaard*

Brisk talkers are usually slow thinkers. There is, indeed, no wild beast more to be dreaded than a communicative man having nothing to communicate.
*Jonathan Swift*

Outside noisy, inside empty.
*Chinese Proverb*

Mastering discretion is greater than employing eloquence.
*Chinese Proverb*

Keep your mouth from being rash, and let not your throat be quick to bring forth speech before God... your words should be few.
*The Book of Ecclesiastes*

He who curbs his tongue shows sense.
*The Book of Proverbs*

Unless you are forced by necessity, be careful in your conversations never to say anything which, if repeated, might displease others. For often, at times and in ways you could never foresee, those words may do you great harm. In this matter, I warn you, be very careful. Even prudent men go wrong here, and it is difficult not to.
*Francesco Guicciardini*

What is said in private is heard like a peal of thunder in heaven.
*Chinese Proverb*

Bushes have ears, walls have eyes.
*Jamaican Proverb*

If either necessity or contempt induces you to speak ill of another, at least be careful to say things that will offend only him. For instance, if you want to insult a particular person, do not speak ill of his country, his family, or his relatives. It is great folly to offend many if you only want to insult one man.
*Francesco Guicciardini*

Let your heart overflow; but restrain your mouth.
*Ptah-Hotep*

The babbling tongue, if a bridle it finds not, often for itself sings ill.
*The Havamal*

For one word a man is often deemed to be wise, and for one word he is often deemed to be foolish. We should be careful indeed of what we say.
*Confucius*

He who guards his lips guards his life, but he who speaks rashly will come to ruin.
*The Book of Proverbs*

Be wary of speech when a learned man listens carefully to you.
*Ptah-Hotep*

A man of knowledge uses words with restraint.
*The Book of Proverbs*

No one would talk much in company if he realized how often he himself mis-understands others.
*Goethe*

Before you utter a word you are the master; afterwards you're a fool.
*Yiddish Proverb*

Suffer not thy tongue to run before thy thought.
*Chilon*

Never exaggerate...avoid offending the truth, in part to avoid the cheapening of your judgment. Exaggeration wastes distinction, and testifies to the paucity of your understanding.
*Baltasar Gracian*

Never trust your tongue when your heart is bitter.
*Samuel J. Hurwitt*

Mark your words, as a matter of caution when with rivals, and as a matter of decency, when with the rest. There is always time to add a word, but none in which to take one back.
*Baltasar Gracian*

Whatever you may fail to guard, guard well your tongue, for flawed speech unfailingly invokes anguish and affliction.
*Tiruvalluvar*

A man should be careful never to tell tales of himself to his own disadvantage; people may be amused, and laugh at the time, but they will be remembered, and brought up against him upon some subsequent occasion.
*Samuel Johnson*

How often do we supply our enemies with the means of our own destruction.
*Aesop*

Your friend has a friend, and your friend's friend has a friend; be discreet.
*The Talmud*

The great thing is to know when to speak and when to keep quiet.
*Seneca the Younger*

I have often repented speaking but never of holding my tongue.
*Xenocrates*

It is a rare fortune of these days that one may think what one likes and say what one thinks.
*Tacitus*

As we must account for every idle word, so we must for every idle silence.
*Franklin*

In regard to his language the superior man is never careless in any respect.
*Confucius*

Exaggerations carry with them a cartload of demons.
*The Book of Changes*

A single word can change a man forever.
*Nan Guo Zi*

The cautious guest who comes to the table speaks sparingly.
*The Havamal*

Do not speak for other men; speak for yourself.
*Thoreau*

A pause giving time for thought was the truly courteous way of beginning and conducting a conversation.
*Chief Luther Standing Bear*

Let not your tongue cut your throat.
*Arabian Proverb*

To listen well is to speak well.
*Ptah-Hotep*

Speak not nor act before you have reflected.
*Pythagoras*

Kindness is to use one's will to guard one's speech and conduct so as not to injure anyone.
*Omaha Teaching*

Always when you are about to say anything, first weigh it in your mind; for with many the tongue outruns the thought. Let there be but two occasions for speech – when the subject is one which you thoroughly know and when it is one on which you are compelled to speak. On these occasions alone is speech better than silence; on all others, it is better to be silent than to speak.
*Isocrates*

Never answer a question until it is asked.
*American legal maxim*

Be always alert against the four failings of speech: speaking falsely, speaking ill of others, backbiting, and talking too much. These tendencies must be controlled.
*Sai Baba*

Brevity is the soul of wit.
*Shakespeare*

Always speak well and truthfully. Never be critical. Never speak truth in a way that hurts others.
*Swami Muktananda*

Never make a promise in haste.
*Gandhi*

Conversation is the art of telling people a little less than they want to know.
*Franklin P. Jones*

Judge the nature of your listeners and speak accordingly.
*Tiruvalluvar*

Things are often spoke and seldom meant.
*Shakespeare*

He who has control over his tongue is greater than a hero in battle.
*Swami Shivananda*

Those who speak ill of others to you will speak ill of you to others.
*German Proverb*

A word can't be recalled once spoken.
*Okinawan Proverb*

I must say it is prudent not to talk about your own affairs except when necessary. And when you do speak of them, say no more than is necessary for your argument or your purpose, always.
*Francesco Guicciardini*

A prudent man keeps his knowledge to himself, but the heart of fools blurts out folly.
*The Book of Proverbs*

Let not your tongue say what your head may pay for.
*Italian Proverb*

Mend your speech a little, lest it may mar your fortune.
*Shakespeare*

Everyone is disgusted by a man who offends one and all with meaningless chatter.
*Tiruvalluvar*

If any man think it a small matter to bridle his tongue, he is much mistaken.
*Plutarch*

Many a time I wish I had held my peace.
*Thomas a' Kempis*

When involved in verbal arguments, it is good to reply, "I will think about it and then answer." Even when stating an opinion, make allowance by saying, "I would like to think it over."
*Tsunetomo Yamamoto*

One offensive word is enough to leave a permanent scar that may become a seed for revenge.
*Taisou*

As he knew not what to say, he swore.
*Byron*

The foolish and wicked practice of profane cursing and swearing is a vice so mean and low that every person of sense and character detests and despises it.
*George Washington*

Let a man never allow an obscene word to pass out of his mouth.
*The Talmud*

Listen much; speak only to the point.
*Bias*

It is better to keep one's mouth shut and be thought a fool than to open it and resolve all doubt.
*Lincoln*

Say little but do much.
*Mishnah, Abot*

What you cannot say briefly you do not know.
*Danish Proverb*

Listen! Or your tongue will make you deaf.
*Cherokee Saying*

It is a great misfortune not to have sense enough to speak well, and judgment enough to speak little.
*Erasmus*

By a lie, a man…annihilates his dignity as a man.
*Immanuel Kant*

Exchange of words with a witless ape you must not ever make.
*The Havamal*

You cannot talk to a frog in a well about the vast sea; he is limited to his area of space. A summer insect has no knowledge of snow; it knows nothing beyond its own season.
*Chiu Shu*

If better were within, better would come out.
*Scottish Proverb*

Whatever is in the heart will come up to the tongue.
*Persian Proverb*

Words are the voice of the heart.
*Confucius*

Those who know do not talk; those who talk do not know.
*Chinese Proverb*

Harsh words and poor reasoning never settle anything.
*Chinese Proverb*

Speak up for the dumb, for the rights of all the unfortunate.
*The Book of Proverbs*

True eloquence consists in saying all that is required and only what is required.
*La Rochefoucauld*

Don't' tell your complaint to one who has no pity.
*Irish Proverb*

To speak of "mere words" is much like speaking of "mere dynamite."
*C. J. Ducasse*

Use soft words and hard arguments.
*English Proverb*

Tact is the art of making a point without making an enemy.
*Isaac Newton*

If indeed you must be candid, be candid beautifully.
*Kahlil Gibran*

When people talk, listen completely. Most people never listen.
*Ernest Hemingway*

Many attempts to communicate are nullified by saying too much.
*Robert Greenleaf*

Words are, of course, the most powerful drug used by mankind.
*Rudyard Kipling*

Talk low, talk slow, and don't say too much.
*John Wayne*

# SILENCE

生

Be able to be alone. Lose not the advantage of solitude, and the society of thyself.
*Sir Thomas Browne*

Cultivate solitude and quiet and a few sincere friends, rather than mob merriment, noise and thousands of nodding acquaintances.
*William Powell*

Sages of the past cultivated introspection and not speech...The eternal bliss of nirvana comes from the mind at rest.
*Bodhidharma*

Conversation enriches the understanding but solitude is the school of genius.
*Edward Gibbon*

The silent man was ever to be trusted, while the man ever ready with speech was never taken seriously.
*Chief Luther Standing Bear*

The quieter you become, the more you can hear.
*Baba Ram Dass*

All the miseries of mankind come from one thing, not knowing how to remain alone.
*Blaise Pascal*

One can acquire everything in solitude – except character.
*Stendhal*

I never found a companion that was so companionable as solitude.
*Thoreau*

Talents are best nurtured in solitude.
*Goethe*

Blessed are those who have chosen their solitude...
*Jesus*

Silence is a great help to a seeker after truth...In the attitude of silence, the soul finds the path in clearer light, and what is elusive and deceptive resolves itself into crystal clearness.
*Gandhi*

I lived in solitude in the country and noticed how the monotony of a quiet life stimulates the creative mind.
*Einstein*

The thoughtful soul to solitude retires.
*Omar Khayyam*

Live in silence.
*Rumi*

I have seen nothing more conducive to righteousness than solitude.
*Dhu-Nun*

Silence is the language of the self-realized.
*Sai Baba*

The heart of a wise man lies quiet like clear water.
*Cameroon Proverb*

No one betrays himself by silence.
*German Proverb*

Quietness is the sign of a sage.
*Sakya Pandit*

Talking comes by nature, silence by understanding.
*English Proverb*

The silent man is most trusted.
*Danish Proverb*

Give thy thoughts no tongue.
*Shakespeare*

To the silent and wise does ill come seldom.
*The Havamal*

When wrathful words arise a closed mouth is soothing.
*Irish Proverb*

Silence can be more profitable to you than abundant speech.
*Ptah-Hotep*

One who keeps silent, endures.
*Swahili Proverb*

Silence is the safest and best.
*The Havamal*

It is wise to be silent when occasion requires...
*Plutarch*

In silence man can most readily preserve his integrity.
*Meister Eckhart*

Silence, when nothing need be said, is the eloquence of discretion.
*Christian Nestell Bovee*

The Indian believes profoundly in silence – the sign of perfect equilibrium. Silence is the absolute poise or balance of body, mind and spirit... What are the fruits of silence? They are self-control, true courage or endurance, patience, dignity, and reverence. Silence is the cornerstone of character.

*Ohiyesa*

Silence in times of suffering is best.
*John Dryden*

Wise men say nothing in dangerous times.
*John Selden*

Let the wise man take refuge in his silence...
*Baltasar Gracian*

Where the river is deepest it makes the least noise.
*Italian Proverb*

Silence is the means of avoiding misfortune.
*Sakya Pandit*

Silence is the safest policy if you are unsure of yourself.
*La Rochefoucauld*

Sometimes you have to be silent in order to be heard.
*Swiss Proverb*

The tree of silence yields the fruit of inner peace.
*Peruvian Proverb*

Where speech will not succeed, it is better to be silent.
*Sri Guru Granth Sahib*

Those with little learning have great pride; grown wise, they are quiet.
*Sakya Pandit*

The man I meet with is not often so instructive as the silence he breaks.
*Thoreau*

Often it is best for the unwise man to sit in silence. His ignorance goes unnoticed unless he tells too much.
*The Havamal*

For the ignorant there is no better rule than silence and if he knew its advantage he would not be ignorant.
*Saadi*

Silence is an answer to a wise man.
*Euripides*

82

Speech is silver, silence is golden.
*Thomas Carlyle*

Silence is the best answer to the stupid.
*Egyptian Proverb*

Silence is a friend who will
never betray.
*Confucius*

Silence is more eloquent than words.
*Thomas Carlyle*

What is silence...It is the Great Mystery.
The holy silence is God's voice.
*Ohiyesa*

If anyone asks what is the shortest and
surest way of disposing ourselves to
advance continually in the spiritual life, I
shall reply that it is to remain carefully self-
gathered within, for it is there properly that
one sees the gleam of the true light.
*Tauler*

To retire from the world, that is to retire
into oneself, is to aid in the dispersion of
all doubts.
*Tolstoy*

The silent person is often worth listening
to.
*Japanese Proverb*

One has great respect for the silent man.
*Ptah-Hotep*

The silent mouth is sweet to hear.
*Irish Proverb*

Keep your mouth shut when required.
*Chinese Proverb*

Great eloquence is silent.
*Lao Tzu*

Into the closed mouth the fly does not get.
*Philippine Proverb*

Silence is deep as Eternity...
*Thomas Carlyle*

The first stage of worship is silence.
*Hadith*

I regret often that I have spoken; never that
I have been silent.
*Syrus*

Be silent, or say something better than
silence.
*German Proverb*

Ordinarily be silent.
*Epictetus*

Two things alone are fitting, instructive
words or a grave silence.
*Buddha*

He who walks in silence quarrels with
nobody.
*African Proverb*

The innermost chamber opens to the man
of silence.
*The Instruction of Ke'gemni*

When two men quarrel, he who is first
silent is the better man.
*The Talmud*

The silence of a stupid man looks like
wisdom.
*Syrus*

The word is silver, silence gold.
*Spanish Proverb*

Silence is wisdom.
*English Proverb*

# SECRETS

生

You surrender your freedom where you deposit your secret.
*Spanish Proverb*

He who tells his secrets to another, makes himself his slave... secrets, therefore, should never be heard, and never spoken.
*Baltasar Gracian*

The only way to keep a secret is to say nothing.
*French Proverb*

Don't tell your secret even to a fence.
*Irish Proverb*

You have everything to gain from managing your affairs secretly. And you will gain even more if you can do it without appearing secretive to your friends.
*Francesco Guicciardini*

A secret that should be concealed in the mind is uttered by a fool.
*Indian Proverb*

Where you tell your secret you surrender your freedom.
*Portuguese Proverb*

What you want to keep secret, tell no one. If you could not control your urge to tell, how can you expect silence from anyone else?
*Seneca*

One may know your secret never a second. If three, a thousand will know.
*The Havamal*

On matters which you would keep secret, speak to no one save when it is equally expedient for you who speak and for those who hear that the facts should not be published.
*Isocrates*

How can we expect somebody else to keep our secret if we cannot keep it ourselves.
*La Rochefoucauld*

Keep whatever you hear to yourself. Never divulge another's secrets.
*Swami Muktananda*

Tell no one anything you want kept secret, for there are many things that move men to gossip. Some do it through foolishness, some for profit, others through vanity, to seem in the know. And if you unnecessarily told your secret to another, you need not be surprised if he does the same, since it matters less to him than to you that it be known.
*Francesco Guicciardini*

It is no secret that is known to three.
*Irish Proverb*

Confide in your friends about matters which require no secrecy as if they were secrets; for if you fail you will not injure yourself, and if you succeed you will have a better knowledge of their character.
*Isocrates*

The ricordo that warns against revealing secrets unless forced by necessity applies to everyone. For you become a slave to those who know your secrets...Even when necessity forces you to tell them, you should do so as late as possible. For when men have lots of time, they will think a thousand and one evil thoughts.
*Francesco Guicciardini*

There is no secret between two people.
*Swahili Proverb*

# ADVICE

Who is a wise man? He who learns of all men.
*The Talmud*

If you wish to know the road up the mountain, ask the man who goes back and forth on it.
*Zenrin*

Write down the advice of him who loves you, though you like it not at present.
*English Proverb*

A wise son heeds his father's instruction.
*The Book of Proverbs*

Ignore an old man's advice and one day be a begger.
*Chinese Proverb*

Many receive advice, only the wise profit from it.
*Syrus*

Counsel before action.
*Dutch Proverb*

To accept good advice is but to increase one's own ability.
*Goethe*

Receive an old man's counsel and a learned man's knowledge.
*Greek Proverb*

Every man, however wise, needs the advice of some sagacious friend in the affairs of life.
*Plautus*

Hear all sides and you will be enlightened. Hear one side, and you will be in the dark.
*Wei Zheng*

He who does not seek advice is a fool.
*Kahlil Gibran*

Ask opinions of those individuals who spend their time studying and learning.
*Taisou*

Seek the counsel of the aged, for their eyes have looked on the faces of the years and their ears have hearkened to the voices of Life. Even if their counsel is displeasing to you, pay heed to them.
*Kahlil Gibran*

Ask advice from those who evidence good self-discipline.
*Leonardo da Vinci*

Never give advice unless asked for it.
German Proverb

We give advice but we do not influence people's conduct.
*La Rochefoucauld*

Being a good listener spares one the burden of giving advice.
*Lao Tzu*

He that gives good advice builds with one hand; he that gives good counsel and example builds with both; but he that gives good admonition and bad example builds with one hand and pulls down with the other.
*Francis Bacon*

Advice is seldom welcome. Those who need it most, like it least.
Samuel Johnson

Give neither advice nor salt until you are asked for it.
English Proverb

If your words are worthless, don't give advice.

*Chinese Proverb*

Don't cast your pearls before swine.

*Jesus*

To give counsel to a fool is like throwing water on a goose.

*Danish Proverb*

Wise men don't need advice. Fools don't take it.

*Franklin*

He is an incorrigible ass who will never listen to others.

*Baltasar Gracian*

Be wary of the man who urges an action in which he himself incurs no risk.

*Joaquin Setanti*

He who builds according to every man's advice will have a crooked house.

*Danish Proverb*

Do not ask advice from the ignorant.

*Indain Proverb*

It is not safe to trust the advice of a man in difficulties.

*Aesop*

If you see a man who shows you what is to be avoided, who administers reproofs, and is intelligent, follow that wise man as you would one who tells of hidden treasures.

*Buddha*

Know or listen to those who know.

*Baltasar Gracian*

Wisdom is found in those who take advice.

*The Book of Proverbs*

Whatever advice you give, be short.

*Horace*

It is rare to find one who can give good counsel.

*Sakya Pandit*

Don't follow any advice, no matter how good, until you feel as deeply in your spirit as you think in your mind that the counsel is wise.

*David Seabury*

Do not ask the way from a blind man.

*Han Wen'gong*

Advice is like snow; the softer it falls the longer it dwells upon and the deeper it sinks into the mind.

*Samuel Coleridge*

Whenever you purpose to consult with anyone about your affairs, first observe how he has managed his own; for he who has shown poor judgment in conducting his own business will never give wise counsel about the business of others.

*Isocrates*

Ask for advice, and then use your brain.

*Norwegian Proverb*

Hear sixty advisers, but be guided by your own convictions.

*The Talmud*

Ask advice from everyone, but act with your own mind.

*Yiddish Proverb*

Harsh counsels have no effect. They are like hammers which are always repulsed by the anvil.

*Clause Adrien Helvetius*

Advice is not disliked because it is advice, but because so few people know how to give it.

*Leigh Hunt*

# ANGER

生

Whoever grows angry amid troubles applies a drug worse than the disease and is a physician unskilled about misfortunes.
*Sophocles*

If you're always getting angry, you'll turn your nature against the Way.
*Bodhidharma*

An angry man opens his mouth and shuts his eyes.
*Cato*

If you are angry, people will focus on your anger instead of your problem.
*Stephen Pollan*

To carry a grudge is like being stung to death by one bee.
*William H. Walton*

Malice drinks one-half of its own poison.
*Seneca*

Holding on to anger is like holding on to a hot coal with the intent of throwing it at someone else; you are the one who gets burned.
*Buddha*

Anger is a killing thing: it kills the man who angers, for each rage leaves him less than he had been before – it takes something from him.
*Louis L'Amour*

A quick-tempered man does foolish things...
*The Book of Proverbs*

Anger makes a fool out of the wise.
*Yiddish Proverb*

When anger speaks, wisdom veils her face.
*Chinese Proverb*

A hot tempered man must pay the penalty; if you rescue him, you will have to do it again.
*The Book of Proverbs*

Anger hears no counsel.
*German Proverb*

In proportion as anger comes, sense departs.
*Turkish Proverb*

Of all the bad things by which mankind are curst, their own bad tempers surely are the worst.
*Richard Cumberland*

The angry and the weak are their own enemies.
*Russian Proverb*

One second of rage, or one of stupid self-satisfaction brings more in its wake than many hours of listlessness. They occasion in a moment, what to correct afterwards requires a lifetime.
*Baltasar Gracian*

An angry man knows no reason.
*Philippine Proverb*

Anger breeds confusion. To be clear-minded you must avoid being angry.
*The Bhagavad Gita*

Angry men make themselves beds of nettles.
*English Proverb*

Anger is the wind that blows out the lamp of the mind.
*Robert G. Ingersoll*

87

My life is in the hands of any fool who makes me lose my temper.
*Dr. John Hunter*

The end of anger is sorrow.
*Seneca*

Frequent fits of anger produce in the soul a propensity to be angry.
*Plutarch*

He that corrects out of passion raises revenge sooner than repentance.
*William Penn*

If a man be his own guard, let him guard himself against rage. Left unguarded, his own wrath will annihilate him.
*Tiruvalluvar*

To be angry is to revenge the faults of others on ourselves.
*Alexander Pope*

A bad temper carries with it its own punishment.
*Aesop*

If you are angry with powerful and malicious men, you will only hurt yourself. What reason is there to be angry with the virtuous and the wise?
*Sakya Pandit*

The angry man will defeat himself in battle as well as in life.
*Samurai Maxim*

Anger brings out destruction.
*Kok Yim Ci Yuen*

Passion often makes fools of the wisest men...
*La Rochefoucauld*

What do evil thoughts of injury do? They injure you and not your enemy.
*Nagarjuna*

The three poisons are greed, anger and delusion.
*Bodhidharma*

The three gates of hell that destroy the self are desire, anger, and greed; one must relinquish all three.
*The Bhagavad Gita*

Anger is a momentary madness, so control your passion or it will control you.
*Horace*

Anger dwells only in the bosom of fools.
*Einstein*

Let us not throw away any of our days upon useless resentment...It is best not to be angry; best, in the next place, to be quickly reconciled.
*Samuel Johnson*

Anger is a weed; hate is the tree.
*Saint Augustine*

Anger is the stone cast into the wasp's nest.
*Indian Proverb*

An angry man is a brother of the madman.
*Lebanese Proverb*

Anger, envy, greed, intolerance – are all so many holes in the pot – and the waters of peace leak out through them.
*Sai Baba*

We must interpret a bad temper as a sign of inferiority.
*Alfred Adler*

Envy, mockery, contempt, anger, revenge, and the other effects which are related to hatred or arise from it, are evil.
*Baruch Spinoza*

Anger begins in folly, and ends in repentance.
*Pythagoras*

Anger shows the character of a man.
*The Talmud*

When angry, count to ten before you speak; if very angry, a hundred.
*Thomas Jefferson*

Forgive, son; men are men, they must err.
*Euripides*

The first rule is to keep an untroubled spirit. The second is to look things in the face and know them for what they are.
*Marcus Aurelius*

Forgiving those who hurt us is the key to personal peace.
*G. Weatherly*

To be wronged is nothing unless you continue to remember it.
*Confucius*

The stupid neither forgive nor forget; the naïve forgive and forget; the wise forgive, but do not forget.
*Thomas Szasz*

The weak can never forgive. Forgiveness is the attribute of the strong.
*Gandhi*

Those who are free of resentful thoughts surely find peace.
*Buddha*

Judge not, that ye be not judged.
*Jesus*

It is in pardoning that we are pardoned.
*Saint Francis of Assisi*

A gentle answer turns away wrath, but a harsh word stirs up anger.
*The Book of Proverbs*

Let us forget and forgive injuries.
*Cervantes*

It is to a man's honor to avoid strife; but every fool is quick to quarrel.
*The Book of Proverbs*

He who conquers his anger has conquered an enemy.
*German Proverb*

If you are patient in one moment of anger, you will escape a hundred days of sorrow.
*Chinese Proverb*

…wise men turn away anger.
*The Book of Proverbs*

To respond immediately to an angry person is like throwing fuel on a fire.
*Spanish Proverb*

When anger arises, think of the consequences.
*Confucius*

The anger of a prudent man never shows.
*Burmese Proverb*

Don't bear a grudge and don't record it.
*Japanese Proverb*

…renounce wrath and observe justice.
*Mahabharata*

A fool gives full vent to his anger, but a wise man keeps himself under control.
*The Book of Proverbs*

Dominate the rush of passion. Yield not to the impulsion of a turbulent heart.
*Fo-shu-hing-tsan-king*

There are no justified resentments.
*Wayne Dyer*

Stop looking for occasions to be offended… Become a person who refuses to be offended by any one, any thing, or any set of circumstances.
*Wayne Dyer*

Whoever suppresseth his anger, when he hath in his power to show it, God will give him a great reward.

*Mohammad*

Do not give way to anger. To master emotions is greater than to be mastered by them.

*Buddha*

Someone despises me. That's their problem. Mine: not to do or say anything despicable. Someone hates me. Their problem. Mine: to be patient and cheerful with everyone... never let the gods catch us feeling anger or resentment.

*Marcus Aurelius*

I was going around the world with the clouds when God spoke to my thoughts and told me to... be at peace with all.

*Cochise*

Perfect peace means that type of peace derived as a result of the absence of desire, anger, greed, and hatred.

*Sai Baba*

Hesitation is the best cure for anger.

*Eric Sevareid*

Master anger.

*Periander of Corinth*

Moderation in temper is always a virtue, but moderation in principle is always a vice.

*Thomas Paine*

Assume silence when anger comes into your consciousness... Do not try to remind yourself of things which will inflame the mind and feelings even more.

*Sai Baba*

As quickly as you discover yourself roused, let intelligence blow the retreat.

*Baltasar Gracian*

The wise conquer by strength, rather than anger. The malevolent fail by their own rage.

*Nagarjuna*

Let cold deliberation take the place of sudden outburst...Fine proof of judgment to keep your head when the fools have lost theirs: every flair of temper is a step downwards from the rational...it is necessary always to ride with the tight rein of attention...

*Baltasar Gracian*

If you quell your own anger, your real enemy will be slain.

*Nagarjuna*

Let your anger set with the sun and not rise again with it.

*Irish Proverb*

Do not bear a grudge from the anger you felt.

*The Kabbalah*

If you allow compassion to spring from your heart, the fire of anger will die right away.

*Thich Nhat Hanh*

Don't try to put out a fire by throwing on more fire. Don't wash a wound with blood!

*Rumi*

After a violent quarrel; be at peace with him that is hostile to you.

*Ptah-Hotep*

Bad temper and anger shorten the years.

*Yiddish Proverb*

Two things never to be angry about: what you can help and what you cannot.

*Scottish Proverb*

A quick temper does not bring success.

*Japanese Proverb*

Neither anger nor fear shall find lodging in your mind.
*Dekanawidah*

Do not harbor anger or vengeance.
*Sai Baba*

Never lose your temper and fly into a rage.
*Swami Muktananda*

Act nothing in a furious passion. It is putting to sea in a storm.
*Thomas Fuller*

Give up anger…Whoever restrains rising anger like a chariot gone astray, that one I call a real driver; others merely hold the reins.
*The Dhammapada*

Be not easily moved to anger.
*The Talmud*

Nothing should disturb you.
*The Kabbalah*

Postpone today's anger until tomorrow.
*Filipino Proverb*

The anger of the prudent never shows.
*Burmese Proverb*

Be aware of bodily anger and control the body… Be aware of the tongues' anger and control your tongue… Be aware of the mind's anger and control your mind.
*The Dhammapada*

Tolerant men are never stupid, and stupid men are never tolerant.
*Chinese Proverb*

Anger and lust are your great enemies; they sap your strength.
*Swami Muktananda*

Be not angry.
*Mohammad*

Anger dies quickly with a good man.
*English Proverb*

God loves those who swallow down their anger.
*Mohammad*

A man who never opens his mouth in anger can close his eyes in peace.
*Chinese Proverb*

The strongest among you is the one who controls his anger.
*Hadith*

He is strong who withholds himself from anger.
*Mohammad*

A heedful man stands always on the side of reason, and never that of passion…
*Baltasar Gracian*

An angry man is again angry with himself when he returns to reason.
*Syrus*

A gentleman does not bear a grudge.
*Chinese Proverb*

If you get angry easily, it may be because the seed of anger in you has been watered frequently over many years, and unfortunately you have allowed it or even encouraged it to be watered.
*Thich Nhat Han*

Only one who can swallow an insult is a man.
*Chinese Proverb*

Anger at a petty offense is unworthy of a superior man, but indignation for a great cause is righteous wrath.
*Mencius*

Anger is the thing that gives no life.
*Hawaiian Proverb*

Forgive all who have offended you, not for them, but for yourself.
*Harriet Uts Nelson*

When a thought of anger or cruelty or a bad and unwholesome inclination awakes in a man, let him immediately throw it from him, let him dispel it, destroy it, prevent it from staying with him.
*Buddhist Maxim*

One must be vigilant, without a moment's carelessness, against cravings, anger, greed, attachment, impatience, hatred, and pride.
*Sai Baba*

To err is human, to forgive divine.
*Alexander Pope*

To give vent occasionally to feelings of pleasure or anger is very comforting, but it is harmful. Therefore, it is wise not to do it, even though it is very hard.
*La Rochefoucauld*

Forget anger toward all who have offended you, for it gives rise to teeming troubles.
*Tiruvalluvar*

Reason is the light in the darkness, as anger is darkness amidst light. Be wise – let reason, not impulse, be your guide.
*Kahlil Gibran*

Get rid of all bitterness, rage and anger, brawling and slander, along with every form of malice. Be kind and compassionate to one another, forgiving each other...
*The Apostle Paul*

Those who remember that we must come to an end in this world, their quarrels cease at once.
*The Dhammapada*

It is no use being in a rage against things, that makes no difference to them.
*Marcus Aurelius*

If you forgive men when they sin against you, your heavenly Father will also forgive you. But if you do not forgive men their sins, your Father will not forgive your sins.
*Jesus*

Consider how much more often you suffer from your anger and grief than from those very things for which you are angry and grieved.
*Marcus Aurelius*

He who loses his temper is in the wrong.
*French Proverb*

In anger the will power is charged with evil and the man becomes dangerous to himself and to others.
*Omaha Maxim*

Never forget God, even for a moment. See only oneness, and anger and fear will depart.
*Swami Muktananda*

Anger brings loss.
*Swahili Proverb*

The evil man fails by being angry.
*Nagarjuna*

Anger is the most dangerous of all passions - the most unmannerly - Reason deliberates before it judges - but anger passes sentence without deliberation...it leaves no place for counsel, or friendship, honesty, or good manners...it falls many times upon the wrong person; upon the innocent, tears all to pieces. It is most certain that we might govern our anger, if we would; for the same thing that angers us at home, gives us no offense at all abroad; and what is the reason? We are patient in one place, and not in another.
*Seneca*

Anger profits nobody.
*The Talmud*

# HATE

生

Nothing on earth consumes a man more quickly than the passion of resentment.
*Nietzsche*

Hatred is self-punishment.
*Hosea Ballou*

The bitter heart eats its owner.
*Tswana Proverb*

That he may vanquish hate, let the disciple live with a soul delivered from all hate and show towards all beings love and compassion.
*Majjhima Nikaya*

The hatred we bear our enemies injures their happiness less than our own.
*Jean Antoine Petit-Senn*

Forgiveness is the finding again of a lost possession – hatred an extended suicide.
*Friedrich Schiller*

Love all and hate none.
*Hazrat Khuaja*

For hatred does not cease by hatred at any time: hatred ceases by love – this is the eternal law.
*The Pali Cannon*

Do not wrong or hate your neighbor, for it is not he that you wrong; you wrong yourself.
*Shawnee Maxim*

Hate is a prolonged form of suicide.
*Harry Emerson Fosdick*

Hatred can be overcome only by love.
*Gandhi*

He who loves according to the guidance of reason strives as much as possible to repay the hatred, anger, or contempt of others toward himself with love and generosity.
*Baruch Spinoza*

Though men devise disunity and deliberately harm you, the highest path plots no hateful retribution.
*Tiruvalluvar*

Let us live in joy, not hating those who hate us. Among those who hate us, we live free of hate.
*The Dhammapada*

Excessive hatred brings us down below the level of those we hate.
*La Rochefoucauld*

The man who has properly understood that everything follows from the necessity of the divine nature, and comes to pass accordingly to the eternal laws and rules of nature, will in truth discover nothing which is worthy of hatred...
*Baruch Spinoza*

He who sees all beings in the Self, and the Self in all beings, hates none.
*The Upanishads*

That man alone can be called truly religious or moral whose mind is not tainted with hatred or selfishness.
*Gandhi*

"They insulted me; they hurt me; they defeated me; they cheated me." In those who harbor such thoughts, hate will never cease. For hate is never conquered by hate. Hate is conquered by love. This is an eternal law.
*The Dhammapada*

Thou shall not hate thy brother in thy heart.
*The Book of Leviticus*

There is no pollution like hatred.
*Buddha*

Let not one even whom the whole world curses, nourish against it any feeling of hatred.
*Sutta Nipata*

He who nurses vengeance is not called wise.
*Swahili Proverb*

It is a sin peculiar to man to hate his victim.
*Tacitus*

To master emotions is greater than to be mastered by them. Hatred is wretched.
*Buddha*

It is easy to hate and it is difficult to love. This is how the whole scheme of things works. All good things are difficult to achieve; and bad things are very easy to get.
*Confucius*

Fear of something is at the root of hate for others, and hate within will eventually destroy the hater.
*George Washington Carver*

The wicked envy and hate; it is their way of admiring.
*Victor Hugo*

Anger may repast with thee for an hour, but not repose for a night; the continuance of anger is hatred, the continuance of hatred turns malice.
*Francis Quarles*

Forget like a child any injury done by somebody immediately. Never keep it in the heart. It kindles hatred.
*Swami Sivananda*

For the poison of hatred seated near the heart doubles the burden for the one who suffers the disease; he is burdened with his own sorrow, and groans on seeing another's happiness.
*Aeschylus*

Hatred is active, and envy passive dislike; there is but one step from envy to hate.
*Goethe*

Hatred is an affair of the heart; contempt that of the head.
*Arthur Schopenhauer*

Hatred is gained as much by good works as by evil.
*Niccolo Machiavelli*

Hatred is settled anger.
*Cicero*

Hatred is something peculiar. You will always find it strongest and most violent where there is the lowest degree of culture.
*Goethe*

Hatred, in the course of time, kills the unhappy wretch who delights in nursing it in his bosom.
*Giacomo Casanova*

94

# REVENGE

生

This is certain, that man that studies revenge keeps his own wounds green, which otherwise would heal and do well.
*Francis Bacon*

If you seek your own good, never wish others ill.
*Swami Muktananda*

Malice sucks up the greater part of its own venom, and poisons itself.
*Montaigne*

Do evil thoughts of retaliation injure oneself or one's enemy?
*Nagarjuna*

You bite in the form of a snake, and suffer as the person bitten.
*Swami Muktananda*

Never thirst for revenge.
*Swami Muktananda*

Abandon your animosities…
*Robert E. Lee*

He who has injured you was either stronger or weaker than you. If weaker, spare him; if stronger, spare yourself.
*Seneca*

Though unjustly aggrieved, it is best to suffer the suffering and refrain from unrighteous retaliation.
*Tiruvalluvar*

Living well is the best revenge.
*George Herbert*

Those who are free of resentful thoughts surely find peace.
*Buddha*

Love your enemies, do good to those who hate you, bless those who curse you, and pray for those who mistreat you, so that you may be children of your Father in Heaven.
*Jesus*

If you avenge yourself in such a manner that the injured party does not know whence the injury comes, you cannot be said to have done it for any reason but hatred or rancor. It is more honest to do it openly and in such a manner that everyone knows who did the deed. For then you can be said to have acted not so much out of hatred or the desire for revenge, as for the sake of honor. That is to say, you have done it so that others will know you are the sort of man who does not take insults.
*Francesco Guicciardini*

If you would be revenged of your enemy, govern yourself.
*Franklin*

If you wish to injure an enemy, make yourself perfect in all good qualities.
*Sakya Pandit*

There is no revenge like unto that of forgetting, for it is to bury them in the dust of their own nothingness.
*Baltasar Gracian*

Forgiveness is the noblest vengeance.
*H. G. Bohn*

Revenge is always the delight of a mean spirit, of a weak and petty mind.
*Juvenal*

There is no revenge so complete as forgiveness.
*Josh Billings*

The remedy for wrongs is to forget them.
*Syrus*

Do not say, "I'll do to him as he has done to me; I'll pay that man back for what he did."
*The Book of Proverbs*

Do not repay anyone evil for evil. Be careful to do what is right in the eyes of everybody. If it is possible, as far as it depends on you, live at peace with everyone. Do not take revenge, my friends, but leave room for God's wrath, for it is written: "It is mine to avenge; I will repay," says the Lord.
*Jesus*

Those who when offended, do not give offense, when hearing slighting remarks, do not retaliate, they are the friends of God, they shall shine forth like the sun in its glory.
*The Talmud*

Doing an injury puts you below your enemy; revenging one makes you but even with him; forgiving it sets you above him.
*Franklin*

Whatever may be the motive of an insult, it is always best to overlook it; for folly scarcely can deserve resentment, and malice is punished by neglect.
*Ben Johnson*

It is often better not to see an insult than to avenge it.
*Seneca*

The best way to avenge yourself is not to become like the wrongdoer.
*Marcus Aurelius*

Seek no revenge for another's wrongdoings; his misdeeds will ultimately exact their own penalty on him.
*Rose Chatcuff*

No man need seek revenge, for his enemy's body will arrive at his door soon enough.
*Chinese Proverb*

Revenge a wrong by forgiving it.
*English Proverb*

The just suffer injury without returning it; they hear reproach without replying; they act only out of love and keep the serenity of their souls in the midst of torments.
*Maimonides*

Revenge is an act of passion; vengeance of justice. Injuries are revenged; crimes are avenged.
*Samuel Johnson*

Revenge is not always sweet, once it is consummated we feel inferior to our victim.
*Emile M. Cioran*

Revenge is often like biting a dog because the dog bit you.
*Austin O'Malley*

Revenge only engenders violence, not clarity and true peace. I think liberation must come from within.
*Sandra Cisneros*

Revenge proves its own executioner.
*John Ford*

Revenge... is like a rolling stone, which, when a man hath forced up a hill, will return upon him with a greater violence, and break those bones whose sinews gave it motion.
*Albert Schweitzer*

Two wrongs will not make one right.
*English Proverb*

# FEAR

生

The Lord is my light and my salvation; whom shall I fear? The Lord is the strength of my life; of whom shall I be afraid?
*The Psalms*

It is folly to fear what one cannot avoid.
*Danish Proverb*

Fear is met and destroyed with courage.
*James F. Bell*

Do the thing we fear, and the death of fear is certain.
*Emerson*

Action conquers fear.
*Peter Nivio Zarlenga*

Knowledge is the antidote for fear.
*Emerson*

You gain strength, courage and confidence by every experience in which you really stop to look fear in the face…You must do the thing which you think you cannot do.
*Eleanor Roosevelt*

Reason and sense remove anxiety.
*Horace*

In the heavenly world is no fear whatsoever.
*The Katha Upanishad*

Where fear is present, wisdom cannot be.
*Lactantius*

All fear is a sign of want of faith.
*Gandhi*

When we understand that we cannot be destroyed, we are liberated from fear.
*Thich Nhat Hanh*

The death of fear is in doing that what you fear to do.
*Sequichie Comingdeer*

Neither anger nor fear shall find lodging in your mind.
*Dekanawidah*

Have a vision not clouded by fear.
*Cherokee Maxim*

Be just, and fear not.
*Shakespeare*

The first duty of man is that of subduing fear. We must get rid of fear, we cannot act until then.
*Thomas Carlyle*

Nothing is so much to be feared as fear.
*Thoreau*

To live in fear and falsehood is worse than death.
*Zend-Avesta*

Still your mind; have no fear.
*Swami Muktananda*

If evils come not, then our fears are vain; and if they do, fear but augments the pain.
*Franklin*

Do not let your hearts be troubled, and do not let them be afraid.
*Jesus*

…continuous fear does not allow one to be happy.
*Boethius*

He who fears something gives it power over him.
*Moorish Proverb*

He who fears he will suffer, already suffers from his fear.

*Montaigne*

Fear causes anger and wastes time, health, and character.

*Sai Baba*

One has to face fear or forever run from it.

*Hawk*

Fear makes the wolf bigger than he is.

*German Proverb*

Knowing that the individual self, eater of the fruit of action, is the universal Self, maker of past and future, he knows he has nothing to fear.

*The Katha Upanishad*

I fear no man, and I depend on the Great Spirit.

*Koniaronk*

We are more often frightened than hurt; and suffer more from imagination than from reality.

*Seneca*

There is no worse counselor than fear.

*Chilean Proverb*

All fear is bondage.

*English Proverb*

Who lives in fear will never be a free man.

*Horace*

Fear is the proof of a degenerate mind.

*Virgil*

Fear always springs from ignorance.

*Emerson*

Whenever we're afraid, its because we don't know enough. If we understood enough, we would never be afraid.

*Earl Nightingale*

That which is feared lessons by association.

*Nagarjuna*

Collective fear stimulates herd instinct, and tends to produce ferocity toward those who are not regarded as members of the herd.

*Bertrand Russell*

Death is not the biggest fear we have; our biggest fear is taking the risk to be alive — the risk to be alive and express what we really are.

*Don Miguel Ruiz*

Fear grows in darkness; if you think there's a bogeyman around, turn on the light.

*Dorothy Thompson*

Nothing in life is to be feared. It is only to be understood.

*Marie Curie*

Ultimately we know deeply that the other side of every fear is a freedom.

*Marilyn Ferguson*

Worry gives a small thing a big shadow.

*Swedish Proverb*

Fear arises from impotence of mind, and therefore is of no service to reason...

*Baruch Spinoza*

# YOUR
# MIND
# &
# THOUGHTS

生

We are the masters of our fate, the captains of our souls, because we have the power to control our thoughts.
*Napoleon Hill*

The mind is the master over every kind of fortune: itself acts in both ways, being the cause of its own happiness and misery.
*Seneca*

We are what we think. All that we are arises with our thoughts. With our thoughts, we make the world.
*Buddha*

Thoughts are energy. And you can make your world or break your world by your thinking.
*Susan L. Taylor*

It is the mind that rules the body.
*Sojourner Truth*

The universe is change; our life is what our thoughts make it.
*Marcus Aurelius*

What the mind of man can conceive and believe, the mind of a man can achieve.
*Napoleon Hill*

As a man thinks in his heart, so is he.
*The Book of Proverbs*

Mindfulness means to be present, to be aware of what is going on… Every mental formation – anger, jealousy, despair, etc. – is sensitive to mindfulness the way all vegetation is sensitive to sunshine.
*Thich Nhat Hanh*

What a man thinks of himself, that it is which determines, or rather indicates his fate.
*Thoreau*

Human beings, by changing the inner attitudes of their minds, can change the outer aspects of their lives.
*William James*

It is the mind that wins or loses.
*Nepalese Proverb*

You should keep your mind pure, for what a person thinks, he becomes – this is the eternal mystery.
*The Maitri Upanishad*

Understand that what you think about expands.
*Wayne Dyer*

Change your thoughts, and you change your world.
*Norman Vincent Peale*

It is the mind that leads a man to power, not strength of body.
*Crow Maxim*

Your thoughts create your reality because your thoughts determine how you respond to situations in your daily life.
*Wayne Dyer*

Who is ready to believe, is easy to deceive.
*German Proverb*

It is the mind which makes a man, or mars him.
*Sai Baba*

Like water which can clearly mirror the sky and the trees only so long as its surface is undisturbed, the mind can only reflect the true image of the Self when it is tranquil and wholly relaxed.
*Indra Devi*

Do not let trifles disturb your tranquility of mind…Ignore the inconsequential.
*Grenville Kleiser*

When his mind is tranquil, perfect joy comes to the man of discipline.
*The Bhagavad Gita*

Quiet minds cannot be perplexed or frightened but go on in fortune or misfortune at their own private pace, like a clock during a thunderstorm.
*Robert Louis Stevenson*

Don't let worldly thoughts and anxieties trouble your mind.
*Ramakrishna*

Even as the troubled surface of rolling waters cannot properly reflect the full moon, but only gives broken images of it, so a mind troubled by the desires and passions of the world cannot fully reflect the light of the Ineffable.
*Ramakrishna*

The best cure for the body is a quiet mind.
*Napoleon Bonaparte*

Quiet your mind; leave the world to its fate.
*Swami Muktananda*

Only in quiet waters things mirror themselves undistorted. Only in a quiet mind is adequate perception of the world.
*Margolis*

Control your mind and remain undisturbed. That is the secret of perfect peace.
*Sai Baba*

Concentrate all your thoughts upon the work at hand.
*Alexander Graham Bell*

A concentrated mind will pierce a rock.
*Japanese Proverb*

When by a constant practice a man is capable of effecting mental concentration, then wherever he may be, his mind will always lift itself above his surroundings and will repose in the Eternal.
*Ramakrishna*

The superior man is committed to focus.
*Hsun Tzu*

Control the mind. Restrain it with discipline; never let it distract you. Make your intellect one-pointed; keep agitation far away.
*Swami Muktananda*

As the fletcher whittles and makes straight his arrows, so the master directs his straying thoughts.
*Buddha*

When we direct our thoughts properly, we can control our emotions.
*W. Clement Stone*

Be master of your thoughts.
*The Book of Golden Precepts*

Sharpen your mind and show your dignity.
*Matsura Seizan*

Be master of the mind rather than mastered by the mind.
*Zen Maxim*

Still waters run deep.
*English Proverb*

The treasure that is precious is the quality of evenmindedness in all situations.
*Sai Baba*

There is no thought in any mind, but it quickly tends to convert itself into a power.
*Emerson*

Whatever we plant in our subconscious mind and nourish with repetition and emotion will one day become reality.
*Earl Nightingale*

Let no man imagine that he has no influence. Whoever he may be, and wherever he may be placed, the man who thinks becomes a light and a power.
*Henry George*

All that a man does outwardly is but the expression and completion of his inward thought. To work effectively, he must think clearly; to act nobly, he must think nobly. Intellectual force is a principle element of the soul's life, and should be proposed by every man as the principle end of his being.
*William Ellery Channing*

Every single thought you have can be assessed in terms of whether it strengthens or weakens you.
Wayne Dyer

Actions are made of thoughts.
*The Upanishads*

Thoughts are forces.
*Ralph Waldo Trine*

The very first step in self-restraint is the restraint of thoughts....There is nothing more potent than thought – deed follows word and word follows thought.
*Gandhi*

No problem can withstand the assault of sustained thinking.
*Voltaire*

The mind is its own place, and in itself can make heaven of hell, a hell of heaven.
*John Milton*

Belief is easier than investigation.
*Serbo-Croatian Proverb*

Little things affect little minds.
*Benjamin Disraeli*

If you wish to know the mind of a man, listen to his words.
*Chinese Proverb*

Think much, say little.
*French Proverb*

It is a man's own fault, it is from want of use, if his mind grows torpid in old age.
*Samuel Johnson*

Thinking is not knowing.
*Portuguese Proverb*

Think today and speak tomorrow.
*English Proverb*

People who think deeply and seriously are on bad terms with the public.
*Goethe*

The more and the better one thinks about things, the better they are understood and carried out.
*Francesco Guicciardini*

Think like a man of action, act like a man of thought.
*Thomas Mann*

It is we who entertain thoughts, and it is we ourselves who repulse them.
*Gandhi*

Who dares not speak his free thoughts is a slave.
*Euripides*

It is clear that thought is not free if the professions of certain opinions make it impossible to earn a living.
*Bertrand Russell*

Iron rusts from disuse, stagnant water loses its purity and in cold weather becomes frozen; so does inaction sap the vigors of the mind.
*Leonardo da Vinci*

The primary indication…of a well ordered mind is a man's ability to remain in one place and linger in his own mind.
*Seneca*

Second thoughts are ever wiser.
*Euripides*

A small brain cannot comprehend the workings of a great mind.
*Zhuang Zi*

Thinking is the talking of the soul with itself.
*Plato*

Whatever is noble, whatever is right, whatever is pure, whatever is lovely, whatever is admirable – if anything is excellent or praiseworthy – think about such things.
*The Apostle Paul*

Think, and most about that which is most important…An intelligent man thinks about everything, though with discrimination, digging deepest where there are prospect, and treasure.
*Baltasar Gracian*

Let your thought not be separated from God.
*The Kabbalah*

Think of three things: whence you came, where you are going, and to whom you must account.
*Franklin*

It is not enough to have a good mind. The main thing is to use it well.
*Rene Descartes*

Give yourself more to thinking than to reading, for reading without thinking will make you vain, rather than knowing.
*Charles Simmons*

Think for yourself. Whatever is happening at the moment, try to think for yourself.
*Jean Ribound*

Every head must do its own thinking.
*African Proverb*

No man has the right to constrain another to think like himself.
*Giordano Bruno*

Think with the whole body.
*Taisen Deshimaru*

All truly wise thoughts have already been thought thousands of times; but to make them truly ours, we must think them over again honestly, until they take root in our personal experience.
*Goethe*

It is wrong always, everywhere, and for everyone, to believe anything upon insufficient evidence.
*William James*

No man can think for me.
*Chief Joseph*

The mind is a clear and polished mirror and our continual duty is to keep it pure and never allow dust to accumulate on it.
*Hindu Maxim*

Their life is so practical, so confused, so excited, so active, that little time remains for them for thought.
*Tocqueville*

If people are taught how to think and not always what to think, a false concept will be guarded against.
*Georg Christoph Lichenberg*

Think for yourselves and let others enjoy the right to do the same.
*Voltaire*

The landscape lies far and fair within, and the deepest thinker is the farthest traveled.
*Thoreau*

The evil life is really the thoughtless life...
The Dhammapada

Think of who created thought...Move outside the tangle of fear-thinking.
*Rumi*

Speak not nor act before you have reflected.
*Pythagoras*

Guard your thoughts like a city gate.
*Chinese Proverb*

A vacant mind is open to all suggestions as hollow building echoes all sounds.
*Chinese Proverb*

The whole dignity of man is in thought. Labor then to think right.
*Pascal*

A bad thought is the most dangerous of thieves.
*Buddha*

Have no vicious thoughts.
*Confucius*

Guard well your thoughts; our thoughts are heard in Heaven.
*Edward Young*

Sinful thoughts are even more dangerous than sin itself.
*The Talmud*

Ponder all things, and establish high your mind.
*Pythagoras*

When a thought rises in us, let us see whether it has not its roots in the inferior worlds.
*Antoine the Healer*

The highest possible stage in moral culture is when we recognize that we ought to control our thoughts.
*Charles Darwin*

Except our own thoughts, there is nothing absolutely in our power.
*Rene Descartes*

In courage desire greatness and in thought desire carefulness.
*Liu Su*

Like the chariot yoked with wild horses, the wise should restrain the mind attentively.
*The Upanishads*

As rain makes its way into a badly roofed house, so passion makes its way into an unreflecting mind.
*The Dhammapada*

If we are not responsible for the thoughts that pass our doors, we are at least responsible for those we admit and entertain.
*Charles B. Newcomb*

Do not be thoughtless; watch your thoughts.
*The Dhammapada*

The mind should be kept independent of any thoughts that arise within it.
*The Diamond Sutra*

The mind deludes itself. In matters of the mind, you must stay on your guard.
*Takuan Soho*

Banish bad thoughts from your mind.
*Swami Muktananda*

103

Mediocre minds usually dismiss anything which reaches beyond their own understanding.
*La Rochefoucauld*

This mind is the source of all virtues.
*Bodhidharma*

Whatever a man does he must do first in his mind.
*Albert Szent-Gyorgyi*

Think ahead…it is reflection and foresight that assure freedom to life.
*Baltasar Gracian*

No matter where the body is, the mind is free to go elsewhere.
*W. H. Davies*

Deliberate often – decide once.
*Latin proverb*

By performing all actions with a balanced mind, you will free yourself from conflicts.
*Swami Muktananda*

The superior man keeps his mind on his own duties.
*Confucius*

It is necessary to the happiness of man that he be mentally faithful to himself.
*Thomas Paine*

Whatever you think, be sure it is what you think.
*T. S. Eliot*

Freethinkers are those who are willing to use their minds without prejudice and without fearing to understand things that clash with their own customs, privileges, or beliefs. This state of mind is not common, but it is essential for right thinking; where it is absent, discussion is apt to become worse than useless.
*Tolstoy*

We are what we think.
*Buddha*

This inner speech, your thoughts, can cause you to be rich or poor, loved or unloved, happy or unhappy, attractive or unattractive, powerful or weak…
*Ralph Charell*

Thought is the sculptor who can create the person you want to be.
*Thoreau*

Your thoughts are the source of virtually everything in your life.
*Wayne Dyer*

All that we are is the result of what we have thought: It is founded on our thoughts and is made up of our thoughts.
*The Dhammapada*

The things you think about determine the quality of your mind. Your soul takes on the color of your thoughts.
*Marcus Aurelius*

Could we rightly comprehend the mind of man nothing would be impossible to us upon the earth.
*Paracelsus*

If you wear shoes to protect your feet, the pebbles in the road cannot affect you. Likewise, if you remain calm under all conditions, the pebbles in the road of life cannot cause you pain.
*Narada*

You must be single minded. Drive for the one thing on which you have decided.
*George S. Patton*

As you change your handwriting by constant practice, so you can change your mind pattern by constant practice of positive and constructive thoughts.
*Swami Shivananda*

I can control my thoughts as necessary; then how can I be troubled? What is outside my mind means nothing to it.
*Marcus Aurelius*

Restrain the mind. Withdraw the sense; master them.
*Swami Muktananda*

Mediocre minds usually dismiss anything which reaches beyond their own understanding.
*La Rochefoucauld*

The secret of patience is to do something else in the meantime.
*Spanish Proverb*

A man who does not think for himself does not think at all.
*Oscar Wilde*

In order to improve the mind, we ought less to learn than to contemplate.
*Rene Descartes*

One's mind should not agonize over anything.
*Kok Yim Ci Yuen*

Every thought you entertain is a force that goes out; and every thought comes back laden with its kind.
*Ralph Waldo Trine*

Each time that the mobile and inconstant mind goes outward, it should be controlled, brought back into oneself and made obedient.
*The Bhagavad Gita*

Great thoughts reduced to practice become great acts.
*William Hazlitt*

Be careful of your thoughts; they are the beginning of your acts.
*Lao Tzu*

To return, time after time, to the same annoyance, is a sort of insanity.
*Baltasar Gracian*

A man would do well to carry a pencil in his pocket, and write down the thoughts of the moment. Those that come unsought for are commonly the most valuable, and should be secured, because they seldom return.
*Francis Bacon*

They are never alone that are accompanied with noble thoughts.
*Sir Philip Sidney*

To enjoy good health, to bring true happiness to one's family, to bring peace to all, one must first discipline and control one's own mind.
*Buddha*

Rule your mind, or it will rule you.
*Horace*

Keep your mind pure, clean, and content.
*Swami Muktananda*

# EDUCATION
# &
# KNOWLDEGE

Learning through practice is like pushing a cart up a hill: if you slack off, it will slip backwards.

*Japanese Proverb*

In all our studies, continuous concentration and diligence are the hallmark of success.

*Gichin Funakoshi*

Learning is not attained by chance; it must be sought for with ardor and attended to with diligence.

*Abigail Adams*

Question attentively, and then meditate at leisure over what you have learned.

*Confucius*

Apply your heart to instruction and your ears to words of knowledge.

*The Book of Proverbs*

All wish to be learned but no one is willing to pay the price.

*Juvenal*

Knowledge is a treasure, but practice is the key to it.

*English Proverb*

Not the school, nor the teachers, but the student is the preponderant factor in education.

*James Weldon Johnson*

The force of attention properly guided and directed towards the inner life allows us to analyze our soul and will shed light on many things. The forces of the mind resemble scattered rays; concentrate them and they illuminate everything. That is the sole source of knowledge we possess; to conquer this knowledge there is only one method, concentration.

*Vivekananda*

He that studies books alone will know how things ought to be; and he who studies men will know how they are.

*Charles Caleb Colton*

The man who graduates today and stops learning tomorrow is uneducated the day after.

*Newton D. Baker*

I wasn't born knowing what I teach you. Being fond of the past, I sought it through diligence.

*Confucius*

As a human being one should train one's mind and one's ability to the fullest.

*Miyamoto Musashi*

It is much better to learn one thing well than to know many things partially.

*Menander*

Without attention while you are learning, all the time you employ at your book is thrown away; and your shame will be the greater if you should be ignorant, when you had such opportunities of learning. An ignorant man is insignificant and contemptible; nobody cares for his company, and he can just be said to live, and that is all.

*Lord Chesterfield*

Study as if you were never to master it; as if in fear of losing it.

Confucius

What you don't understand, you don't possess.

*Goethe*

The recipe for perpetual ignorance is: Be satisfied with your opinions and content with your knowledge.

*Elbert Hubbard*

Scholarly knowledge tends, on the whole, to be remote from life and only return to it via a detour.

*Goethe*

How different theory is from practice! So many people understand things well but either do not remember or do not know how to put them into practice! The knowledge of such men is useless. It is like having a treasure stored in a chest without ever being able to take it out.

*Francesco Guicciardini*

There is a difference between memory and understanding.

*Montaigne*

People who don't understand and think they can do so without study are no different from those deluded souls who can't tell white from black.

*Bodhidharma*

It is still worse to be ignorant of your ignorance.

*Saint Jerome*

Knowledge is not enough, we have to apply it.

*Goethe*

You have to study a great deal to know a little.

*Charles de Secondat*

The worth of a book is to be measured by what you carry away from it.

*James Bryce*

Ignorance is the starless, moonless night of the mind.

*Chinese Proverb*

The most useful piece of learning for the uses of life is to unlearn what is untrue.

*Antisthenes*

Knowledge, if it does not determine action, is dead to us.

*Plotinus*

A child educated only at school is an uneducated child.

*George Santayana*

All that you learn, learn perfectly.

*Tiruvalluvar*

He who loves to ask extends his knowledge.

*Shu Ching*

The intellect of most men is barren.

*Thoreau*

It is just as important to have studied men, as to have studied books.

*Baltasar Gracian*

An education isn't how much you have committed to memory. It's knowing where to go to find out what you need to know, and it's knowing how to use the information you get.

*William Feather*

I have never let my schooling interfere with my education.

*Mark Twain*

Learning without thought is labor lost.

*Confucius*

Education is the ability to listen to almost anything without losing your temper or your self-confidence.

*Robert Frost*

Education is that which remains when one has forgotten everything he learned in school.

*Einstein*

Whoever acquires knowledge but does not practice it is as one who ploughs but does not sow.

*Saadi*

Is anyone educated in whom the powers of conscious reasoning are untrained or underdeveloped, however great may be the store of accumulated knowledge?

*Joseph Odell*

The supreme end of education is expert discernment in all things – the power to tell the good from the bad, the genuine from the counterfeit, and to prefer the good and the genuine to the bad and the counterfeit.

*Samuel Johnson*

The only real security that a person can have in this world is a reserve of knowledge, experience, and ability.

*Henry Ford*

Real education must ultimately be limited to men who insist on knowing. The rest is mere sheep-herding.

*Ezra Pound*

Seek knowledge from the cradle to the grave.

*Muhammad*

Learn all you can.

*Sitting Bull*

Knowledge is power.

*Thomas Hobbes*

Educated men are as much superior to uneducated men as the living are to the dead.

*Aristotle*

Only the educated are free.

*Epictetus*

In the fields of observation chance favors only the prepared mind.

*Louis Pasteur*

All men naturally desire knowledge.

*Aristotle*

Knowledge and human power are synonymous.

*Francis Bacon*

There is no knowledge that is not power.

*Emerson*

With knowledge, doubt increases.

*Goethe*

Knowledge is of two kinds; we know a subject ourselves or we know where we can find information upon it.

*Samuel Johnson*

The discerning heart seeks knowledge.

*The Book of Proverbs*

Learning is a treasure which follows its owner everywhere.

*Chinese Proverb*

Education is the best provision for old age.

*Aristotle*

Those who do not study are simply cattle in clothing.

*Chinese Proverb*

The more a person knows the more luck he will have.

*Burmese Proverb*

Chance favors the trained mind.

*Louis Pasteur*

First learn, then form opinions.

*Hebrew Proverb*

Questioning is the door to knowledge.
*Irish Proverb*

Knowledge is the antidote to fear.
*Emerson*

Treasures laid up in the mind do not decay.
*Japanese Proverb*

The best weapon is education.
*Welsh Proverb*

Knowledge is, indeed, that which, next to virtue, truly and essentially raises one man above another.
Joseph Addison

Among all the things, knowledge is truly the best thing.
*The Hitopadesa*

Education...is the great equalizer of conditions of men.
*Horace Mann*

Knowledge is long, and life is short, and he who does not know, does not live.
*Baltasar Gracian*

What does a frog in the well know about oceans?
*Chinese Proverb*

Learned men delight in knowledge; the ignorant do not.
*Sakya Pandit*

Genius without education is like silver in the mine.
*Franklin*

Know, or hearken to him who knows. You cannot live without knowledge, either your own, or borrowed, but there be many who do not know that they know nothing, and others who think that they know, but know nothing.
*Baltasar Gracian*

It is the mark of an educated mind to be able to entertain a thought without accepting it.
*Aristotle*

The doer alone learneth.
*Friedrich Nietzsche*

Failure is instructive. The person who really thinks learns quite as much from his failures as from his successes.
*John Dewey*

Though a man be learned, if he does not apply his knowledge, he resembles the blind man, who, lamp in hand, cannot see the road.
*Nagarjuna*

Acquire knowledge though you may die next year... It will become a precious thing.
*Sakya Pandit*

Wear your learning, like your watch, in a private pocket. Do not pull it out merely to show that you have one. If asked what time it is, tell it; but do not proclaim it hourly and unasked, like the watchman.
*Lord Chesterfield*

What is now proved was once only imagined.
*William Blake*

A man's learning is an imperishable and precious wealth. No other possession is as golden.
*Tiruvalluvar*

The future belongs to those who prepare for it.
*Emerson*

Like unproductive barren land is the man who has neglected learning. All that can be said about him is that he exists.
*Tiruvalluvar*

109

If a man empties his purse into his head, no one can take it from him.
*Franklin*

As men are to wild beast, so are the masters of brilliant texts to other men.
*Tiruvalluvar*

The important thing is not to stop questioning.
*Einstein*

There is hardly any place or any company where you may not gain knowledge, if you please; almost everybody knows some one thing, and is glad to talk about that one thing.
*Lord Chesterfield*

The years teach much which the days never know.
*Emerson*

The whole object of education is or should be, to develop the mind. The mind should be a thing that works.
*Sherwood Anderson*

We should not take heed to what many say but what the specialist will say.
*Plato*

The child will always attend more to what a teacher does than to what the same teacher says.
*William James*

Self-education is, I firmly believe, the only kind of education there is.
*Isaac Asimov*

True teaching liberates the student from his teacher.
*Ernest Holmes*

A teacher affects eternity; he can never tell where his influence stops.
*Henry Brooks Adams*

A teacher who can arouse a feeling for one single good action…accomplishes more than he who fills our memory with rows on rows of natural objects, classified with name and form.
*Goethe*

You cannot teach a man anything. You can only help him to discover it within himself.
*Galileo Galilei*

Much does he gain who learns when he loses.
*Italian Proverb*

Without character – devoted rugged strength of soul – no man has the right to teach…The great teacher never fails to leave a profound mark on young men and women.
*David Starr Jordan*

The true aim of every one who aspires to teach should be, not to impart his own opinions, but to kindle minds.
*Frederick William Robertson*

The highest function of the teacher consists not so much in imparting knowledge as in stimulating the pupil in its love and pursuit.
*Henri Frederic Amiel*

Better than a thousand days of diligent study is one day with a great teacher.
*Japanese Proverb*

A student should not be taught more than he can think about.
*Alfred North Whitehead*

When the student is ready, the master appears.
*Japanese Proverb*

Teachers open the door, but you must enter by yourself.
*Chinese Proverb*

110

The superior man uses learning as a means of self-improvement. The lesser man uses learning as a means of showing off.
Hsun Tzu

Educate the heart – educate the heart. Let us have good men.
Hiram Powers

Education begins at home. You can't blame the school for not putting into your child what you don't put into him.
Geoffrey Holder

The very spring and root of honesty and virtue lie in good education.
Plutarch

The foundation of every state is the education of its youth.
Diogenes

A human being is not, in any proper sense, a human being till he is educated.
Horace Mann

The ignorant classes are the dangerous classes.
Henry Ward Beecher

Education has for its object the formation of character.
Herbert Spencer

Liberty cannot be preserved without a general knowledge among the people.
John Adams

Education is a danger…Every educated person is a future enemy.
Nazi Leader

Ignorance is rough; and nothing refines more than learning.
Baltasar Gracian

What is not increased diminishes.
Rumi

Intelligence is worth more than all the possessions in the world.
Minokhired

The ignorant is a child.
Laws of Manu

The plague of ignorance overflows all the earth.
Hermes

There is a stain worse than all stains, the stain of ignorance.
The Dhammapada

Ignorance is the field in which all other difficulties grow.
Patanjali

There is in this world no purification like knowledge.
The Bhagavad Gita

He alone is truly a man who is illumined by the light of the true knowledge.
Ramakrishna

To educate a man in mind and not in moral is to educate a menace to society.
Theodore Roosevelt

Knowledge without integrity is dangerous and dreadful.
Samuel Johnson

The more intelligent a man is, the more originality he discovers in men. Ordinary men see no difference between men.
Pascal

The ignorant in comparison of the learned, are worse than dead.
Stefano Guazzo

Education begins the gentleman, but reading, good company, and reflection must finish him.
John Locke

Learning is the only wealth tyrants cannot despoil… The true wealth of a nation lies not in its gold or silver but in its learning, wisdom, and in the uprightness of its sons.
*Kahlil Gibran*

Knowledge without wisdom is a load of books on the back of an ass.
*Japanese Proverb*

Character development is the great, if not sole, aim of education.
*O'Shea*

The fate of empires depends on the education of youth.
*Aristotle*

The preservation of the means of knowledge among the lowest ranks is of more importance to the public than all the property of all the rich men in the country.
*John Adams*

Learning is as necessary to a nation as water is to a fish.
*Chinese Proverb*

Of what use is a man who has acquired little knowledge?
*Sakya Pandit*

In the conditions of modern life the rule is absolute; the race which does not value trained intelligence is doomed.
*Alfred North Whitehead*

If a nation expects to be ignorant and free, in a state of civilization, it expects what never was and never will be.
*Thomas Jefferson.*

Be not proud because you are learned.
*Ptah-Hotep*

Teach the young people how to think, not what to think.
Sidney Sugarman

A man may be so much of everything that he is nothing of anything.
*Samuel Johnson*

The true university of these days is a collection of books.
*Thomas Carlyle*

Public schools are the nurseries of all vice and immorality.
*Henry Fielding*

The mind which studies is not disquieted.
*Lao Tzu*

A single conversation across the table with a wise man is worth a month's study of books.
*Chinese Proverb*

The test of a first-rate intelligence is the ability to hold two opposed ideas in the mind at the same time, and still retain the ability to function.
*F. Scott Fitzgerald*

Man's mind stretched to a new idea never goes back to its original dimensions.
*Oliver Wendell Holmes*

What greater or better gift can we offer the republic than to teach and instruct our youth?
*Cicero*

I am learning all the time. The tombstone will be my diploma.
*Eartha Kitt*

The mistakes of others are good teachers.
*Estonian Proverb*

There is no education like adversity.
*Benjamin Disraeli*

The roots of education are bitter but the fruit is sweet.
*Aristotle*

Nothing in education is so astonishing as the amount of ignorance it accumulates in the form of inert facts.

*Henry Brooks Adams*

Education... has produced a vast population able to read but unable to distinguish what is worth reading.

*George Macaulay Trevelyan*

We are too civil to books. For a few golden sentences we will turn over and actually read a volume of four or five hundred pages.

*Emerson*

Read first the best books. The important thing for you is not how much you know, but the quality of what you know.

*Desiderius Erasmus*

Learning which does not advance each day will daily decrease.

*Chinese Proverb*

Live always in the best company when you read.

*Sydney Smith*

The things taught in schools and colleges are not an education, but the means of education.

*Emerson*

We are drowning in information and starving for knowledge.

*Rutherford Rogers*

It is far better for us to possess only a few maxims of philosophy that are nevertheless always at our command and in use than to acquire vast knowledge that notwithstanding serves no useful purpose.

*Demetrius the Cynic*

To be conscious that you are ignorant is a great step to knowledge.

*Benjamin Disraeli*

We should not ask who is the most learned, but who is the best learned.

*Montaigne*

Education is the power to think clearly, the power to act well in the world's work, and the power to appreciate life.

*Brigham Young*

We do not know one-millionth of one percent about anything.

*Thomas Edison*

The more a man enters the light of understanding, the more aware he is of his own ignorance.

*Symeon the New Theologian*

Most of the learning in use, is of no great use.

*Franklin*

Learning colors a man more than the deepest dye.

Chinese Proverb

Even noble souls can become corrupted with wrong education.

*Plato*

A wise man should have money in his head, but not in his heart.

*Jonathan Swift*

Whoso neglects learning in his youth, loses the past and is dead for the future.

*Euripides*

A man without knowledge, a world in darkness.

*Baltasar Gracian*

Learning acquired in youth is an inscription on stone.

*Indian Proverb*

Learning is wealth that can't be stolen.

*Philippine Proverb*

The only thing more expensive than education is ignorance.
*Franklin*

Those who know the least obey the best.
*Farquhar*

It is only the ignorant who despise education.
*Syrus*

Employ all the leisure you have in listening to the well-informed; so you shall learn without difficulty what they have learned by long labor.
*Isocrates*

To know is to control.
*Scott Reed*

Men learn while they teach.
*Seneca*

It is a miracle that curiosity survives formal education.
*Einstein*

The illiterate of the 21st century will not be those who cannot read and write, but those who cannot learn, unlearn, and relearn.
*Alvin Toffler*

Children require guidance and sympathy far more than instruction.
*Annie Sullivan*

We cannot hold a torch to light another's path without brightening our own.
*Ben Sweetland*

The aim of education should be to teach us rather how to think, than what to think, rather to improve our minds, so as to enable us to think for ourselves, than to load the memory with thoughts of other men.
*Bill Beattie*

Human beings, who are almost unique in having the ability to learn from the experience of others, are also remarkable for their apparent disinclination to do so.
*Douglas Adams*

114

# TIME & LIFE

生

Don't hurry, don't worry. You're only here for a short visit. So be sure to stop and smell the flowers.
*Walter C. Hagen*

It's a very short trip. While alive, live.
*Malcolm Forbes*

We should live as though our life would be both long and short.
*Bias*

Brief is the space of life allotted to you; pass it as pleasantly as you can, not grieving from noon till eve.
*Euripides*

Since it is not granted to live long, let us transmit to posterity some memorial that we have at least lived.
*Pliny the Younger*

Life is short, and time passes quickly...
*Vincent van Gogh*

Live mindful of how brief your life is.
*Horace*

Ah! The clock is always slow; it is later than you think.
*Robert W. Service*

Men flourish only for a moment.
*Homer*

Our existence as embodied beings is purely momentary. What are a hundred years in eternity?
*Gandhi*

A day is long, but a lifetime is short.
*Russian Proverb*

Man's life is like a drop of due on a leaf.
*Slovenian Proverb*

Life is like a bubble that may vanish at anytime.
*Philippine Proverb*

Time passes like the wind.
*Portuguese Proverb*

Don't you know that your life, whether long or short, consists of only a few breaths?
*Farid-uddin Attar*

Life is short and we have never too much time for gladdening the hearts of those who are traveling the dark journey with us.
*Henri Frederick Amiel*

Write it on your heart that every day is the best day in the year.
*Emerson*

Nothing is swifter than the years.
*Ovid*

The life given to us by nature is short; but the memory of a well-spent life is eternal.
*Cicero*

Life is short and no one knows what the next moment will bring.
*Dogen*

Time in its flight passes secretly and deceives living beings; nothing goes more swiftly than the years.
*Leonardo da Vinci*

The cost of a thing is the amount of what I will call life which is required to be exchanged for it, immediately or in the long run.
*Thoreau*

What is life? It is the flash of a firefly in the night. It is the breath of a buffalo in the wintertime. It is the little shadow which runs across the grass and loses itself in the sunset.

*Crowfoot*

This is how you should think of this fleeting world: a star at dawn, a bubble in a stream; a flash of lightning in a summer cloud, a flickering lamp, a phantom, and a dream.

*Buddha*

We are always getting ready to live, but never living.

*Emerson*

The fool with all his other thoughts has this also: he is always getting ready to live.

*Epicurus*

There are those of us who are always about to live. We are waiting until things change, until there is more time, until we are less tired, until we get a promotion, until we settle down – until, until, until. It always seems as if there is some major event that must occur in our lives before we begin living.

*George Sheehan*

For of all sad words of tongue or pen, the saddest are these: "It might have been!"

*John Greenleaf Whittier*

Do not boast about tomorrow, for you do not know what a day may bring forth.

*The Book of Proverbs*

Do not worry about tomorrow, for tomorrow will worry about itself. Each day has enough trouble of its own.

*Jesus*

Defer not till tomorrow to be wise. Tomorrow's sun to thee may never rise.

*William Congreve*

He who postpones the hour of living rightly is like the rustic who waits for the river to run out before he crosses.

*Horace*

We are not alive for very long, so we should not put off listening to the inner voice of our heart.

*Lieh Tzu*

Once a person says "This is who I really am, what I am all about, what I was really meant to do," it is easier to decide how to spend one's time.

*David Viscott*

Life will always be to a large extent what we ourselves make it.

*Samuel Smiles*

Return to the root and you will find the meaning.

*Sengstan*

True wisdom lies in gathering the precious things out of each day as it goes by.

*E. S. Bouton*

Live rather than avoid death.

*Jean-Jacques Rousseau*

Use your eyes as if tomorrow you would be stricken blind.

*Helen Keller*

Live all you can; it's a mistake not to. It doesn't so much matter what you do in particular, so long as you have your life. If you haven't had that, what have you had?

*Henry James*

Take a deep breath of life and consider how it should be lived.

*Don Quixote's Creed*

The art of life lies in a constant re-adjustment to our surroundings.

*Okakura Kakuzo*

116

Know the true value of time; snatch, seize, and enjoy every moment of it. No idleness, no laziness, no procrastination: never put off till tomorrow what you can do today.
*Lord Chesterfield*

Do your best every day and your life will gradually expand into satisfying fullness.
*Horatio W. Dresser*

The moment that any life, however good, stifles you, you may be sure it isn't your real life.
*Arthur Christopher Benson*

Since we all must die sooner or later, let us enjoy life while we can!
*Otoma no Tabito*

Beware lest you lose the substance by grasping at the shadow.
*Aesop*

The days come and go like muffled and veiled figures sent from a distant friendly party, but they say nothing, and if we do not use the gifts they bring, they carry them as silently away.
*Emerson*

The proper function of man is to live, not to exist. I shall not waste my days in trying to prolong them.
*Jack London*

I recommend you to take care of the minutes, for the hours will take care of themselves.
*Philip Dormer Stanhope*

One should build as if one were to live forever, and live as if one were to die tomorrow.
*German Proverb*

Let not the opportunity pass, for it may not return.
*Kuai Tong*

Begin at once to live, and count each separate day as a separate life.
*Seneca*

The greatest use of a life is to spend it on something that outlasts it.
*William James*

Spend your time in nothing which you know must be repented of.
*Richard Baxter*

Living is not the good, but living well. The wise man therefore lives as long as he should, not as long as he can. He will think of life in terms of quality, not quantity.
*Seneca*

No life ever grows great until it is focused, dedicated, and disciplined.
*Harry Emerson Fosdick*

To be able to look back on one's past life with satisfaction is to live twice.
*Macus Valerius Martialis*

The whole life of man is but a point of time; let us enjoy it, therefore, while it lasts, and not spend it to no purpose.
*Plutarch*

You will find rest from vanities if you go about every act in life as though it were your last.
*Marcus Aurelius*

This world is like snow exposed to sun, which continues to melt until it disappears altogether, while the next life is like a precious stone that never passes away.
*Al-Ghazzali*

Live all you can; it's a mistake not to.
*Henry James*

Life is not a problem to be solved, but a reality to be experienced.
*Soren Kierkegaard*

It matters not where or how far you travel, the farther commonly the worse, but how much alive you are.
*Thoreau*

When you are intent upon a journey, after you purchase your ticket and board the train – whether you sit quietly, lie down, read or meditate, the train will take you to the destination. So, too, at birth each living thing has received a ticket to the event of death and is now on the journey.
*Sai Baba*

Life demands to be lived.
*H. L. Mencken*

Remember this, that very little is needed to make a happy life.
*Marcus Aurelius*

Death twitches my ear. "Live," he says, "I am coming."
*Virgil*

You must live your life from start to finish; no one can do it for you.
*Hopi Maxim*

Our lives are in the hands of the Great Spirit.
*Tecumseh*

Everybody who lives dies. But not everybody who dies has lived.
*Dhaggi Ramanashi*

Live as you will wish to have lived when you are dying.
*Christian Furchtegott Gellert*

Time is the most valuable thing a man can spend.
*Diogenes*

A man who dares to waste one hour of life has not discovered the value of life.
*Charles Darwin*

One life: a little gleam of time between two eternities.
*Thomas Carlyle*

As is a tale, so is life; not how long it is but how good it is, is what matters.
*Seneca*

Every day is a page of your life's history.
*Arabian Proverb*

New day, new fate.
*Bulgarian Proverb*

Live as if you had at once to say farewell to life and the time you now have were an unexpected gift.
*Marcus Aurelius*

Life is either a daring adventure or nothing.
*Helen Keller*

To Zen, time and eternity are one.
*D. T. Suzuki*

A life well spent is long.
*Leonardo da Vinci*

Do not look back on happiness or dream of it in the future. You are only sure of today; do not let yourself be cheated out of it.
*Henry Ward Beecher*

Life is not lost by dying; life is lost minute by minute, day by day, in all the thousand small, uncaring ways.
*Stephen Saint Vincent Benet*

He is blessed over all mortals who loses no moment of the passing life.
*Thoreau*

Lost time is never found again.
*Franklin*

Seize the day, put no trust in tomorrow.
*Horace*

This day will not come again. Each minute is worth a priceless gem.
*Takuan Soho*

Wasting of time is an abomination to the spirit...
*Ptah-Hotep*

To lose time is most displeasing to him who knows most.
*Dante*

For time lost may never be recovered.
*Geoffrey Chaucer*

Misspending a man's time is a kind of self-homicide.
*George Savile*

Lost, yesterday, somewhere between sunrise and sunset, two golden hours, each set with sixty diamond minutes. No reward is offered, for they are gone forever.
*Horace Mann*

Procrastination is the thief of time.
*Edward Young*

Life is half spent before we know what it is.
*English Proverb*

Time does not wait for man.
*Japanese Proverb*

Like the waves of a river that flow slowly on and return never back, the days of human life pass and come not back again.
*Buddha*

Idle men are dead all their life long.
*Thomas Fuller*

Most of the time we are only partially alive. Most of our faculties go on sleeping because they rely on habit which can function without them.
*Marcel Proust*

Brothers, time waits for no man... So don't waste your time. Life is precious; if you miss this chance, it may take a billion eons before you receive a human body again.
*Yun-Men*

Once gone, a day will never return. Therefore, one must strive to do good in every moment.
*The Jain scriptures*

The days and the months are indeed passing, and the years play no favorites!
*Confucius*

If we do not enjoy ourselves today, the days and months will pass us by.
*The Book of Songs*

Even if someone lives to be a hundred years old, a great part of that time is spent in the infirmities of childhood and old age. A huge part is consumed by sleep at night and worries by day. Much of it is wasted in sorrow and fear. Only a small fraction remains for enjoying being alive – so don't waste it.
*Tang Zhu*

I expect to pass through this life but once. If, therefore, there be any kindness I can show or any good thing I can do to any fellow being, let me do it now and not defer or neglect it, as I shall not pass this way again.
*William Penn*

We never live; we are always anticipating living.
*Voltaire*

It has been my observation that most people get ahead during the time that others waste.
*Henry Ford*

There is no distance on this earth as far away as yesterday.
*Robert Nathan*

Employ your time well if you mean to gain leisure.
*Franklin*

The mass of men lead lives of quiet desperation.
*Thoreau*

It is one life whether we spend it in laughing or weeping.
*Japanese Proverb*

Reckon not upon a long life: think every day the last, and live always beyond thy account.
*Sir Thomas Browne*

What time would it be if all the clocks were stopped?
*Zen Question*

To live is the rarest thing in the world. Most people exist, that is all.
*Oscar Wilde*

The shorter my possession of life is, the deeper and fuller I must make it.
*Montaigne*

When something enjoyable comes your way – enjoy it completely!
*Lieh Tzu*

Time is the most valuable thing that a man could waste.
*Theophrastus*

Does't thou love life? Then do not squander time, for that is the stuff life is made of.
*Franklin*

Time is a shadow that passes away.
*Apocrypha*

Life is the childhood of our immortality.
*Goethe*

Life on earth passes away, it is not long.
*The Teaching for Merikare*

Life is short.
*Hippocrates*

Time is flying never to return.
*Virgil*

The short bloom of our brief and narrow life flies fast away. While we are calling for flowers and wine and women, old age is upon us.
*Juvenal*

Is not life a hundred times too short for us to bore ourselves?
*Friedrich Nietzsche*

As if you could kill time without injuring eternity!
*Henry David Thoreau*

Talk of the year ahead and the devil laughs.
*Japanese Proverb*

Man is born to live and not to prepare to live.
*Boris Pasternak*

Use your eyes as if tomorrow you would be stricken blind.
*Helen Keller*

Every day should be passed as if it were to be our last.
*Syrus*

While we live, let us live.
*D. H. Lawrence*

Oh, how much good time you lose over a bad matter!
*Seneca*

Use your best vase today, for tomorrow it may, perchance, be broken.
*The Talmud*

For years fleet away with the wings of the dove.
*Byron*

Time is the wisest counselor.
*Pericles*

Live dangerously and you live right.
*Goethe*

May you live all the days of your life.
*Jonathan Swift*

Each day a day goes by.
*Carlo Goldoni*

While living I want to live well.
*Geronimo*

You may delay, but time will not.
*Franklin*

Plunge boldly into the thick of life!
*Goethe*

Opportunities lost can never be regained.
*Pliny the Elder*

Even a full life is short.
*The Katha Upanishad*

Life is short, time is fleeting.
*Sai Baba*

If we could see the miracle of a single flower clearly, our whole life would change.
*Buddha*

Life is just a chance to grow a soul.
*A. Powell Davies*

Life is a process of becoming, a combination of states we have to go through. Where people fail is that they wish to elect a state and remain in it. This is a kind of death.
*Anais Nin*

Life without liberty is like a body without spirit.
*Kahlil Gibran*

There are as many nights as days, and the one is just as long as the other in the year's course. Even a happy life cannot be without a measure of darkness and the word 'happy' would lose its meaning if it were not balanced by sadness.
*Carl Jung*

Only when we are no longer afraid do we begin to live.
*Dorothy Thompson*

That it will never come again is what makes life so sweet.
*Emily Dickinson*

The life I touch for good or ill will touch another life and that in turn another, until who knows where the trembling stops or in what far place my touch will be felt.
*Frederick Buechner*

A useless life is an early death.
*Goethe*

# The NOW

生

If not now, then when?
*Hillel*

Seize this very moment!
*John Anster*

Enjoy the present hour.
*Martial*

You must concentrate upon and consecrate yourself wholly to each day, as though a fire were raging in your hair.
*Deshimaru*

To sensible men, every day is a day of reckoning.
*John W. Gardner*

Act well at the present moment, and you have performed a good action to all eternity.
*Johann Kasper Lavater*

Time is not a line, but a series of now-points.
*Taisen Deshimaru*

Reality is a staircase going neither up nor down, we don't move; today is today, always is today.
*Octavio Paz*

This is not a dress rehearsal. This is it.
*Tom Cunningham*

Seize the Day.
*Horace*

If we are ever to enjoy life, now is the time, not tomorrow or next year...Today should always be our most wonderful day.
*Thomas Dreier*

He who lives in the present lives in eternity.
*Ludwig Wittgenstein*

With the past, I have nothing to do; nor with the future. I live now.
*Emerson*

Every man's life lies within the present, for the past is spent and done with, and the future is uncertain.
*Marcus Aurelius*

Look not mournfully into the past, it comes not back again. Wisely improve the present, it is thine.
*Henry Wadsworth Longfellow*

Now is all we have.
*Wayne Dyer*

The secret of health for both mind and body is...to live the present moment wisely and earnestly.
*Buddha*

We cannot put off living until we are ready. The most salient characteristic of life is its coerciveness: it is always urgent, "here and now," without any possible postponement. Life is fired at us point-blank.
*Jose Ortega y Gasset*

One instant is eternity; eternity is in the now.
*Wu-Men*

We do not remember days, we remember moments.
*Cesare Pavese*

Live now, believe me, wait not till tomorrow; gather the roses of life today.
*Pierre de Ronsard*

122

The world is an eternal present, and the present is now; what was is no more and who can say what will come or whether tomorrow morning the dawn will arise.
*Anaximander*

The present is the most precious moment. Use all the forces of your spirit not to let that moment escape you.
*Tolstoy*

Whatever does not annoy you in the present is a meaningless pain in expectation.
*Epicurus*

One of the illusions of life is that the present hour is not the critical decisive hour. Write it on your heart that every day is the best day of the year. He only is right who owns the day, and no one owns the day who allows it to be invaded by worry, fret and anxiety. Finish every day, and be done with it. You have done what you could.
*Emerson*

"Today" means boundless and in-exhaustible eternity.
*Philo*

God himself culminates in the present moment.
*Thoreau*

The present is all we have to live in; or to lose.
*Marcus Aurelius*

Respond to the constantly changing circumstances in the immediacy of the moment. What else can you do?
*Chuang Tzu*

Tao is not far away from where you are. Those who go looking for it elsewhere always return to here and now.
*Lao Tzu*

You must live in the present, launch yourself on every wave, find your eternity in each moment.
*Thoreau*

There exists only the present instant...a Now which always and without end is itself new. There is no yesterday, or any tomorrow, but only Now, as it was a thousand years ago, and as it will be a thousand years later.
*Meister Eckhart*

Be fully in the moment; open yourself to the powerful energies dancing around you.
*Ernest Hemmingway*

The whole of life is now, is today, is this eternal moment.
*Rumi*

One today is worth two tomorrows.
*Franklin*

Enjoy the present hour, be mindful of the past; and neither fear nor wish the approaches of the last.
*Franklin*

No one can confidently say that he will still be living tomorrow.
*Euripides*

One must not ruin the things present with desire for things absent.
*Epicurus*

Never leave that till tomorrow which you can do today.
*Franklin*

Life is what happens to us while we are making other plans.
*Thomas La Mance*

Study as if you were to live forever. Live as if you were to die tomorrow.
*Isidore of Seville*

While walking, examine the walking; while sitting, the sitting.
*Zen Maxim*

Tomorrow life is too late; live today.
*Martial*

Delay not to seize the hour.
*Aechylus*

Act – act in the living present!
*Henry Wadsworth Longfellow*

It's not that "today is the first day of the rest of my life," but that now is all there is of my life.
*Hugh Prather*

Yesterday is ashes; tomorrow wood. Only today does the fire burn brightly.
*Eskimo Proverb*

The present is an eternal now.
*Abraham Cowley*

The future is purchased by the present.
*French Proverb*

Bear tomorrow's sorrow tomorrow, drink today's wine today.
*Chinese Proverb*

You cannot step twice into the same river, for other waters are continually flowing on.
*Heraclitus*

Each of us lives only now, this brief instant.
*Marcus Aurelius*

By always saying, "Further on!"
He's become estranged from "here":
Because of a false fantasy
He's driven from reality.
*Rumi*

Fill the unforgiving minute with sixty seconds worth of distance run.
*Rudyard Kipling*

Every second is of infinite value.
*Goethe*

"Now" is the watchword of the wise.
*Charles H. Spurgeon*

Nothing is worth more than this day.
*Goethe*

We waste our lives in procrastination.
*Epicurus*

Tomorrow I will live, the fool does say.
*Martial*

How wonderful it is that nobody need wait a single moment before starting to improve the world.
*Anne Frank*

The best things in life are nearest: Breath in your nostrils, light in your eyes, flowers at your feet, duties at your hand, the path of right just before you. Then do not grasp at the stars, but do life's plain, common work as it comes, certain that daily duties and daily bread are the sweetest things in life.
*Robert Louis Stevenson*

Life can be found only in the present moment. The past is gone, the future is not yet here, and if we do not go back to ourselves in the present moment, we cannot be in touch with life.
*Thich Nhat Hanh*

Every moment of life is the last.
*Basho*

124

# EXPERIENCE

Any experience can be transformed into something of value.
*Vash Young*

You know more of the road by having traveled it than by all the conjectures and descriptions in the world.
*William Hazlitt*

Has any man ever attained to inner harmony by pondering the experience of others? Not since the world began! He must pass through the fire.
*Norman Douglas*

You cannot create experience, you undergo it.
*Albert Camus*

The knowledge of the world is only to be acquired in the world and not in a closet.
*Lord Chesterfield*

The person who has lived the most is not the one with the most years, but the one with the richest experience.
*Jean Jacques Rousseau*

There are many truths of which the full meaning cannot be realized until personal experience has brought it home.
*John Stuart Mill*

Wisdom is the daughter of experience.
*Leonardo da Vinci*

Nothing is a waste of time if you use the experience wisely.
*Auguste Rodin*

Shun the teachings of those speculators whose arguments are not confirmed by experience.
*Leonardo da Vinci*

It isn't quite the same thing to comment on the bull ring and to be in the bull ring.
*Spanish Proverb*

The Creator made us to learn by trial and error.
*Mohican Elder*

Having the idea is not living the reality, of anything.
*Rumi*

Without experience we will not gain full knowledge.
*Chinese Proverb*

Young men should realize that experience teaches a great deal – and more to large minds than to small.
*Francesco Guicciardini*

The successful man will profit from his mistakes and try again in a different way.
*Dale Carnegie*

Experience is a good school, but the fees are high.
*Heinrich Heine*

Anything that we have to learn to do we learn by the actual doing of it.
*Aristotle*

Everyone is a prisoner of his own experiences. No one can eliminate prejudges – just recognize them.
*Edward Roscoe Murrow*

There are but few proverbial sayings that are not true, for they are all drawn from experience itself, which is the mother of all sciences.
*Cervantes*

The words printed here are concepts. You must go through the experiences.
*Saint Augustine*

You learn to speak by speaking, to study by studying, to run by running, to work by working; and just so, you learn to love by loving. All those who think to learn in any other way deceive themselves.
*Saint Francis de Sales*

Good judgment comes from experience, and often experience comes from bad judgment.
*Rita Mae Brown*

A man who carries a cat by the tail learns something he can learn in no other way.
*Mark Twain*

Every moment is an experience.
*Jake Roberts*

Experience is one thing you can't get for nothing.
*Oscar Wilde*

Experience is the child of thought, and thought is the child of action.
*Benjamin Disraeli*

Few people even scratch the surface, much less exhaust the contemplation of their own experience.
*Randolph Bourne*

I think we are a product of all our experiences.
*Sanford I. Weill*

The only source of knowledge is experience.
*Einstein*

People become house builders through building houses, harp players through playing the harp.
*Aristotle*

126

# RELATIONSHIPS

If you live in the river you should make friends with the crocodile.
*Indian Proverb*

Don't spit in the well: you'll be thirsty by and by.
*Russian Proverb*

People, by and large, will relate to the image you project.
*Chyatee*

Don't neglect your own field to plow your neighbor's.
*English Proverb*

He labors in vain who tries to please everybody.
*Latin Proverb*

Keep away from people who try to belittle your ambition. Small people always do that, but the really great make you feel that you, too, can become great.
*Mark Twain*

If you call one wolf, you invite the pack.
*Bulgarian Proverb*

Try to please all and you end by pleasing none.
*Aesop*

Take good care of the bull if you wish him to plough well for you.
*Greek Proverb*

You can't please everybody.
*Aesop*

To feed men and not to love them is to treat them as if they were barnyard cattle. To love them and not to respect them is to treat them as if they were household pets.
*Mencius*

The seven principles of conduct with people are forbearance, forgiveness, humility, generosity, compassion, good counsel, justice, and fairness.
*Al-Sadiq*

No snowflake in an avalanche ever feels responsible.
*Stanislaus Leszcynski*

If you are seeking the favor of men, be careful never to give a flat refusal to anyone who makes a request of you. Rather you should give evasive answers, for it may happen that someone who asked for something will not need it later. Or else circumstances may arise that make your excuses seem convincing. Furthermore, many men are foolish and easily swayed by words. Even without doing what you could not or would not do, you can often leave a person well satisfied by answering him cleverly, whereas if you had refused him outright, he would dislike you no matter how things turned out subsequently.
*Francesco Guicciardini*

Deal gently with people, and be not harsh; cheer them and condemn them not.
*Mohammad*

See yourself in others, then whom can you hurt? What harm can you do?
*Buddha*

The person who knew you when you were young will seldom respect you as an adult.
*Lebanon Maxim*

Let no one imagine that people have been waiting for him as a savior!
*Goethe*

People generally – and inexperienced men always – are more easily moved by the hope of gain than by the danger of loss. And yet the contrary should be true, for the desire to keep is more natural than the desire to gain.

*Francesco Guicciardini*

Though few men can do it, it is very wise to hide your displeasure with others, so long as it does you no shame or harm. For it often happens that later you will need the help of these people, and you hardly get it if they already know you dislike them. It has happened to me very often that I have had to seek help from someone towards whom I was very ill disposed. And, he believing the contrary, or at least not knowing the truth, served me without hesitation.

*Francesco Guicciardini*

In every way evil company should be abandoned, because it gives occasion to passion, wrath, folly, dissipation, loss of decision, and loss of energy. These propensities are at first a bubbling froth, but they become as if oceans.

*The Narada Sutra*

You can better rely on someone who needs you or who happens to have a common objective than on someone you have benefited. For men are generally not grateful. If you do not want to be deceived, make your calculations according to this rule.

*Francesco Guicciardini*

Let your good judgment rule and ponder seriously before breaking bonds that have served you well.

*Pushmataha*

Most people are other people. Their thoughts are someone else's opinions, their lives a mimicry, their passions a quotation.

*Oscar Wilde*

A man who dislikes everybody is much more unhappy than a man nobody likes.

*La Rochefoucauld*

Do not trust to the cheering, for those persons would shout as much if you and I were going to be hanged.

*Oliver Cromwell*

Men will never disappoint us if we observe two rules:
1. To find out what they are;
2. To expect them to be just that

*George Iles*

Love all, trust few.

*Shakespeare*

A righteous man is cautious in friendship.

*The Book of Proverbs*

Beware of him who regards not his reputation.

*English Proverb*

Beware of the person with nothing to lose.

*Italian Proverb*

Don't put your affairs into the hands of someone who has failed to manage his own.

*Maltese Proverb*

It is the foolish sheep that makes the wolf its confessor.

*Italian Proverb*

Vows made in storms are forgotten in calms.

*English Proverb*

Think not those faithful who praise all your words and actions, but those who kindly reprove your faults.

*Socrates*

Avoid those who always praise you.

*African Proverb*

For be aware that if the companion be defiled, also the one rubbing up against them must be defiled, even though one happens to be clean.

*Epictetus*

When we live habitually with the wicked, we become necessarily their victims or their disciples; on the contrary, when we associate with virtuous we form ourselves in imitation of their virtues, or at least lose, every day, something of our faults.

*Agapet*

You are judged by the company you keep.

*Aesop*

Associate not with the wicked man, even if you can learn from him.

*The Talmud*

A man with bad qualities infects others.

*Sakya Pandit*

If you touch pitch, it will stick to your fingers; even so, if you associate with evil companions, you will acquire their vices.

*The Talmud*

The swan does not belong among hawks…or a clever man among fools.

*Nagarjuna*

If a man is by nature wicked, avoid him even though he is learned.

*Sakya Pandit*

The rotten apple spoils his companion.

*Franklin*

Do not mix with undesirable company or cultivate bad habits just for the sake of having fun.

*Sai Baba*

Stay away from the bad people and cultivate a preference for wise people.

*Takuan Soho*

No reply should be given to the words of the wicked. Be at a great distance from them; that is for your own good. If need be, break off relationships with such people.

*Sai Baba*

Fly from the company of the wicked – fly and turn not back.

*Plato*

It is no great misfortune to have one's kindness repaid by ingratitude, but it is intolerable to be beholden to a scoundrel.

*La Rochefoucauld*

Whoever associates with fools suffers a long time.

*The Dhammapada*

Embrace the snake and it will bite you.

*Bulgarian Proverb*

Keep your distance from unvirtuous people.

*Takuan Soho*

Who with the wolf associates, to howl learns.

*Spanish Proverb*

If you lie down with dogs you'll rise with fleas.

*George Herbert*

A man is known by the company he keeps.

*M. Coverdale*

Those who play with cats must expect to be scratched.

*Cervantes*

Every man is like the company he is wont to keep.

*Euripides*

Good and Evil will never mix.

*Swahili Proverb*

Keep far away from an evil neighbor, and don't become friendly with the wicked.
*Mishnah, Abot*

Ever associate with the good. Associate not with the wicked man, even if thou canst learn from him.
*The Talmud*

Keep good company, and you'll be counted one of them.
*Scottish Proverb*

By associating with good and evil persons a man acquires the virtues and vices which they possess, even as the wind blowing over different places takes along good and bad odors.
*The Panchatantra*

Associate yourself with men of good quality if you esteem your own reputation, for 'tis better to be alone than in bad company.
*George Washington*

A man becomes like those whose society he loves.
*Hindu Proverb*

Better to live alone; with a fool there is no companionship.
*The Pali Canon*

He that walks with the wise will be wise.
*The Book of Proverbs*

What do righteousness and wickedness have in common? Or what fellowship can light have with darkness?
*The Apostle Paul*

Beyond all other men make yourself the friend of him who is distinguished by his virtue. Yield always to his gentle warnings and observe his honorable and useful actions.
*Pythagoras*

Keep bad men company and you'll soon be of their number.
*English Proverb*

Do not make friends with a hot-tempered man; do not associate with one easily angered.
*The Book of Proverbs*

The wolf will hire himself out very cheaply as a shepherd.
*Russian Proverb*

Keep company with good men, and you'll increase their company.
*Italian Proverb*

If you see a wise person who shows you your faults, who shows what is to be avoided, follow that wise person as you would one who reveals hidden treasures.
*The Dhammapada*

Shun evil company.
*Irish Proverb*

One must look at a man's company.
*Turkish Proverb*

If they do not want you in their company, go aside.
*African Proverb*

Meddle with dirt and some of it will stick to you.
*Danish Proverb*

Deal solely with men of honor: with such only may you be involved, and such only may you be involved. What they have done is the best pledge of what they will do.
*Baltasar Gracian*

Regard not an evil prince.
Regard not deceitful relatives.
Regard not a lustful woman.
Regard not a great sinner.
*Nagarjuna*

130

The company of just and righteous men is better than wealth and a rich estate.
*Euripides*

Intimacy in the society of the holy,
Conversation in the society of the learned,
And the friendship of the unselfish,
These will cause no regrets.
*Nagarjuna*

After three days even the most welcome guest becomes a bore.
*Japanese Proverb*

When good friends become neighbors they should erect a high fence between them.
*Chinese Proverb*

A frequent guest becomes a burden.
*Yiddish Proverb*

Even welcome guests becomes a parasite on the third day.
*Japanese Proverb*

Even if you don't like your guest, welcome them with a smile.
*Philippine Proverb*

The first day indeed a guest; the second, a nuisance; the third, a pest.
*Hebrew Proverb*

Relations and friends should be visited but not lived with.
*Swedish Proverb*

Eat and drink with your relatives; do business with strangers.
*Greek Proverb*

No reply should be given to the words of the wicked.
*Sai Baba*

Someone who lies for you will also lie against you.
*Bosnian Proverb*

Whoever gossips to you will gossip of you.
*Spanish Proverb*

Most men are either stupid or evil, and to take up with such people involves too great a risk.
*Francesco Guicciardini*

The man who thinks he can find enough in himself to be able to dispense with everybody else makes a great mistake, but the man who thinks he is indispensable to others makes an even greater.
*La Rochefoucauld*

If you have doubts about someone, your true and best security consists in having things so arranged that he cannot hurt you even if he wants to. For security founded on the will and discretion of others is worthless, seeing how little goodness and faith is to be found in men.
*Francesco Guicciardini*

Men are so false, so insidious, so deceitful and cunning in their wiles, so avid in their own interest, and so oblivious to other's interests, that you cannot go wrong if you believe little and trust less.
*Francesco Guicciardini*

Never have a companion who casts you in the shade.
*Baltasar Gracian*

Never forget what a man says to you when he is angry.
*Henry Ward Beecher*

It is more important to study men than books.
*La Rochefoucauld*

If you have offended a man, do not trust or confide in him, even in a business deal which, if successful, would bring him profit and honor.
*Francesco Guicciardini*

The knowledge of mankind is a very useful knowledge for everybody...You will have to do with all sorts of characters; you should therefore know them thoroughly, in order to manage them ably.
*Lord Chesterfield*

If you wish to please people, you must begin by understanding them.
*Charles Reade*

Why blast a sparrow with a cannon?
*Chinese Proverb*

We probably wouldn't worry about what people think of us if we could know how seldom they do.
*Olin Miller*

The more I see of man, the more I like dogs.
*De Stael*

One can't live for everyone, more especially not for those with whom one wouldn't care to live.
*Goethe*

Don't be tricked into thinking that there are no crocodiles just because the water is still.
*Malaysian Proverb*

Don't judge a dog by its hair.
*Finnish Proverb*

The passions are the most effective orators for persuading. They are a natural art that have infallible rules; and the simplest man with passion will be more persuasive than the most eloquent with it.
*La Rochefoucauld*

All sails do not suit every ship.
*Icelandic Proverb*

Mind, not only what people say, but how they say it.
*Lord Chesterfield*

When two dogs fight for a bone, a third runs away with it.
*Dutch Proverb*

People hate those who make them feel their own inferiority.
*Lord Chesterfield*

Let sleeping tigers lie.
*Chinese Proverb*

Remove a tree and you remove its shade.
*Chinese Proverb*

All for one, one for all.
*Alexandre Dumas*

The nail that sticks out is certain to be knocked back in.
*Japanese Proverb*

A dwarf standing on the shoulders of a giant may see farther than a giant himself.
*Robert Burton*

In seeking to save another, beware of drowning yourself.
*Sir Francis Osborne*

The fish eyes the bait, never the hook.
*Chinese Proverb*

There is no indispensable man.
*Franklin Delano Roosevelt*

You may force a horse to the water, but you cannot make him drink.
*Dutch Proverb*

Superiority has always been detested.
*Baltasar Gracian*

Listen to what they say about others, and you'll know what they say about you.
*Cuban Proverb*

Faces we see, hearts we know not.
*Spanish Proverb*

The pebble in the brook secretly thinks itself a precious stone.

*Japanese Proverb*

A little fire is quickly trodden out. Which being suffered, rivers cannot quench.

*Shakespeare*

The best of us have our bad sides; and it is as imprudent as it is ill-bred to exhibit them.

*Lord Byron*

Every fire is the same size when it begins.

*Seneca Proverb*

The fire that seems extinguished often slumbers beneath the ashes.

*Pierre Corneille*

The graveyards are full of indispensable men.

*Charles de Gaulle*

There are more bad men than good...Therefore, except for those whom you know to be good from experience or from a completely trustworthy source, it is wise to deal with all people with your eyes wide open... don't trust anyone unless you are sure you can.

*Francesco Guicciardini*

Early impressions are hard to eradicate from the mind. When once wool has been dyed purple, who can restore it to its previous whiteness?

*Saint Jerome*

It is with books as with men: a very small number play a great part, the rest are lost in the multitude.

*Voltaire*

A book whose sale is forbidden, all men rush to see, and prohibition turns one reader into three.

*Italian Proverb*

One should desire the company of the good and virtuous.

*Sai Baba*

Every man becomes, to a certain degree, what the people he generally converses with are.

*Lord Chesterfield*

He who walks with the wise grows wise; but a companion of fools suffers harm.

*The Book of Proverbs*

He does a good day's work who rids himself of a fool.

*French Proverb*

If you do not meet a sage following the same road as yourself, then walk alone.

*The Dhammapada*

Expect nothing from others.

*Swami Muktananda*

Trust, but verify.

*Russian Proverb*

The fool, who is really a two-faced brute, should be especially avoided.

*Nagarjuna*

He that causes strife comes himself to sorrow. Do not take such a one for your companion.

*Ptah-Hotep*

Tell me thy company, and I'll tell thee what thou art.

*Cervantes*

Association with the evil man is unbecoming, whether he be pleasant or obnoxious.

*Nagarjuna*

Things that have a common quality ever quickly seek their kind.

*Marcus Aurelius*

133

Judge not the play before the play is done.
*Francis Quarles*

A little truth helps the lie go down.
*Italian Proverb*

Betters have their betters.
*Japanese Proverb*

There are finer fish in the sea than have ever been caught.
*Irish Proverb*

It is good to have an end to journey toward; but it is the journey that matters, in the end.
*Ursula K. Le Guin*

When your hand is in the dog's mouth withdraw it gently.
*Irish Proverb*

If a man is lacking in good fellowship, no speech has any influence over him.
*The Instruction of Ke'gemni*

A runaway monk never speaks well of his monastery.
*Italian Proverb*

He who is wise never consorts with fools.
*Baltasar Gracian*

The wise man does not befriend the faithless, the avaricious and the slanderous, or the one who stirs up strife, the wise avoid the wicked.
*Buddha*

The superior person will prudently pick the community he will live within, and will choose the proper people to associate with.
*Confucius*

Absence lessons moderate passions and intensifies great ones, as the wind blows out a candle but fans up a fire.
*La Rochefoucauld*

If the wine drinker has a deep gentleness in him, he will show that, when drunk. But if he has hidden anger and arrogance, those appear.
*Rumi*

The following are mad:
He who tries to teach simpletons,
Contradicts the wise,
Is moved by empty speeches,
Believes whores,
Entrust secrets to the garrulous.
*Goethe*

To expect bad people not to injure others is crazy. It's to ask the impossible. And to let them behave like that to other people, but expect them to exempt you is arrogant.
*Marcus Aurelius*

The greatest difficulties are situated where we're not looking for them.
*Goethe*

Until you have rectified yourself, you cannot rectify others.
*Chinese Proverb*

Nothing is more disagreeable than a majority; for it consists of a few powerful people in the lead, rogues who are adaptable, weak people who assimilate with the rest, and the crowd that trundles along behind without the slightest notion of what it's after.
*Goethe*

If you want to be loved by your superiors, show respect and reverence for them – and, in fact, rather too much than too little. For nothing offends a superior more than to think he is not receiving the respect and reverence he believes he is due.
*Francesco Guicciardini*

No gratitude is to be expected from the wicked.
*Aesop*

Be careful not to do anyone the sort of favor that cannot be done without at the same time displeasing others. For injured men do not forget offenses; in fact, they exaggerate them.
*Francesco Guicciardini*

The leopard does not change his spots.
*Shakespeare*

Too many captains run the ship aground.
*Greek Proverb*

Familiarity breeds contempt.
*Aesop*

We find few guilty of ingratitude while we are still in a position to help them.
*La Rochefoucauld*

Love seems the swiftest, but it is the slowest of all growths. No man or woman really knows what perfect love is until they have been married a quarter of a century.
*Mark Twain*

It seems essential, in relationships and all tasks, that we concentrate only on what is most significant and important.
*Soren Kierkegaard*

If there is such a thing as a good marriage, it is because it resembles friendship rather than love.
*Michel de Montaigne*

When marrying, ask yourself this question: Do you believe that you will be able to converse well with this person into your old age? Everything else in marriage is transitory.
*Friedrich Nietzsche*

Don't marry someone you would not be friends with if there was no sex between you.
*William Glasser*

The question of sex will take care of itself.
*Helen Frankenthaler*

The world is full of pots jeering at kettles.
*La Rochefoucauld*

# FAMILY
# &
# FILIAL DUTY

生

From children you must expect childish acts.
*Danish Proverb*

Childhood shows the man, as morning shows the day.
*John Milton*

The young rely on their fathers, the old on their children.
*Vietnamese Proverb*

Children learn from their parents.
*Japanese Proverb*

You must not expect old heads upon young shoulders.
*English Proverb*

Children do not understand the hearts of parents.
*Japanese Proverb*

Most young people think they are being natural when really they are just ill-mannered and crude.
*La Rochefoucauld*

In whatever they do, children should consult their elders.
*Philippine Proverb*

Outside the bedroom a husband and wife should treat each other like guests.
*Chinese Proverb*

Husbands, love your wives and don't be harsh with them.
*The Apostle Paul*

Women should mind what their husbands, not what their in-laws, think.
*Chinese Proverb*

Choose a wife from a position lower than your own and choose friends from a higher status.
*Japanese Proverb*

Like father, like son.
*English Proverb*

If you would be wise, provide for your house, and love your wife in your arms. Fill her stomach, clothe her back; oil is the remedy for her limbs. Gladden her heart during your lifetime, for she is an estate profitable to his lord. Do not be harsh, for gentleness masters her more than strength. Give to her that for which she sighs and that toward which her eye looks.
*Ptah-Hotep*

He who does not honor his wife dishonors himself.
*Spanish Proverb*

In every woman there is a Queen. Speak to the Queen, and the Queen will answer.
*Norwegian Proverb*

When you have your own children you will understand your obligation to your parents.
*Japanese Proverb*

Many a shabby colt makes a fine horse.
*Irish Proverb*

Honor your father and your mother, as the Lord your God has commanded you, so that you may live long and that it may go well with you in the land the Lord your God is giving you.
*The Book of Deuteronomy*

Unblessed is the son who does not honor his parents; but if reverent and obedient to them, he will receive the same from his own children.

*Euripides*

If anyone does not provide for his relatives, and especially for his immediate family, he has denied the faith and is worse than an unbeliever.

*The Apostle Paul*

The family should pursue harmony, the individual diligence.

*Chinese Proverb*

The filial duty of feeding one's parents is known even to the crows.

*Japanese Proverb*

Father and mother are the most precious jewels on earth.

*Philippine Proverb*

To understand your parent's love you must raise children yourself.

*Chinese Proverb*

You must apply yourself seriously to your work, serve your parents with filial piety, behave with propriety towards your wife...Furthermore, as a parent you should conduct yourself with dignity and in accordance with what is right.

*Takuan Soho*

Filial piety is the source of many good deeds and the beginning of all virtue.

*Japanese Proverb*

Parents should be worshipped (respected and loved) as visible representatives of the Godhead; they are responsible for their children's very existence and for seeing to their children's welfare in the world. For this reason children should respect and honor parents.

*Sai Baba*

Your Lord has decreed that you shall not serve any but Him and to be kind to parents. Whether one or both of them attains old age with you, do not scorn them nor chide them but speak to them graciously and humble yourself gently to them with compassion and say "O my Lord, have mercy on them as they cherished me in childhood."

*Mohammad*

Show parents respect with love and devotion. It is a tribute you should offer them for the great chance they gave you to come into this world...

*Sai Baba*

Serve and revere your parents.

*Hadith*

He who is neglectful toward his parents is hated not only by humanity but also by the gods.

*Demosthenes*

Don't quarrel with your parents even if you are on the right.

*Plato*

Be grateful to your parents for all of the care and sacrifice they have undergone for your sake.

*Sai Baba*

Conduct yourself toward your parents as you would have your children conduct themselves toward you.

*Isocrates*

Do not do anything to bring tears to the eyes of your parents. Honor them and obey them. Do not condemn them as being "old fashioned."

*Sai Baba*

To abandon kindly parents can turn into a source of regret.

*Gampopa*

The young must respect the old, especially their fathers, who well deserve it for their age and for many other reasons. From your father you have received life and instruction on how to acquire virtue. With his labor, solicitude, and zeal, your father has brought you to manhood...If you owe gratitude to those who help you when in need and misery, you will certainly owe more to the one who, insofar as he could, did not let you want in the least.
*Leon Battista Alberti*

A wise son heeds his father's instruction.
*The Book of Proverbs*

Let the young not be slow in helping all elders in their age and weakness... Let them, therefore, be diligent and prompt in giving them comfort, pleasure and rest in their old age.
*Leon Battista Alberti*

He (Cato) never said anything obscene in front of his son, no more than if he had been in the presence of the holy Vestal Virgins.
*Plutarch*

The son disgraces the father by bad conduct.
*African Proverb*

Let a son receive the word of his father, not being heedless of any rule of his.
*Ptah-Hotep*

It is the duty of the young to share with their fathers and elders their every wish, thought, and plan to ask counsel of many on everything, especially of those who, to our knowledge, love and cherish us more than others.
*Leon Battista Alberti*

A torn jacket is soon mended; but hard words bruise the heart of a child.
*Henry Wadsworth Longfellow*

Can a crab teach his children how to walk a straight line?
*Malay Proverb*

Rather than dream of jade or gold pray for virtue among your children and grandchildren.
*Chinese Proverb*

Fathers, do not embitter your children, or they will become discouraged.
*The Apostle Paul*

A superior man never loses his son's love.
*Japanese Proverb*

A change needed in a grandchild has to begin with the grandfather.
*African Proverb*

Be ever gentle with the children God has given you. Watch over them constantly; reprove them earnestly, but not in anger.
*Elihu Burritt*

It is a wise father that knows his own child.
*English Proverb*

A father...He should make himself worthy of respect by his virtue and abilities, and worthy of love by his kindness and gentle manners.
*Montaigne*

Honor the old, teach the young.
*Danish Proverb*

The first great gift we can bestow on others is a good example.
*Sir Charles Morell*

Internal dissension may seem as small as a split sesame seed, yet there is enough power in it to destroy.
*Tiruvalluvar*

Better than birth is upbringing.
*Japanese Proverb*

138

Children have more need of models than of critics.

*Joseph Joubert*

A child learns more by imitation than in any other way.

*George Sanderlin*

He preaches well that lives well.

*Cervantes*

A father will do well, as his son grows up... to talk familiarly with him... The sooner you treat him as a man, the sooner he will begin to be one: and if you admit him into serious discourses... with you, you will...raise his mind above the usual amusements of youth, and those trifling occupations which it is commonly wasted in... Nothing cements and establishes friendship and good-will so much as confident communication... When your son sees you open your mind to him he will know he has a friend and... father.

*John Locke*

Harsh counsels have no effect. They are like hammers which are always repulsed by the anvil.

*Clause Adrien Helvetius*

That which we are, we are all the while teaching, not voluntarily, but involuntarily.

*Emerson*

Parents can tell, but not teach, unless they practice what they preach.

*Ezra Taft Benson*

As iron is worn away by frequent filing, a family's strength is eroded by incessant inner frictions.

*Tiruvalluvar*

Whatever you would have your children become, strive to exhibit in your own lives and conversations.

*Lydia H. Sigourney*

Do your duty; learn and teach....Educate your children; learn and teach.

*The Upanishads*

If you do bad things your children will follow you and do the same. If you want to raise good children, be decent yourself.

*Chris*

Cultivate peace at home.

*Petalesharo*

In regards to your son's behavior, it is wrong for a parent to scold a child for misdeeds if the parent has not corrected his own mind. You must first of all conduct yourself properly. Then, if you admonish your son, his behavior will improve naturally and your younger son will be sure to learn from his brother's example and improve his behavior as well. It is truly auspicious when father and sons become virtuous together.

*Takuan Soho*

Remember that your children are not your own, but are lent to you by the Creator.

*Mohawk Maxim*

Praise the young and they will blossom.

*Irish Proverb*

Keep your son from those that make light of what is commanded, for it is they that make him rebellious. Those who are guided do not go astray – but those that lose their bearings; they cannot find a straight course.

*Ptah-Hotep*

Stretch hide while it is still green.

*Swahili Proverb*

Nothing sinks a young man into low company, both of women and men, so surely as timidity, and diffidence of himself.

*Lord Chesterfield*

Even without noticing his father's conduct the son imitates him.
*Nagarjuna*

The head of the family must first of all be on the watch for the first sparks of vice to appear among his children's appetites and must put them out immediately if he does not wish to be compelled later to extinguish the flames of corrupt desire at greater cost, with sorrow and tears.
*Leon Battista Alberti*

Trust not too surely for early harvest, nor trust too soon in your son. The field needs good weather; the son needs wisdom, and often is either denied.
*The Havamal*

Austerity and harshness make one angry and scornful toward his elders more often than obedient. A noble spirit suffers when treated as a servant rather than a son.
*Leon Battista Alberti*

Diogenes struck the father when the son swore.
*Robert Burton*

Dignity, of course, must be kept; a father should never let himself sink to the level of familiarity or become the boon companion of his son – that merely breeds contempt and self-confidence in the youth, who, feeling himself curbed by no law, comes to pursue with headstrong passion whatever takes his fancy. On the other hand he should be no formal or rigid moralist, afraid of giving his son ample proof of courteous and warm-hearted consideration, or shy of taking affectionately and even with a certain rapture to his heart the child, who is a living image of himself, than which nothing in life is sweeter to a parent.
*Jacopo Sadoleto*

When your son is young, discipline him.
Arabic Proverb

It is a father's duty to test his sons' intellect in many ways.
*Leon Battista Alberti*

All children must look after their own upbringing. Parents can only give good advice or put them on the right paths, but the final forming of a person's character lies in their own hands.
*Anne Frank*

A wise son brings joy to his father.
*The Book of Proverbs*

To make your children capable of honesty is the beginning of education.
*John Ruskin*

A wise son heeds his father's instruction.
*The Book of Proverbs*

Where there is agreement between father and son the family will prosper; where there is agreement between brother and brother the family will survive.
*Chinese Proverb*

The parents can see best the character of the child.
*Japanese Proverb*

Children's children are a crown to the aged, and parents are the pride of the children.
*The Book of Proverbs*

Happy will that house be in which the relationships are formed from character.
*Emerson*

The child is father of the man.
*William Wordsworth*

Youth may stray afar yet return at last.
*French Proverb*

Few men have been admired by their own households.
*Montaigne*

140

Respect the child. Be not too much his parent. Trespass not on his solitude.

*Emerson*

A father must see where his son is headed from the earliest age and must not allow him to proceed on an unsafe and little-praised path. He must not allow his sons to have their way against his wishes or become accustomed to dishonest ways. The father must always appear as a father; he must be severe, but not hateful, loving, but not too familiar. Let all fathers and elders remember that authority maintained through force is always less stable then that maintained through love. No fear can last forever; love is enduring.

*Leon Battista Alberti*

Do but gain a boy's trust; convince him by your behavior that you have his happiness at heart; let him discover that you are the wiser of the two; let him experience the benefits of following your advice and the evils that arise from disregarding it; and fear not you will readily enough guide him.

*Herbert Spencer*

The head of a family must be vigilant and observant above all. He must know the family's acquaintances, examine all customs both within and without the house, and correct and mend the evil ways of any member of the family with words of reason rather than anger... He must be severe, firm, and stern when necessary, and he must always keep in mind the well-being, peace, and tranquility of his entire family as the ultimate purpose of all his efforts and counsels for the guidance of the family in virtue and honor.

*Leon Battista Alberti*

The best thing to give to your...father, deference; to a mother, conduct that will make her proud of you; to yourself, respect; to all men, charity.

*Francis Maitland Balfour*

When the parents die in extreme age a dutiful son should be merry.

*Chinese Proverb*

Youth and age will not agree.

*English Proverb*

What I learned constructive about women is that no matter how old they get, always think of them the way they were on the best day they ever had.

*Ernest Hemingway*

Choose a wife to please yourself, not others.

*Rumanian Proverb*

If a widow has children or grandchildren, these should learn first of all to put their religion into practice by caring for their own family and so repaying their parents and grandparents, for this is pleasing to God.

*The Apostle Paul*

Children of good parents will have happy marriages; parents of good children will have splendid funerals.

*Chinese Proverb*

Duty to parents is higher than the mountains, deeper than the sea.

*Japanese Proverb*

A young man owes respect and gratitude to his father and elders.

*Leon Battista Alberti*

A son that listens carefully, he listens carefully: he reaches honor and reverence. Pass on the teachings that they may work well. Let that which you speak implant true and just things in the life of your children.

*Ptah-Hotep*

A fool spurns his father's discipline, but whoever heeds correction shows prudence.

*The Book of Proverbs*

The child of a snake is also a snake.
*African Proverb*

Noble fathers have noble children.
*Euripides*

The voice of parents is the voice of gods, for to their children they are Heaven's lieutenants.
*William Shakespeare*

There is a transcendent power in example. We reform others unconsciously when we walk uprightly.
*Madame Swetchine*

If you love your son you must let him travel.
*Japanese Proverb*

A good man leaves an inheritance for his children's children.
*The Book of Proverbs*

To spend the prime of youth mostly in vulgar amusements, can be a later source of much regret.
*Gampopa*

There is no child who is a doer of good to his parents who God will not look at with great favor.
*Hadith*

Fathers must strive with their whole being, with all their diligence and wisdom, to make their children honest and high-principled... it is mainly up to the father to make the children honest, virtuous, and honorable.
*Leon Battista Alberti*

Children, obey your parents in everything, for this pleases the Lord.
*The Apostle Paul*

The value of the father is known after his death.
*Indian Proverb*

If we would amend the world we should mend ourselves and teach our children to be not what we are but what they should be.
*William Penn*

How pleasant it is for a father to sit at his child's board. It is like an aged man reclining under the shadow of an oak which he has planted.
*Voltaire*

To enjoy good health, to bring true happiness to one's family, to bring peace to all, one must first discipline and control one's own mind. If a man can control his mind he can find the way to Enlightenment, and all wisdom and virtue will naturally come to him.
*Buddha*

A man should never neglect his family for business.
*Walt Disney*

In dwelling, live close to the ground. In thinking, keep to the simple. In conflict, be fair and generous. In governing, don't try to control. In work, do what you enjoy. In family life, be completely present.
*Lao Tzu*

Having children makes you no more a parent than having a piano makes you a pianist.
*Michael Levine*

As states subsist in part by keeping their weaknesses from being known, so is it the quiet of families to have their chancery and their parliament within doors, and to compose and determine all emergent differences there.
*John Donne*

# Dear Dad

Dear Dad,

I am writing this to you, though you have been dead thirty years...

I feel I must say some things to you, things I didn't know when I was a boy in your house...

It's only now, after passing through the long hard school years, only now, when my own hair is gray, that I understand how you felt.

I must have been a...trial to you...I believed my own petty wisdom...

Most of all, I want to confess my worst sin against you. It was the feeling I had that you "did not understand."

When I look back over it now, I know that you did understand. You understood me better than I did myself...

And how patient you were with me! How full of long-suffering, and kindness!

And how pathetic, it now comes home to me, were your efforts to get close to me...

What was it held me aloof? I don't know. But it is tragic – that wall that rises between a boy and his father...

I wish you were here now, across the table from me, just for an hour, so that I could tell you how there's no wall any more; I understand you now, Dad, and, how I love you, and wish I could go back and be your boy again...

Well, it won't be long, Dad, till I am over there, and I believe you'll be the first one to take me by the hand and help me...

I know that among the richest, most priceless things on earth, and the thing least understood, is that mighty love and tenderness and craving to help, which a father feels toward his boy.

For I have a boy of my own...

Up there somewhere in the Silence, hear me, Dad, and believe me.

*Dr. Frank Crane*

# THE ELDERLY

生

Seek the friendship of the elderly.
*Strabo*

To succeed, consult three old people.
*Chinese Proverb*

Seek ye counsel of the aged, for their eyes
have looked on the faces of the years and
their ears have hearkened to the voices of
Life. Even if their counsel is displeasing
to you, pay heed to them.
*Kahlil Gibran*

Old men see things clearly.
*Chinese Proverb*

It is the duty of the elders to show the rising
generation, by the example of their own
lives, that spiritual discipline and study has
made them more joyful and courageous in
the adventure of life. Youth always imitates
those who are older.
*Sai Baba*

When young, seek to listen to elder's
conversations.
*Strabo*

Ignore an old man's advice and one day be
a beggar.
*Chinese Proverb*

To be able to look back on one's past life
with satisfaction is to live twice.
*Marcus Valerius Martialis*

Reverence your elder, for the man excelling
in age excels in wisdom.
*African Proverb*

The poverty of having no one coming to
visit them is the poverty that older people
feel the most.
*Mother Teresa*

As the old cock crows the young cock
learns.
*Irish Proverb*

With the ancient is wisdom; and in length
of days understanding.
*The Book of Job*

Do not consider useless the advice of an
old person.
*Spanish Proverb*

Every time an old man dies it is as a library
has burnt down.
*Chiek Oumar*

The old pipe gives the sweetest smoke.
*Irish Proverb*

To live long is to see much.
*Swahili Proverb*

The old should be treated with due respect.
*Okinawan Proverb*

The young should respect their elders
above all things.
*Confucius*

Humanity means loving men. Righteousness means respecting the aged.
*Ying Tang*

We must respect the elderly with words and
actions.
*Plato*

We respected our old people above others
in the tribe. To live to be so old they must
have been brave and strong...and we
aspired to be like them. We never allowed
our old people to want for anything.
*Buffalo Child Long Lance*

Nothing is less worthy of honor than an old man who has no other evidence of having lived long except his age.
*Seneca*

The family that has an old person in it possesses a precious jewel.
*Chinese Proverb*

As you respect old people you will be yourself blessed with longevity.
*Vietnamese Proverb*

It is good for even old men to learn wisdom.
*Aeschylus*

To honor an old man is showing respect to God.
*Mohammad*

Old people's speech is not to be dishonored.
*Namibia Proverb*

Respect old people, and be gentle with children.
*Okinawan Proverb*

For good judgment ask old people.
*Japanese Proverb*

To shun an elder's word is to refuse good advice.
*African Proverb*

Learn your way from old people.
*Estonian Proverb*

Good sense comes only with age.
*Irish Proverb*

Old people are everyone's treasures.
*Okinawan Proverb*

To one who always reveres and respects the aged four things increase: life, health, happiness, and power.
*The Dhammapada*

An old broom knows the dirty corners best.
*Irish Proverb*

Much talking is unbecoming in an elder.
*African Proverb*

Old people like for others to listen to them....To listen to someone who has no one to listen to him is a very beautiful thing.
*Mother Teresa*

A good youth, a good old man.
*Greek Proverb*

Old friends pass away, new friends appear. It is just like the days. An old day passes, a new day arrives. The important thing is to make it meaningful: a meaningful friend - or a meaningful day.
*The Dalai Lama*

The older the fiddle the sweeter the tune.
*Irish Proverb*

# AGING

Do not take the faults of youth into old age...
*Goethe*

Acquire something during your youth to provide for your losses during old age. If you intend for your old age to feed on wisdom, so act during your youth that you may not lack food during your old age.
*Franklin*

Take kindly to the counsel of the years; gracefully surrender the things of youth.
*Max Ehrmann*

You are young, my son, and, as the years go by, time will change and even reverse many of your present opinions. Refrain therefore awhile from setting yourself up as a judge of the highest matters.
*Plato*

Education is the best provision for the journey to old age.
*Aristotle*

Take care that old age does not wrinkle your spirit even more than your face.
*Montaigne*

The excesses of our youth are drafts upon our old age, payable with interest, about thirty years after date.
*Charles Caleb Colton*

To know how to grow old is the master work of wisdom, and one of the most difficult chapters in the great art of living.
*Henri Frederic Amiel*

Men wish to live long, but when they grow old, are afraid of old age. To be afraid of old age and to wish for long life is the poor logic of a foolish man.
*Nagarjuna*

One finds many grey hairs but few wise words.
*Swedish Proverb*

With ancient is wisdom; and in length of days understanding.
*The Book of Job*

Men...who have no resources in themselves...find every age burdensome. There is a quiet, pure, and cultivated life which produces a calm and gentle old age. The qualities best adapted to it are culture and active exercise of the virtues. If they have been maintained at every period...the harvest they produce is wonderful.
*Cicero*

Increase your wisdom, even in your declined age.
*Nagarjuna*

The more sand that has escaped from the hourglass of our life, the clearer we should see through it.
*Jean Paul*

The mature person accepts his situation...He makes sure that his own conduct is correct and seeks nothing from others; thus he is never disappointed. He has no complaints against heaven and no blame toward other people. Therefore the mature person lives in perfect serenity...
*Tzu-Ssu*

A hero in his old age never lets go of his principle.
*Cao Cao*

It is good even for old men to learn wisdom.
*Aeschylus*

The short bloom of our brief and narrow life flies fast away. While we are calling for flowers and wine and women, old age is upon us.

*Juvenal*

Kill the elk in your youth if you would lie on its skin in your old age.

*Finnish Proverb*

You've only got to grow old to be more lenient; I see no fault committed of which I too haven't been guilty.

*Goethe*

Old age and the passage of time teach us everything.

*Sophocles*

Just as a good day's work leads to pleasant sleep, so a life well spent leads to a pleasant death.

*Franklin*

When men grow virtuous in their old age they are merely making a sacrifice to God of the devil's leavings.

*Jonathan Swift*

The harvest of old age is the memory and rich store of blessings laid up in earlier life.

*Cicero*

The closing years of life are like the end of a masquerade party when the masks are dropped.

*Arthur Schopenhauer*

And in the end, it's not the years in your life that count. It's the life in your years.

*Lincoln*

Old age, believe me, is a good and pleasant thing. It is true you are gently shouldered off the stage, but then you are given such a comfortable front stall as spectator.

*Confucius*

We do not grow absolutely, chronologically. We grow sometimes in one dimension, and not in another; unevenly. We grow partially. We are relative. We are mature in one realm, childish in another. The past, present, and future mingle and pull us backward, forward, or fix us in the present. We are made up of layers, cells, constellations.

*Anais Nin*

I want to die young at a ripe old age.

*Ashley Montagu*

The older I grow the more I distrust the familiar doctrine that age brings wisdom.

*H. L. Mencken*

To hold the same views at forty as we held at twenty is to have been stupefied for a score of years.

*Robert Louis Stevenson*

None are so old as those who have outlived enthusiasm.

*Thoreau*

No man loves life like him that's growing old.

*Sophocles*

# FRIENDS
# &
# ENEMIES

Make him your friend who distinguishes himself by his virtue, and take example from his virtuous and useful actions.
*Pythagoras*

A man cannot be too careful in his choice of enemies.
*Oscar Wilde*

If your enemy falls beneath your foot, crush him.
*Kurdish Proverb*

If evil you know, as evil proclaim it, and make no friendship with foes.
*The Havamal*

Keep your friends close, but your enemies closer.
*Sicilian Proverb*

Though your enemy seems like a mouse, watch him like a lion.
*Italian Proverb*

Beware of an enemy, even though he be only an ant.
*Turkish Proverb*

Go often to the house of thy friend, for weeds choke the unused path.
*Emerson*

Take heed of reconciled enemies.
*English Proverb*

There is no such thing as an insignificant enemy.
*French Proverb*

A friend who leads one astray is an enemy.
*Greek Proverb*

Our friends show us what we can do, our enemies teach us what we must do.
*Goethe*

Gifts from enemies are dangerous.
*English Proverb*

Know how to profit through your enemies.
*Baltasar Gracian*

Reflect on this: efforts and enemies, if left unfinished, can both ravage you like an unextinguished fire.
*Tiruvalluvar*

Every man counts as an enemy, but not every man as a friend. Very few can do us good, but nearly all harm… from friends now spoiled, there emerge the worst of enemies.
*Baltasar Gracian*

When the time comes that foes pose as friends, keep a friendly face but banish their brotherhood from your heart.
*Tiruvalluvar*

He is a good man whose intimate friends are all good, and whose enemies are decidedly bad.
*John Caspar Lavater*

My enemy is not the man who wrongs me, but the man who means to wrong me.
*Democritus*

Be never the first to break with your friend the bond that holds you both; care eats the heart if you can not speak to another all your thoughts.
*The Havamal*

Beware of meat twice boiled, and an old foe reconciled.

*Franklin*

To win one hundred victories in one hundred battles is not the highest skill. To subdue the enemy without fighting is the highest skill.

*Sun Tzu*

Never underestimate an adversary. One could lose one's life if one despises an adversary as unwise and stupid.

*Kazumi Tabata*

Our enemies teach us life's most valuable lessons.

*Chinese Proverb*

The greatest enemies, and the ones we must mainly combat, are within.

*Cervantes*

Forgiving an enemy is a requirement; trusting him is not.

*Venezuelan Proverb*

...enemies can harm you, in times and places you would never have expected.

*Francesco Guicciardini*

You will never destroy a tree without destroying its root.

*Chinese Proverb*

There is no little enemy.

*Franklin*

When you step beyond your own gate, you face a million enemies.

*Gichin Funakoshi*

Prosperity makes friends, adversity tries them.

*Syrus*

In hardship you know your friends.

*Japanese Proverb*

As the yellow gold is tried in fire, so the faith of friendship must be seen in adversity.

*Ovid*

The shifts of fortune test the reliability of friends.

*Cicero*

It is only when the cold season comes that we know the pine and cypress to be evergreens.

*Chinese Proverb*

Trouble is a sieve through which we sift our acquaintances. Those too big to pass through are our friends.

*Arlene Francis*

The shifts of fortune test the reliability of friends.

*Cicero*

You do not really know your friends from your enemies until the ice breaks.

*Icelandic Proverb*

Love him, and keep him for thy friend, who, when all go away, will not forsake thee, nor suffer thee to perish at the last.

*Thomas a' Kempis*

A man must be watchful and wary as well, and fearful of trusting a friend.

*The Havamal*

Have no friends not equal to yourself.

*Confucius*

Avoid friends who are detrimental to your peace of mind.

*Gongs and Drums of Gampopa Precepts*

Avoid that friend who is greedy for wealth.

*Nagarjuna*

Your enemy makes you wise.

*Italian Proverb*

Everybody's friend is nobody's friend.
*Italian Proverb*

He is a friend to none who is a friend to
all.
*Swedish Proverb*

Avoid the society of evil friends and men
of vulgar minds; have pleasure in that of
the giants of wisdom and take as thy friends
those who practice justice.
*The Dhammapada*

He never was a friend who has ceased to
be one.
*French Proverb*

Before you befriend him, consider a man's
character, family background, faults and
faithful allies.
*Tiruvalluvar*

Never trust much to a new friend or an old
enemy.
*Scottish Proverb*

There is no true friendship among
thieves…
*Baltasar Gracian*

The friend that can be bought is not worth
buying.
*Irish Proverb*

To give up friendship with fools and quit
their company – such loss is said to be a
man's greatest gain.
*Tiruvalluvar*

Nothing is as dangerous as an ignorant
friend; a wise enemy is to be preferred.
*Jean De La Fontaine*

The friendship of the base is dangerous.
*Indian Proverb*

One is known by the friends he keeps…
*Baltasar Gracian*

To be intimate with a foolish friend is like
going to bed with a razor.
*Franklin*

Everyone's companion is no one's friend.
*German Proverb*

Many kiss the hand they wish cut off.
*George Herbert*

Three friends benefit us; three harm us. The
upright friend, the devoted, and the learned
benefit us. The fawning friend, the
flattering, and the too eloquent harm us.
*Confucius*

Foolish friends are worse than wise
enemies.
*The Dhammapada*

The unwise man imagines a smiling face,
a friend. Surprised to find how little
support he musters at a meeting.
*The Havamal*

Distrust whatever words may come from
men whose hearts do not beat in harmony
with your own.
*Tiruvalluvar*

The same man cannot be both friend and
flatterer.
*Franklin*

Friendship with the ignorant is as foolish
as arguing with a drunkard.
*Kahlil Gibran*

To say that a man is your friend means
commonly no more than this, that he is not
your enemy.
*Thoreau*

Beware of befriending an enemy's friend.
*The Havamal*

He who has many friends has no friends.
*Aesop*

150

To let friendship die away by negligence and silence is certainly not wise.
*Samuel Johnson*

There is nothing on this earth more to be prized than true friendship.
*Saint Thomas of Aquinas*

Man's best support is a very dear friend.
*Cicero*

There is nothing meritorious but virtue and friendship.
*Alexander Pope*

Friends are an aid to the young, to guard them from error; to the elderly, to attend to their wants and to supplement their failing power of action; to those in the prime of life, to assist them to noble deeds.
*Aristotle*

One loyal friend is worth ten thousand relatives.
*Euripides*

In poverty and other misfortunes of life, true friends are a sure refuge.
*Aristotle*

.

If a man does not make new acquaintances as he advances through life, he will soon find himself left alone. A man, sir, should keep his friendship in a constant repair.
*Samuel Johnson*

We should not join with an enemy who has fought long against us, even though he wants our friendship.
*Sakya Pandit*

The wicked have only accomplices; voluptuaries have companions in debauch, self-seekers have partners, politicians attract partisans; the generality of idle men have attachments; princes have courtiers, and virtuous men alone have friends.
*Voltaire*

If men fathom what it means to have virtuous and wise friends, they will find the means to procure such friendships.
*Tiruvalluvar*

There are three faithful friends – an old wife, an old dog, and ready money.
*Franklin*

Hold tight to friendship with pure men; let go of unfit fellows...
*Tiruvalluvar*

The word friend is common, the fact is rare.
*Phaedrus*

Be slow in choosing a friend, slower in changing.
*Franklin*

One should keep old roads and old friends.
*German Proverb*

If you have one true friend, you have more than your share comes to.
*Thomas Fuller*

The best mirror is an old friend.
*English Proverb*

Make friends only with those gentlemen who are superior men.
*Confucius*

Put not so much in a friend's power that, if hostilely disposed, he can do you an injury.
*Saadi*

Among our people, friendship is held to be the severest test of character. To have a friend, and to be true under any and all trials, is the truest mark of a man.
*Ohiyesa*

Rare though true love may be, true friendship is rarer still.
*La Rochefoucauld*

Friendship exists only between good men, whereas the bad man never achieves true friendship with either a good or a bad man.
*Socrates*

Flattery makes friends, truth enemies.
*Spanish Proverb*

Reprove your friends in secret, praise them openly.
*Syrus*

Speak well of your friend, of your enemy say nothing.
*English Proverb*

Tart words make no friends; a spoonful of honey will catch more flies than a gallon of vinegar.
*Franklin*

Do not imagine that you will make friends by showing your superiority over them.
*William Hazlitt*

The only way to have a friend is to be one.
*Emerson*

Never forget fellowship with pure souls, nor forsake friendship with those who aided you in adversity.
*Tiruvalluvar*

There is a magnet in your heart that will attract true friends. That magnet is unselfishness, thinking of others first...when you learn to live for others, they will live for you.
*Paramahansa Yogananda*

You win the victory when you yield to friends.
*Sophocles*

He used to say that it was better to have one friend of great value than many friends who were good for nothing.
*Diogenes*

Even among intimate friends there should be courtesy.
*Japanese Proverb*

Your acquaintance must fill the empire; your close friends must be few.
*Chinese Proverb*

Better lose a little money than a little friendship.
*Malagasy*

The wise befriend the wise and keep that friendship constant, not opening and closing it like the petaled lotus.
*Tiruvalluvar*

Be slow to fall into friendship, but when you are in, continue firm and constant.
*Socrates*

If you expect your friend to be unoffended by your warts, you'd better pardon his pimples.
*Horace*

Do good to thy friend to keep him, to thy enemy to gain him.
*Franklin*

A true friend whom you trust well and wish for his good will: go to him often, exchange gifts and keep him company.
*The Havamal*

Be slow to give your friendship, but when you have given it, strive to make it lasting.
*Isocrates*

Criticize a friend in secret and praise him openly.
*Leonardo da Vinci*

You will best serve your friends if you do not wait for them to ask your help, but go of your own accord at the crucial moment to lend them aid.
*Isocrates*

Envy and selfishness break off friendships.
*Buddha*

Don't let grass grow on the path of friendship.
*Native American Maxim*

You can judge a person's virtue by his most trusted retainers and close friends.
*Takuan Soho*

Familiar with familiarity, the wise are never annoyed when friends do things without asking.
*Tiruvalluvar*

There are limits to the indulgence which friendship allows.
*Cicero*

Ordinary people are friendly to those who are outwardly similar to them. The wise are friendly with those who are inwardly similar to them.
*Lieh Tzu*

A true friend is the most precious of all possessions and the one we take least thought about acquiring.
*La Rochefoucauld*

Nothing is more precious than friends; therefore, lose no opportunity to make them.
*Francesco Guicciardini*

None lives so alone as he who lives without friends; for friendship doubles the good, and divides the bad.
*Baltasar Gracian*

Have few friends though many acquaintances.
*English Proverb*

...friends are the most precious kind of riches.
*Boethius*

Bad friends will prevent you from having good friends.
*African Proverb*

What men have called friendship is merely association, respect for each other's interests, and exchange of good offices, in fact nothing more than a business arrangement from which self-love is always out to draw some profit.
*La Rochefoucauld*

Prostitutes, thieves and people who make friends to make money are all alike.
*Tiruvalluvar*

There are men who will cherish you in private but censure you in public – avoid their every befriending approach.
*Tiruvalluvar*

Beware a dagger hidden in a smile.
*Shi Nai'an*

Love your friends as if they would some day hate you.
*Bias*

The friendship of an official is as thick as a piece of paper.
*Chinese Proverb*

Even though you become the enemy of a good man, don't become the friend of a bad man.
*Japanese Proverb*

Trust in today's friends as if they might be tomorrow's enemies;
*Baltasar Gracian*

Actions, not words, are the true criterion of the attachment of friends.
*George Washington*

Prosperity is not a just scale; adversity is the only balance to weigh friends.
*Plutarch*

Real friendship is shown in times of trouble...
*Euripides*

Method is more important than strength, when you wish to control your enemies.
*Nagarjuna*

But never a man shall friendship make with one of his foeman's friends.
*The Havamal*

When your enemy falls, don't rejoice; but don't pick him up either.
*Yiddish Proverb*

An open foe may prove a curse; but a pretended friend is worse.
*Franklin*

Trust not your defeated enemy, even though he wishes to become your friend.
*Nagarjuna*

Hold a true friend with both hands.
*Nigerian Proverb*

A friend who is made in a year may be lost in an hour.
*Chinese Proverb*

Good friends settle their accounts speedily.
*Chinese Proverb*

Be your friend's true friend.
*The Havamal*

An hour will destroy what it took an age to build.
*English Proverb*

'Tis best to weigh the enemy more mighty than he seems.
*Shakespeare*

Kill the spider and you will destroy the cobweb.
*Maltese Proverb*

It is one of the severest tests of friendship to tell your friend his faults. So to love a man that you cannot bear to see a stain upon him, and to speak painful truth through loving words, that is friendship.
*Henry Ward Beecher*

True friendship consists not in the multitude of friends, but in their worth and value.
*Ben Johnson*

Few friendships would survive if each one knew what his friend says of him behind his back.
*Blaise Pascal*

It takes a long time to grow an old friend.
*John Leonard*

Forgive your enemies, but never forget their names.
*John F. Kennedy*

An enemy generally says and believes what he wishes.
*Thomas Jefferson*

A doubtful friend is worse than a certain enemy. Let a man be one thing or the other, and we then know how to meet him.
*Aesop*

Your best friend and worst enemy are both in this room right now. It's not your neighbor right or left - and it's not God or the devil - it's you.
*Edwin Louis Cole*

# FOOLS

The wise man does at once what the fool does finally.
*Baltasar Gracian*

A fool always finds one still more foolish to admire him.
*Nicolas Boileau-Despreaux*

Little minds are tamed and subdued by misfortune; but great minds rise above it.
*Washington Irving*

The mob does not deserve to be enlightened.
*Frederick the Great*

The fool has said in his heart, there is no God.
*The Psalms*

Fools die for lack of judgment.
*The Book of Proverbs*

Patriotism is the passion of fools…
*Arthur Schopenhauer*

And the burnt fool's bandaged finger goes wobbling back to the fire.
*Rudyard Kipling*

A fool is busy in everyone's business but his own.
*English Proverb*

A wise man changes his mind; a fool, never.
*Spanish Proverb*

A fool spurns his father's discipline.
*The Book of Proverbs*

A fool can no more see his own folly than he can see his ears.
*Thackeray*

A fool is pleased by beauty alone.
*Russian Proverb*

Fools rush in where angels fear to tread.
*English Proverb*

A fool becomes full of evil even if one gathers it little by little.
*The Dhammapada*

Pride, the never-failing vice of fools.
*Alexander Pope*

The fool plucks at a wasp's nest.
*Philippine Proverb*

Power does not corrupt men; fools, however, if they get into a position of power, corrupt power.
*George Bernard Shaw*

Snakes follow the way of serpents.
*Japanese Proverb*

A fool finds pleasure in evil conduct.
*The Book of Proverbs*

Fools always rush in, for all fools are rash.
*Baltasar Gracian*

A white wall is a fool's paper.
*English Proverb*

Haste is the passion of fools.
*Baltasar Gracian*

Bad men cannot make good citizens.
*Patrick Henry*

Stupidity always goes to extremes.
*Baltasar Gracian*

There is always a majority of fools.
*Heraclitus*

Whatever benefit one may give, the wicked man is never grateful.

*Nagarjuna*

A fool causes damage even by his friendship.

*Sakya Pandit*

A fool sees not the same tree that a wise man sees.

*William Blake*

Life with fools consists in drinking; with the wise man, living's thinking.

*Franklin*

The inferior man is proud but not dignified.

*Confucius*

Don't give cherries to a pig; don't give advice to a fool.

*Irish Proverb*

If you write poetry do not show it to an unintelligent man.

*Chinese Proverb*

Do not answer a fool according to his folly, or you will be like him yourself.

*The Book of Proverbs*

Rotten wood cannot be carved.

*Chinese Proverb*

No amount of rosewater can give a crow white feathers.

*Dayak Proverb*

What does a swallow know of the wild swan's mind?

*Chinese Proverb*

Scissors and fools require careful handling.

*Japanese Proverb*

There is no medicine to cure a fool.

*Japanese Proverb*

To reprimand an obstinate fool or to preach to a dolt is like writing upon the water. Christ healed the blind, the halt, the palsied, and the leprous. But the fool He could not cure.

*Kahlil Gibran*

The multitude is always in the wrong.

*Wentworth Dillon*

It is proof of a base and low mind for one to wish to think with the masses or majority, merely because the majority is the majority. Truth does not change because it is, or is not, believed by a majority of the people.

*Guido Bruno*

The world is made up, for the most part, of fools or knaves, both irreconcilable to truth...

*George Villiers*

Fools have been and always will be the majority of mankind.

*Denis Diderot*

The majority of mankind is lazy-minded, incurious, absorbed in vanities, and tepid in emotion, and is therefore incapable of either much doubt or much faith.

*T. S. Eliot*

Eighty percent of mankind is stuff to fill graves with.

*Ford Madox Ford*

The mob has many heads, but no brains.

*Thomas Fuller*

A vulgar man is captious and jealous; eager and impetuous about trifles. He suspects himself to be slighted, thinks everything that is said is meant at him...A vulgar man's conversation always savors strongly of the lowness of his education and company.

*Lord Chesterfield*

The race of fools is infinite.
*Simonides of Ceos*

The intellect of most men is barren.
*Thoreau*

Fools all who seem it, and the half of those who do not.
*Baltasar Gracian*

Those who do not study are simply cattle in clothing.
*Chinese Proverb*

If a fool is associated with a wise person all one's life, the fools will not perceive the truth, any more than a spoon will taste the soup.
*The Dhammapada*

All the fools get lost because they do not think: they never see the half of things, and knowing neither their loss, nor their profit, they make small effort in either direction.
*Baltasar Gracian*

The first chapter of fools is to esteem themselves wise.
*English Proverb*

Learned fools are the greatest fools.
*German Proverb*

Every fool stands convinced; and everyone convinced is a fool; and the faultier a man's judgment, the firmer his convictions.
*Baltasar Gracian*

Fools follow a perverse path, clothing their well-formed naked body, yet never thinking to conceal their deformed mind.
*Tiruvalluvar*

Counsel given to fools excites but does not pacify. He who pours milk for a snake is only increasing its venom.
*Nagarjuna*

A foolish man who will not learn believes everything a miracle.
*Sakya Pandit*

"We will befriend great men and become like them." Such thoughts seldom intrude upon small minds.
*Tiruvalluvar*

The fool seeks not to acquire knowledge, having no mind for understanding.
*Sakya Pandit*

Experience keeps a dear school, yet fools will learn in no other.
*Franklin*

The man who quarrels with facts is a fool.
*Frank Garbutt*

Many men know a great deal, and are all the greater fools for it. There is no fool so great a fool as a knowing fool.
*Spurgeon*

Most fools think they are only ignorant.
*Franklin*

The recipe for perpetual ignorance is: Be satisfied with your opinions and content with your knowledge.
*Elbert Hubbard*

The Superior man stands in awe of the words of the sages. The inferior man does not stand in awe of them; he is disrespectful to important people; he mocks the words of the sages.
*Confucius*

Fools regard themselves as already awake.
*Chuang Tzu*

He who does not seek advice is a fool.
*Kahlil Gibran*

Shallow men believe in luck.
*Emerson*

The wise man doubts often, and changes his mind; the fool is obstinate and never doubts; he knows all things but his own ignorance.
*Akhenaton*

Change of weather is the discourse of fools.
*Thomas Fuller*

A fool finds no pleasure in understanding but delights in airing his own opinions.
*The Book of Proverbs*

There's not much ivory in a rat's mouth.
*Chinese Proverb*

A narrow mind has a broad tongue.
*Arabian Proverb*

The boaster and the proud person are fools.
*Japanese Proverb*

A fool is known by his speech.
*English Proverb*

A fool's lips bring him strife.
*The Book of Proverbs*

Every fool wants to give advice.
*Italian Proverb*

A secret that should be concealed in the mind is uttered by a fool.
*Indian Proverb*

A fool is his own informer.
*Yiddish Proverb*

The smaller the mind the greater the conceit.
*Aesop*

Outside noisy, inside empty.
*Chinese Proverb*

A fool's talk brings a rod to his back.
*The Book of Proverbs*

A fool exposes his folly.
*The Book of Proverbs*

A fool, grown violent, destroys himself and others through quarreling.
*Sakya Pandit*

Wise men talk because they have something to say; fools because they have to say something.
*Plato*

The mouth of the fool gushes folly.
*The Book of Proverbs*

Half wits talk much but say little.
*Franklin*

The lips of the wise spread knowledge; not so the hearts of fools.
*The Book of Proverbs*

The mouth of the fool invites ruin.
*The Book of Proverbs*

At a feast the fool chatters or he stares and stammers. Just as soon as his jug is full ale unveils his mind.
*The Havamal*

A fool has not enough in him to make a good man.
*La Rochefoucauld*

Good and bad are distinct. Cause and effect are clear... But fools don't believe and fall straight into a hell of endless darkness without even knowing it...They're like blind people who don't believe there's such a thing as light. Even if you explain it to them, they still don't believe, because they're blind.
*Bodhidharma*

Hypocrisy, arrogance, vanity, anger, harshness, ignorance; these characterize a man with foolish traits.
*The Bhagavad Gita*

Every generation a new crop of fools comes on. They think they can beat the orderly universe. They conceive themselves to be more clever than the eternal laws. They snatch goods from Nature's store, and run...And one by one they all come back to Nature's counter, and pay – pay in tears, in agony, in despair; pay as fools before them have paid...Nature keeps books pitilessly. Your credit with her is good, but she collects; there is no land you can flee to and escape her bailiffs...She never forgets; she sees to it that you pay her every cent you owe, with interest.

*Dr. Frank Crane*

To generalize is to be an idiot.
*William Blake*

To be like the parakeet, that says what he knows but doesn't know what he says.
*Spanish Proverb*

Little is needed to make a wise man happy, but nothing can content a fool. That is why nearly all men are miserable.
*La Rochefoucauld*

The foolish person seeks happiness in the distance.
*James Oppenheim*

It belongs to small-mindedness to be unable to bear either honor or dishonor, either good fortune or bad, but to be filled with conceit when honored and puffed up by trifling good fortune, and to be unable to bear even the smallest dishonor and to deem any chance failure a great misfortune, and to be distressed and annoyed at everything. Moreover the small-minded man is the sort of person to call all slights an insult and dishonor, even those that are due to ignorance or forgetfulness. Small-mindedness is accompanied by pettiness, querulousness, pessimism and self-abasement.
*Aristotle*

They are utter fools who accept a thing as convincing proof simply because it is in writing.
*Moses Maimonides*

A fool believes everything.
*English Proverb*

A wise man guides his own course of action; the fool follows another's direction.
*Sakya Pandit*

For none of the fools is satisfied with what one has, but rather is distressed about what one does not have.
*Epicurus*

Sweet words please fools.
*Japanese Proverb*

Thus may poor fools believe false teachers.
*Shakespeare*

The wise pursue understanding; fools follow the reports of others.
*Tibetan Proverb*

A fool and his money are soon parted.
*English Proverb*

One wise man can feed a thousand fools; one fool can scarcely feed himself.
*Chinese Proverb*

A fool will soon use up his money.
*Japanese Proverb*

When a fool goes shopping, the store-keepers rejoice.
*Yiddish Proverb*

Should a fool fall upon a great fortune, strangers will feast while his family starves.
*Tiruvalluvar*

Riches destroy the foolish.
*Buddha*

159

A fool is hotheaded and reckless.
*The Book of Proverbs*

Clothes may disguise a fool, but his words will give him away.
*Aesop*

Wicked men promise much and perform nothing.
*The Talmud*

A great talker may be no fool, but he is one that relies on him.
*Franklin*

What is respected by the great is condemned by the lowly.
*Sakya Pandit*

Fools brag of their knowledge, proud, ignorant, dissolving; staggering to and fro, blind and led by the blind; Dunces think, in their pride, that they have solved every problem; the passionate never learn.
*The Upanishads*

It is sometimes possible to be a fool with brains, but never to be a fool with discrimination.
*La Rochefoucauld*

A wise man doesn't know everything – only a fool does.
*African Proverb*

Fools rejoice at promises.
*Russian Proverb*

We have to live with others, and the stupid make up the majority.
*Baltasar Gracian*

Wise men don't need advice. Fools don't take it.
*Franklin*

The fool doth think he is wise.
*Shakespeare*

160

The majority never had right on its side... Who is it that constitutes the majority of the population of the country? Is it the wise folk or the fools... The stupid people are an overwhelming majority all over the world... The minority is always in the right.
*Henrik Ibsen*

It is the peculiar quality of a fool to perceive the faults of others and to forget his own.
*Cicero*

Summer insects are not equipped to talk about ice; a frog in the well is not equipped to discuss the ocean.
*Chinese Proverb*

The fool who acts like a two-footed beast should be especially avoided.
*Nagarjuna*

How can the wise be understood by the fool?
*Sakya Pandit*

Among those who stand outside virtue, there is no greater fool than he who stands with a lustful heart outside another's gate.
*Tiruvalluvar*

A fool, indeed, has great need of a title; it teaches men to call him count or duke, and thus forget his proper name of fool.
*John Crowne*

Any man can make mistakes, but only an idiot persists in his error.
*Cicero*

It never occurs to fools that merit and good fortune are closely united.
*Goethe*

Like snow in summer or rain in harvest, honor is not fitting for a fool.
*The Book of Proverbs*

There never was a good knife made of bad steel.
*Franklin*

Anger dwells only in the bosom of fools.
*Einstein*

Any fool can criticize, condemn and complain and most fools do.
*Franklin*

While fools shun one set of faults they run into the opposite one.
*Horace*

In the mass of mankind, I fear, there is too great a majority of fools and knaves; who, singly from their number, must to a certain degree be respected, though they are by no means respectable.
*Philip Stanhope*

It is difficult to free fools from the chains they revere.
*Voltaire*

It seems to never occur to fools that merit and good fortune are closely united.
*Goethe*

People who don't see their nature and imagine they can practice thoughtlessness all the time are lairs and fools.
*Bodhidharma*

Prejudices are what fools use for reason.
*Voltaire*

The whole problem with the world is that fools and fanatics are always so certain of themselves, and wiser people so full of doubts.
*Bertrand Russell*

Tricks and treachery are the practice of fools, that don't have brains enough to be honest.
*Franklin*

Though a wicked man appears good in his conduct, it is but hypocrisy.
*Sakya Pandit*

Most men are bad.
*Bias of Priene*

Many foxes grow grey, but few grow good.
*Franklin*

Is pride, the never-failing vice of fools.
*Alexander Pope*

Fools are without number.
*Desiderius Erasmus*

Prejudice is the reason of fools.
*Voltaire*

# THE GOLDEN RULE

生

Look to be treated by others as you have treated others.
*Syrus*

We should behave to our friends as we would wish our friends to behave to us.
*Aristotle*

What is hateful to you do not do to your neighbor. That is the whole of the Torah. The rest is commentary.
*The Talmud*

In everything do to others what you would have them do to you.
*Jesus*

Do not choose for anyone what you do not choose for yourself.
*Persian Proverb*

Do to others as we would that they should do to us.
*Meng Tse*

To do to men what we would have them do to ourselves is what one may call the teaching of humanity.
*Confucius*

Let us act towards others as we would that they should act towards us: let us not cause any suffering.
*The Dhammapada*

What you wish others to do, do yourselves.
*Ramakrishna*

Do not to others what would displease thee done to thyself.
*The Mahabharata*

I would act toward others with a heart pure and filled with love exactly as I would have them act toward me.
*Lalita Vistara*

I desire to act towards others even as I would toward myself.
*Buddha*

Do not do to others what angers you if done to you by others.
*Isocrates*

Do not that to thy neighbor that thou would not suffer from him.
*Pittacus of Lesbos*

Do to others as I would they should do to me.
*Plato*

Actions that are known to harm oneself should never be inflicted upon others.
*Tiruvalluvar*

True politeness...It simply consist in treating others just as you love to be treated yourself.
*Lord Chesterfield*

Whatever is hateful to thee, do not to thy neighbor.
*The Talmud*

You shall love your neighbor as yourself.
*Jesus*

Do not do unto others what is not pleasing to yourself.
*Nagarjuna*

What we do not like for ourselves, we should never do for others.
*Sakya Pandit*

162

Treat others as you would be treated yourself.

*The Sri Guru Granth Sahib*

That nature alone is good which refrains from doing unto another whatsoever is not good unto its own itself.

*Dadistan-i-Dinik*

A man should wander about treating all creatures as he himself would be treated.

*The Sutrakritanga*

Ascribe not to any soul that which thou wouldst not have ascribed to thee.

*Baha'u'llah*

Don't do to others what you wouldn't want done to you.

*Tzu-ssu*

Do unto all men as you would wish to have done unto you, and reject for others what you would reject for yourself.

*Muhammad*

Do not do to others what you would not wish to suffer at their hands, and be to them what you would wish them to be to you.

*Isocrates*

Do not thyself what displeases thee in others.

*Thales*

Love one another and do not strive for another's undoing. Even as you desire good treatment, so render it.

*Handsome Lake*

And if thine eyes be turned toward justice, choose thou for thy neighbor that which thou choosest for thyself.

*Epistle to the Son of the Wolf*

Whatever you feel should not be done to you by others, avoid doing to them.

*Sai Baba*

Hurt not others in ways that you yourself would find hurtful...

*Udana-Varga*

Thou shalt love thy neighbor as thyself.

*The Book of Leviticus*

Whatever is disagreeable to yourself do not do unto others.

*Shayast-na-Shayast*

What you do not wish to be done to yourselves, do not do to other men.

*Confucius*

Every religion emphasizes human improvement, love, respect for others, sharing other people's suffering. On these lines every religion has more or less the same viewpoint and the same goal.

*The Dalai Lama*

Wish for others whatever you wish for yourself.

*Hadith*

We have committed the Golden Rule to memory; let us now commit it to life.

*Edwin Markham*

# COMPASSION
# &
# KINDNESS

生

Never lose a chance of saying a kind word.
*William Makepeace Thackeray*

One kind word warms three winter months.
*Japanese Proverb*

Always set high value on spontaneous kindness.
*Samuel Johnson*

Blessed is he who gives from his substance to the poor; twice blessed is he who accompanies his gift with kind, comforting words.
*The Talmud*

To a person struggling in the sea of life a few uplifting words may be of great help.
*Sai Baba*

By doing service, heart and mind are purified...serve your people with the utmost calm and have a kind word for everyone.
*Sri Anandamayee Ma*

Compare your grieves with those of other men and they will seem less.
*Spanish Proverb*

Speak up for those who cannot speak for themselves, for the rights of all who are destitute. Speak up and judge fairly; defend the rights of the poor and needy.
*King Lemuel*

The greatest gain is to give to others.
*Buddha*

Those who do good because they want to be seen as good are not good.
*Lao Tzu*

It is better to give than to receive.
*Jesus*

Give soon and you give twice.
*Syrus*

We should give as we would receive, cheerfully, quickly, and without hesitation; for there is no grace in a benefit that sticks to the fingers.
*Seneca*

If you have much give of your wealth, if you have little give of your heart.
*Arab Proverb*

The manner of giving is worth more than the gift.
*Pierre Corneille*

They who give have all things; they who withhold have nothing.
*Hindu Proverb*

The wise find joy in generosity and because of it become blessed.
*Buddha*

For it is in giving that we receive.
*Saint Francis of Assisi*

Give and it shall be given to you.
*Jesus*

He who understands the duty of giving truly lives.
*Tiruvalluvar*

The most exquisite pleasure is giving pleasure to others.
*Jean de La Bruyere*

Have complete kindness towards all beings and, also, the spirit of self-sacrifice.
*Sai Baba*

Meet bitterness with kindness.
*Lao Tzu*

Cultivate loving kindness.
*Buddhist Proverb*

What wisdom can you find that is greater than kindness?
*Jean-Jacques Rousseau*

To grant forbearing kindness even to those who aggrieve us is the foremost of virtues.
*Tiruvalluvar*

Kindness is produced by kindness.
*Cicero*

Show kindness to your brothers and make them not fall into suffering.
*Chadana Sutta*

Don't postpone a good deed.
*Irish Proverb*

Kindness gives birth to kindness.
*Sophocles*

Be kind, for everyone you meet is fighting a hard battle.
*Philo*

Kindness affects more than severity.
*Aesop*

The believer is not one who eats his fill when his neighbor beside him is hungry.
*Muhammad*

I expect to pass through life but once. If, therefore, there be any kindness I can show, or any good thing I can do for my fellow being, let me do it now...as I shall not pass this way again.
*William Penn*

No kind deed has ever lacked its reward.
*Hawaiian Proverb*

He who is generous to the poor makes a loan to the Lord; He will repay him his due.
*The Book of Proverbs*

Give to the poor and become praiseworthy.
*Tiruvalluvar*

If we have corn and meat and know of a family that has none, we divide with them.
*Black Hawk*

To give alms is nothing unless you give thought also.
*John Ruskin*

Kind words do not cost much; yet they accomplish much.
*Blaise Pascal*

Giving to the poor is true charity.
*Tiruvalluvar*

If you wish to be perfect, go, sell your possessions, and give the money to the poor.
*Jesus*

What He gives you is not to be kept under lock and key, but to be shared.
*Mother Teresa*

Give the goods you have received to others according to their need.
*Sakya Pandit*

He is truly great who has charity.
*Thomas a'Kempis*

He is not charitable that will not be so privately.
*English Proverb*

Blessed is he who is kind to the needy.
*The Book of Proverbs*

He who oppresses the poor shows contempt for their Maker, but whoever is kind to the needy honors God.
*The Book of Proverbs*

When you give to the needy, do not let your left hand know what your right hand is doing, so that your giving may be in secret. Then your Father, who sees what is done in secret, will reward you.
*Jesus*

Each man should give what he has decided in his heart to give, not reluctantly or under compulsion, for God loves a cheerful giver.
*The Apsotle Paul*

The learned man distributes his wealth.
*Nagarjuna*

All living beings hate pain.
*Sutra-Krit-Anga*

A human being is part of the whole, called by us "the universe." Our task must be to widen our circle of compassion to embrace all living creatures and the whole of nature in its beauty.
*Einstein*

Judge charitably every man and justify him all you can.
*The Talmud*

Day and night the Wise never forget their desire to help others.
*Lao Tzu*

To serve the world is service of God; your highest good lies in serving all.
*Swami Muktananda*

If we always helped one another, no one would need luck.
*Menander*

Have benevolence towards all living things.
*The Tattvartha Sutra*

He who helps his fellow creature in the hour of need, and he who helps the oppressed, him will God help.
*Muhammad*

If we put ourselves in the place of other people, the jealousy and hatred we so often feel about them would disappear…
*Goethe*

Rendering help to another is the function of all human beings.
*The Tattvartha Sutra*

Do not let the ingratitude of many men deter you from doing good to others. To do good without ulterior motive is a generous and almost divine thing in itself.
*Francesco Guicciardini*

Truly I tell you, just as you did it to one of the least of these who are members of my family, you did it to me.
*Jesus*

What is serving God? Tis doing good to man.
*Franklin*

Charity is the greatest virtue.
*The Talmud*

To smile at someone who is sad; to visit even for a little while, someone who is lonely; to give someone shelter from the rain with our umbrella; to read something for someone who is blind: these and others can be small things, very small things, but they are appropriate to give our love of God concrete expression to the poor.
*Mother Teresa*

Real generosity is doing something nice for someone who'll never find out.
*Frank A. Clark*

The greatest tragedy is indifference.
*Red Cross Slogan*

166

Do not tire of being useful to yourself by being useful to others.
*Marcus Aurelius*

Do not avoid doing small favors, for you will seem like one who does great ones.
*Epicurus*

He that does good to another does good also to himself...
*Seneca*

Take the trouble to stop and think of the other person's feelings, his viewpoints, his desires and needs. Think more of what the other fellow wants, and how he must feel.
*Maxwell Maltz*

Consideration of others is the basis of a good life, a good society.
*Confucius*

Regard your neighbor's gain as your own gain, and your neighbor's loss as your own loss.
*Tai Shang Kan Ying P'ien*

I don't know what your destiny will be, but one thing I know: the only ones among you who will be really happy are those who have sought and found how to serve.
*Albert Schweitzer*

In nothing do men approach so nearly to the gods as in doing good to men.
*Marcus Aurelius*

Do all the good you can, in all the ways you can, to all the souls you can, in every place you can, at all the times you can, with all the zeal you can, every time you can.
*John Wesley*

If we could read the secret history of our enemies, we should find in each man's life sorrow and suffering enough to disarm all hostility.
*Henry Wadsworth Longfellow*

Filled with sympathy and benevolence, let the disciple show to all beings love and compassion.
*Majjhima Nikaya*

Nourish in your heart a benevolence without limits for all that lives.
*The Metta Sutta*

Have compassion, have pity for all beings that live.
*Fo-shu-hing-tsan-king*

So should you be good to all creatures, disdaining none. Even the most insignificant creatures should assume importance in your eyes, attend to it. Do good to whomever needs your goodness.
*The Kabbalah*

Bear one another's burdens.
*The Apostle Paul*

No one is useless in this world who lightens the burden of it to anyone else.
*Charles Dickens*

Feel for others as you feel for yourself.
*Indian Proverb*

Each of you should look not only to your own interest, but also to the interest of others.
*The ApostlePaul*

Deal with the faults of others as gently as with your own.
*Chinese Proverb*

The greatest pleasure is to do a good action by stealth and to have it found out by accident.
*Charles Lamb*

It is a man's kindly acts that are remembered of him in the years after his life.
*Ptah-Hotep*

Live and let live is not enough; live and help live is not too much.
*Orison Swett Marden*

So long as you can sweeten another's pain, life is not in vain.
*Helen Keller*

If you want others to be happy, practice compassion. If you want to be happy, practice compassion.
*The Dalai Lama*

What do we live for if not to make life less difficult for each other?
*George Eliot*

We should not regard giving as an obligation, but as a desire.
*Mother Teresa*

The path of duty lies in what is near at hand; and men seek for it in what is remote.
*Japanese Proverb*

Its a hard, sad life for most people. Don't scorn the simple things that give them pleasure.
*D. Sutten*

The little I have seen of this world teaches me to look upon the errors of others in sorrow, not in anger.
*Henry Wadsworth Longfellow*

Nothing is rarer than genuine kindness.
*La Rochefoucauld*

Be kind to people whether they deserve your kindness or not. If your kindness reaches the deserving, good for you; if your kindness reaches the undeserving, take joy in your compassion.
*Hadith*

You can not do a kindness too soon, for you never know how soon will be too late.
*Emerson*

A man is called selfish not for pursuing his own good, but for neglecting his neighbor's.
*Richard Whately*

There ain't nothing but one thing wrong with every one of us, and that's selfishness.
*Will Rogers*

Every person is responsible for all the good within the scope of his abilities...
*Gail Hamilton*

God will not show mercy to him who does not show mercy to others.
*Muhammad*

He whose mind is imbued with compassion for all sentient beings, that is the way of salvation and divine wisdom.
*Nagarjuna*

Service to the hungry, poor, sick, and ignorant, in the proper spirit, is as effective as any other spiritual discipline.
*Ramakrishna*

Compassion is the basis for all morality.
*Arthur Schopenhauer*

Man becomes great exactly in the degree to which he works for the welfare of his fellow man.
*Gandhi*

He can be called a master who has compassion for all that lives.
*The Dhammapada*

When a person is down in the world, an ounce of help is better than a pound of preaching.
*Edward Bulwer-Lytton*

Let your compassion extend to all creatures, neither despising nor destroying them.
*The Kabbalah*

Real generosity is doing something nice
for someone who'll never find out.
*Frank A. Clark*

It is the task of a good man to help those
in misfortune.
*Sophocles*

It was the rule of our life to share the fruits
of our skill and success with our less
fortunate brothers and sisters.
*Ohiyesa*

Our prime purpose in life is to help others.
*The Dalai Lama*

Fill your mind with compassion.
*Buddha*

Our kindly deeds and our generous gifts
go to heaven as messengers, and plead for
us before our heavenly father.
*The Talmud*

Compassion is the basis of morality.
*Arnold Schopenhauer*

Rich gifts wax poor when givers prove
unkind.
*Shakespeare*

Brothers, be good to one another.
*Baha-ullah*

Always be a little kinder than necessary.
*Sir James M. Barrie*

I would rather feel compassion than know
the meaning of it.
*Thomas Aquinas*

The duty of man is to be useful to men; to
a great number if he can, if not, to a small
number, otherwise to his neighbors... in
laboring for oneself, one labors also for
others, since there is formed a man who
can be of use to them.
*Seneca*

Compassion is a foundation for sharing our
aliveness and building a more humane
world.
*Martin Lowenthal*

Remember there's no such thing as a small
act of kindness. Every act creates a ripple
with no logical end.
*Scott Adams*

Constant kindness can accomplish much.
As the sun makes ice melt, kindness causes
misunderstanding, mistrust, and hostility
to evaporate.
*Albert Schweitzer*

When we feel love and kindness toward
others, it not only makes others feel loved
and cared for, but it helps us also to develop
inner happiness and peace.
*The Dalai Lama*

# LOVE

生

Love in its essence is spiritual fire.
*Emanuel Swedenborg*

A new command I give you: Love one
another. As I have loved you, so you must
love one another.
*Jesus*

The way to love anything is to realize that
it may be lost.
*G. K. Chesterson*

Love reckons hours for months, and days
for years, and every little absence is an age.
*John Dryden*

My command is this: Love each other as I
have loved you. Greater love has no one
than this, that he lay down his life for his
friends…Love each other.
*Jesus*

Love is patient, love is kind. It does not
envy, it does not boast, it is not proud. It is
not rude, it is not self-seeking, it is not
easily angered, it keeps no record of
wrongs. Love does not delight in evil but
rejoices with the truth, always hopes,
always perseveres. Love never fails.
*The Apostle Paul*

Love is the truth.
*Antoine the Healer*

At all times love is the greatest thing.
*The Narada Sutra*

Do everything in love.
*The Apostle Paul*

We are shaped and fashioned by what we
love.
*Goethe*

Each man, before he is Austrian, Serb, Turk
or Chinese, is first of all a man, that is to
say a thinking and loving being whose one
mission is to fulfill his destiny during the
short lapse of time that he is to live in this
world. That mission is to love all men.
*Tolstoy*

The teaching of our master consists solely
in this, to be upright in heart and to love
one's neighbor as oneself.
*Confucius*

The principal work of life is love. And one
cannot love in the past or in the future:
one can only love in the present, at this
hour, at the minute.
*Tolstoy*

Love is something eternal.
*Vincent Van Gogh*

The way is not in the sky. The way is in
the heart.
*Buddha*

Do all things with love.
*Og Mandino*

It is impossible to compel oneself to the
love of others. One can only reject that
which prevents love; and that which
prevents is the love of one's material I.
*Tolstoy*

Love is the basis of human understanding.
Love others. If the love is not returned,
examine yourself to see what the trouble
might be.
*Confucius*

Humanity does not embrace only the love
of one's like: it extends over all creatures.
*Chinese Proverb*

It is the duty of men to love even those who injure them.
*Marcus Antoninus*

Love is the nature of God in action.
*Stella Terrill Mann*

Those without love have known nothing of God, for God is love.
*The Gospel of John*

God is love. And in every moment of genuine love we are dwelling in God and God in us.
*Paul Tillich*

To love one's fellow man is Manhood-at its-best.
*Confucius*

One who obeys the will of Heaven will practice universal love.
*Mo Zi*

Humanity means loving men.
*Ying Tang*

True love is when one loves others in the same manner as one loves oneself.
*Kok Yim Ci Yuen*

In conflict it is love that wins. Love is the strongest protection. If you have love, it feels as if Heaven itself is keeping you safe.
*Lao Tzu*

At all times, let love flow between you and others.
*Swami Muktananda*

The sign of a person of wisdom is infinite love.
*Sai Baba*

An emotion which is overpowering one moment and gone the next cannot be called Love.
*Kabir*

Always nurture unconditional love for all beings. This is what it means to be truly human.
*Lao Tzu*

Love should be considered as the very breath of life.
*Sai Baba*

Love is to see what is good and beautiful in everything. It is to learn from everything, to see the gifts of God and the generosity of God in everything. It is to be thankful for all God's bounties… It will be difficult for those who have tasted to tell of it to those who have not.
*Sheikh Muzaffer*

He who would know the secret of both worlds will find that the secret of them both is Love.
*Attar*

Love is the cause of unity in all things.
*Aristotle*

Supreme Consciousness is in everyone, in the form of love.
*Sai Baba*

If reasonable people don't feel the presence of love within the universe, that doesn't mean it's not there.
*Rumi*

Whatever you do, do it with love!
*Sheikh Muzaffer*

One can be loved without knowing it, but one cannot love without knowing it.
*Aristotle*

There is no sort of valor more respected by the gods than this which comes of love.
*Plato*

Make love your gift to others.
*Lao Tzu*

The love for all that lives: all the religions teach it to us, the religion of the Brahmins, of the Buddhists, of the Hebrews, of the Chinese, of the Christians, of the Mohammedans. Therefore the most necessary thing in the world is to learn to love.

*Tolstoy*

Even the crow on the roof can be influenced by love.

*Japanese Proverb*

Love is immortal.

*The Narada Sutra*

It was by love that beings were created and it is commanded to them to live in love and harmony.

*Baha-ullah*

In real love you want the other person's good. In romantic love you want the other person.

*Margaret Anderson*

Love thy neighbor.

*Thales*

Let us not love in word, neither in tongue, but in deed and in truth.

*The Gospel of John*

Love conquers all.

*Voltaire*

It is better to have loved and lost, than not to have loved at all.

*Lord Alfred Tennyson*

Love is something you and I must have. We must have it because our spirit feeds upon it.

*Chief Dan George*

Live in joy, in love, even among those who hate.

*The Dhammapada*

The love we give away is the only love we keep.

*Elbert Hubbard*

The one thing we can never get enough of is love. And the one thing we can never give enough of is love.

*Henry Miller*

Love does not die easily. It is a living thing. It thrives in the face of all of life's hazards, save one — neglect.

*James D. Bryden*

Inner peace and love are God's greatest gifts.

*Sioux Proverb*

If you were all alone in the universe with no one to talk to, no one with which to share the beauty of the stars, to laugh with, to touch, what would be your purpose in life? It is other life, it is love, which gives your life meaning. This is harmony. We must discover the joy of each other, the joy of challenge, the joy of growth.

*Mitsugi Saotome*

Love is like a campfire: It may be sparked quickly, and at first the kindling throws out a lot of heat, but it burns out quickly. For long lasting, steady warmth (with delightful bursts of intense heat from time to time), you must carefully tend the fire.

*Molleen Matsumura*

Love doesn't sit there like a stone. It has to made like bread; remade all the time, made new.

*Ursula LeGuin*

172

# GRATITUDE

It is wrong not to repay the kindness of others, and to rejoice in their misfortunes.
*Qing Zheng*

Do not forget great kindness, even for a single meal.
*Emperor Wen Di*

When you drink of the spring be thankful for the source.
*Chinese Proverb*

Gratitude is a fruit of great cultivation; you do not find it among gross people.
*Samuel Johnson*

When you arise in the morning, give thanks for the morning light, for your life and strength. Give thanks for your food and the joy of living. If you see no reason for giving thanks, the fault lies in yourself.
*Tecumseh*

One never forgets to acknowledge a favor, no matter how small.
*Moral teaching of the Omaha*

Gratitude bestows reverence, allowing us to encounter everyday epiphanies, those transcendent moments of awe that change forever how we experience life and the world.
*John Milton*

To speak gratitude is courteous and pleasant, to enact gratitude is generous and noble, but to live gratitude is to touch Heaven.
*Johannes A. Gaertner*

To educate yourself for the feeling of gratitude means to take nothing for granted, but to always seek out and value the kind that will stand behind the action. Nothing that is done for you is a matter of course. Everything originates in a will for the good, which is directed at you. Train yourself never to put off the word or action for the expression of gratitude.
*Albert Schweitzer*

Saying thank you is more than good manners. It is good spirituality.
*Alfred Painter*

Gratitude is the sign of noble souls.
*Aesop*

Thankfulness is the beginning of gratitude. Gratitude is the completion of thankfulness. Thankfulness may consist merely of words. Gratitude is shown in acts.
*Henri Frederic Amiel*

Let us rise up and be thankful, for if we didn't learn a lot today, at least we learned a little, and if we didn't learn a little, at least we didn't get sick, and if we got sick, at least we didn't die; so, let us all be thankful.
*Buddha*

Everything has its beauty, but not everyone sees it.
*Confucius*

Gratitude is the fairest blossom which springs from the soul.
*Henry Ward Beecher*

There is as much greatness of mind in acknowledging a good turn, as in doing it.
*Seneca*

# HAPPINESS

生

Very little is needed to make a happy life. It is all in your way of thinking.
*Marcus Aurelius*

No man is happy who does not think himself so.
*Syrus*

Most folks are about as happy as they make up their minds to be.
*Lincoln*

He who would be truly happy must think his own lot best, and so live with men, as considering that God sees him, and so speak to God, as if men heard him.
*Seneca*

The happiness of your life depends on the quality of your thoughts; therefore, guard accordingly.
*Marcus Aurelius*

The chief happiness for a man is to be what he is.
*Desiderius Erasmus*

Happiness doesn't depend upon who you are or what you have; it depends solely upon what you think.
*Dale Carnegie*

It is necessary to the happiness of man that he be mentally faithful to himself.
*Thomas Paine*

It is the chiefest point of happiness that a man is willing to be what he is.
*Erasmus*

The possession of wisdom leads to true happiness.
*Porphyry*

The only ones among you who will be really happy are those who will have sought and found how to serve.
*Albert Schweitzer*

Happiness is the result of good conduct.
*The Dhammapada*

If a man speaks or acts with pure thought, happiness follows him like a shadow that never leaves him.
*Buddha*

It is virtuous activities that determine our happiness, and the opposite kind that produce the opposite effect.
*Aristotle*

When you cannot find your peace in yourself it is useless to look for it elsewhere.
*La Rochefoucauld*

Happiness depends upon ourselves.
*Aristotle*

The U.S. Constitution doesn't guarantee happiness, only the pursuit of it. You have to catch up with it yourself.
*Franklin*

One is happy as a result of one's own efforts – once one knows the necessary ingredients of happiness – simple tastes, a certain degree of courage, self-denial to a point, love of work, and, above all, a clear conscience.
*George Sand*

The essence of philosophy is that a man should so live that his happiness shall depend as little as possible on external things.
*Epictetus*

174

Happiness comes from within.
*Swami Shivananda*

Relative happiness, which is happiness depending on anything, must end in grief.
*Sri Anandamayee Ma*

What a fool he must be who thinks that his El Dorado is anywhere but where he lives!
*Thoreau*

Your success and happiness lies in you.
*Helen Keller*

It is foolish for someone to remain thirsty when he is in the midst of water.
*Ethiopian Proverb*

Happiness is when what you think, what you say, and what you do are in harmony.
*Gandhi*

To fill the hour, and leave no crevice...that is happiness.
*Emerson*

Human happiness and moral duty are inseparably connected.
*George Washington*

A happy life consists in tranquility of mind.
*Cicero*

True happiness consists in making others happy.
*Hindu Proverb*

Wisdom is the most important part of happiness.
*Sophocles*

Man is the artificer of his own happiness.
*Thoreau*

He is the happy man whose soul is superior to all happenings.
*Seneca*

Character is the basis of happiness and happiness the sanction of character.
*George Santayana*

The secret of happiness is not in doing what one likes to do, but in liking what one has to do.
*Sir James M. Barrie*

Happiness is not a station you arrive at, but a manner of traveling.
*Margaret Lee Runbeck*

Happiness is that state of consciousness which proceeds from the achievement of one's values.
*Ayn Rand*

Happy is the old age that atones for the follies of youth; but happier still the youth for which old age needs not to blush.
*The Talmud*

People far prefer happiness to wisdom, but this is like wanting to be immortal without getting older.
*Sydney J. Harris*

Happiness has nothing to do with wealth and prestige, but is a result of harmony.
*Lao Tzu*

Happy is he who fears God when in the prime of life.
*The Talmud*

The greatest happiness is tranquility of mind.
*Sakya Pandit*

Everyone is attracted to someone who lives in harmony with Tao, because they are peaceful and happy.
*Lao Tzu*

Permanent happiness can be secured only through the science of God-realization.
*Sai Baba*

Happiness is not only good in itself, but it is healthful.
*Hopi Maxim*

It is indeed foolish to be unhappy now because you may be unhappy at some future time.
*Seneca*

Whatever hour God has blessed you with, take it with grateful hand, nor postpone your joys from year to year, so that, in whatever place you have been, you may say that you have lived happily.
*Horace*

If you work at that which is before you, following right reason seriously, vigorously, calmly, without allowing anything else to distract you, but keeping your divine part pure, as if you were bound to give it back immediately; if you hold to this, expecting nothing, but satisfied to live now according to nature, speaking heroic truth in every word which you utter, you will live happy. And there is no man able to prevent this.
*Marcus Aurelius*

The man who makes everything that leads to happiness depend upon himself, and not upon other men, has adopted the very best plan for living happily.
*Plato*

Many run about after happiness like an absent-minded man hunting for his hat, while it is in his hand or on his head.
*James Sharp*

Happiness is not in our circumstances, but in ourselves... Happiness is something we are.
*John B. Sheerin*

Happiness grows at our own firesides, and is not to be picked in stranger's gardens.
*Douglas Jerrold*

To live happily is an inward power of the soul.
*Marcus Aurelius*

Be cheerful while you are alive.
*Ptah-Hotep*

No man is happy unless he believes he is.
*Syrus*

A man should be happy and in good humor to his dying day.
*The Havamal*

There is no happiness so great as peace of mind.
*The Dhammapada*

God and true happiness are one and the same.
*Boethius*

No evil man is happy.
*Juvenal*

A cheerful heart is good medicine.
*The Book of Proverbs*

He who laughs, lasts.
*Norwegian Proverb*

He who would be healthy, let him be cheerful.
*Welch Proverb*

Laugh if you are wise.
*Martial*

Happiness is that state of consciousness which proceeds from the achievement of one's values.
*Ayn Rand*

Thousands of candles can be lighted from a single candle, and the life of the candle will not be shortened. Happiness never decreases by being shared.
*Buddha*

# CONTENTMENT

生

Think contentment the greatest wealth.
*George Shelley*

Sufficiency's enough for men of sense.
*Epicurus*

A wise man will desire no more than what he may get justly, use soberly, distribute cheerfully, and leave contently.
*Franklin*

He who is contented is rich.
*Lao Tzu*

All fortune belongs to him who has a contented mind.
*The Panchattantra*

Do not set your heart on wealth…Do not strain to seek increases, what you have, let it suffice you.
*Amenemope*

He is richest who is content with the least, for content is the wealth of nature.
*Socrates*

A man should always consider how much he has more than he wants.
*Joseph Addison*

Those who know when they have enough are rich.
*Chinese Proverb*

The sage is happy everywhere, the whole earth is his. Nowhere and in no situation is the sage dissatisfied with his condition.
*Confucius*

He has everything who gives no concern to what does not concern him.
*Baltasar Gracian*

The greatest wealth is to live content with little, for there is never want where the mind is satisfied.
*Lucretius*

Who is rich? He who is satisfied with his lot.
*The Talmud*

To be content with what we possess is the greatest and most secure of riches.
*Cicero*

To be satisfied with a little, is the greatest wisdom; and he that increases his riches, increases his cares; but a contented mind is a hidden treasure, and trouble does not find it.
*Akhenaton*

If I am content with little – enough is as good as a feast.
*Nellie Sequichie*

The surest possession is real contentment.
*Nagarjuna*

Nothing is enough to the man for whom enough is too little.
*Epicurus*

Enjoy your own life without comparing it with that of another.
*The Condorcet*

If all misfortunes were laid in one common heap whence everyone must take an equal portion, most people would be contented to take their own and depart.
*Socrates*

He that finds discontentment in one place is not likely to find happiness in another.
*Aesop*

He is a wise man who does not grieve for the things which he has not, but rejoices for those which he has.
*Epictetus*

Let not your mind run on what you lack as much as on what you have already.
*Marcus Aurelius*

A prudent man will think more important what fate has conceded him than what it has denied.
*Baltasar Gracian*

Remember this – that very little is needed to make a happy life.
*Marcus Aurelius*

He who knows that enough is enough will always have enough.
*Lao Tzu*

I have learned, in whatsoever state I am, therewith to be content.
*The Apostle Paul*

For a man who is contented with little, wealth is inexhaustible. He who continually seeks and is never satisfied will experience a constant rain of sorrow.
*Sakya Pandit*

It has always been our belief that the love of possessions is a weakness to be overcome. Its appeal is to the material part, and if allowed its way it will in time disturb the spiritual balance for which we all strive.
*Ohiyesa*

Content makes poor men rich; Discontent makes rich men poor.
*Franklin*

Be content with such things as you have.
*The Book of Hebrews*

He is well paid who is well satisfied.
*Shakespeare*

Contentment consist not in adding more fuel, but in taking away some fire.
*Thomas Fuller*

Health is the greatest possession. Contentment is the greatest treasure. Confidence is the greatest friend. Non-being is the greatest joy.
*Lao Tzu*

The world is full of people looking for spectacular happiness while they snub contentment.
*Doug Larson*

There is no austerity equal to a balanced mind, and there is no happiness equal to contentment; there is no disease like covetousness, and no virtue like mercy.
*Chanakya*

True contentment is a thing as active as agriculture. It is the power of getting out of any situation all that there is in it. It is arduous and it is rare.
*G. K. Chesterson*

He is poor who does not feel content.
*Japanese Proverb*

# The SPIRIT

We must walk in balance on the earth – a foot in spirit and a foot in the physical.
*Lynn Andrews*

The soul of the soul is the Holy Ancient One.
*The Kabbalah*

Until you have found God in your own soul, the whole world will seem meaningless to you.
*Rabindranath Tagore*

Just as the soul is the life of the body, so God is the life of the soul.
*Saint Augustine*

I have been here since the beginning, and I shall be until the end of days; for there is no ending to my existence. The human soul is but a part of a burning torch which God separated from Himself at Creation.
*Kahlil Gibran*

The soul is veiled by the body, God is veiled by the soul.
*Farid-uddin Attar*

There is a natural body and there is a spiritual body.
*The Apostle Paul*

Either we have an immortal soul, or we have not. If we have not, we are beasts; the first and wisest of beasts it may be; but still beasts.
*Samuel Taylor Coleridge*

The spirit is the true self.
*Cicero*

The knower of the Atman does not identify himself with his body. He rests within it, as if within a carriage.
*Shankara*

It is not that we have a soul, we are a soul.
*Amelia E. Barr*

All things in this world have souls or spirits.
*Edward Goodbird*

Do not become attached to this temporary physical body; use the body as a tool. Consider yourself as separate from this destructive body, which has been created out of the blending of the five elements.
*Sai Baba*

The spirit neither disappears nor diminishes nor changes when the body is destroyed.
*Sheik Badruddin*

We believe that the spirit pervades all creation and that every creature possesses a soul in some degree...
*Ohiyesa*

There are two kinds of beauty, one being of the soul and the other of the body. That of the soul is revealed through intelligence, modesty, right conduct, generosity, and good breeding...
*Cervantes*

We are in this world, but not of it.
*Sufi Maxim*

All souls are immortal.
*Socrates*

The voice of which tells us we are immortal is the voice of God within us.
*Pascal*

It is perfectly certain that the soul is immortal and imperishable, and our souls will actually exist in another world.
*Socrates*

Your true nature is not lost in moments of delusion, nor is it gained at the moment of enlightenment. It was never born and can never die.
*Huang-Po*

The spirit never perishes, only the body decays.
*Mou Zi*

Birthless and deathless and changeless remains the spirit, dead though the house of it seems.
*The Bhagavad Gita*

Every distortion of the spirit is more deforming than one of the body, because it degrades a superior beauty.
*Baltasar Gracian*

Not yet settled in a permanent home, the soul takes temporary shelter in a body.
*Tiruvalluvar*

As a draft animal is yoked in a wagon, even so the spirit is yoked in this body.
*Thomas Hobbes*

The soul has not been and will never be, it always is.
*Tolstoy*

The soul of man is immortal and imperishable.
*Plato*

The disembodied spirit is immortal; there is nothing of it that can grow old or die.
*Thomas Hobbes*

It is the general belief of the Indian that after a man dies his spirit still lives.
*Chased-By-Bears*

The true self transcends life and death. It existed before the birth of one's parents. It has been in existence since before the separation of heaven and earth... The true self has no form and cannot be seen as we ordinarily see things with the eyes.
*Takuan Soho*

First, be fixed in the consciousness that you are the immortal soul, which is indestructible, which is holy, which is pure and divine.
*Sai Baba*

The soul bound is man; free, it is God.
*Ramakrishna*

The soul is infinite, universal, detached.
*The Upanishads*

180

# GOD

When you have shut your doors, and darkened your room, remember never to say that you are alone, for you are not alone; but God is within, and your genius is within, and what need have they of light to see what you are doing?

*Epictetus*

The most beautiful of all emblems is that of God, whom Timaeus of Locris describes under the image of "A circle whose centre is everywhere and whose circumference is nowhere."

*Voltaire*

God enters by a private door into every individual.

*Emerson*

God dwells where we let God in.

*Menachem Mendel*

Live innocently; God is here.

*Linnaeus*

He who sees me everywhere
and sees everything in me
will not be lost to me,
and I will not be lost to him.

I exist in all creatures
So the disciplined man devoted to me
Grasps the oneness of life;
Wherever he is, he is in me.

*The Bhagavad Gita*

The eyes of the Lord are everywhere, keeping watch on the wicked and the good.

*The Book of Proverbs*

Be aware that God fashioned everything and is within everything.

*The Kabbalah*

The Eternal is in every man, but all men are not in the Eternal; there lies the cause of their suffering.

*Ramakrishna*

There is nothing in which God does not exist.

*The Hermetic Writings*

We must conclude that nothing is outside of God... everything that exists, large and small - they exist solely through the divine energy that flows to them and clothes itself in them... God's presence fills the entire world.

*The Kabbalah*

Apprehend God in all things, for God is in all things.

*Meister Eckhart*

Know that you are always in God's Presence.

*The Kabbalah*

This universe is nothing but Brahman. See Brahman everywhere, under all circumstances, with the eye of the spirit and a tranquil heart.

*Shankara*

Suppose that a warrior forgot he was already wearing his pearl on his forehead, and sought for it somewhere else: he might search through the whole world without finding it.

*Huang-Po*

In the heart of all things, of whatever is in the universe, dwells the Lord.

*The Upanishads*

The universe is the body of one Being.

*Lao Tzu*

You are bearing God about with you, you poor wretch, and know it not! Do you suppose I am speaking of some external God, made of silver or gold? It is within yourself that you bear Him, and do not perceive that you are defiling Him with impure thoughts and filthy actions.
*Epictetus*

One Universe made up of all that is; and one God in it all, and one principle of Being, and one Law, the Reason, shared by all thinking creatures, and one Truth.
*Marcus Aurelius*

All things are the works of the Great Spirit. We should know that He is within all things: the trees, the grasses, the rivers, the mountains, and all the four-legged animals, and the winged peoples; and even more important, we should understand that He is also above all these things and peoples.
*Black Elk*

We do not walk alone. The Great Being walks beside us.
*Polinggaysi Qoyawayma*

The center of the universe is everywhere.
*Black Elk*

I searched for God, and found only myself. I searched for myself, and found only God.
*Sufi Proverb*

I saw my Lord with the eye of my heart. I said, "Who are you?" He said, "You."
*Al-Hallaj*

There is One that made all this, who shows us everything.
*Yuki*

The Lord of the universe, the Witness of all, never sleeps. He is ever-wakeful. He knows all your actions, good or bad; He is aware of your every thought.
*Swami Muktananda*

He is the first and the last, the manifest and the hidden: and He knows all things.
*Mohammed*

God is a sea of infinite substance.
*Saint John of Damascus*

God and all the attributes of God are eternal.
*Benedict Spinoza*

Eternal and supreme is the Infinite Spirit.
*The Bhagavad Gita*

God is love.
*The Gospel of John*

I am the source of all the gods and great sages.
*The Bhagavad Gita*

Your God permeates everything... He is the Lord of all. Everything is the Absolute.
*Swami Muktananda*

He is supreme Light hidden under every veil.
*Zohar*

He is the soul of all conscious creatures, who constitutes all things in this world, those which are beyond our sense and those which fall within their range.
*Ashwaghosha*

He is the principle of supreme Wisdom.
*Zohar*

For what is God? He is the soul of the universe.
*Seneca*

God is a circle whose center is everywhere and whose circumference is nowhere.
*Empedocles*

Tao is the Whole, the essential reality.
*Chuang Tzu*

182

God is not some person outside ourselves or away from the universe. He pervades everything and is omniscient as well as omnipotent... Being immanent in all beings; he hears everything and reads our innermost thoughts...God is not a person. He is the all-pervading, all powerful spirit.

*Gandhi*

He is the creator of the universe, and as it were the Father of all things in common, and a portion of Him pervades everything.

*Zeno*

There are innumerable definitions of God, because his manifestations are in-numerable... To me God is truth and love. God is ethics and morality; God is fearlessness... He is the searcher of the hearts. He knows us and our hearts better than we do ourselves...

*Gandhi*

There is only one Universal Way, but from different perspectives it is given different names.

*Lao Tzu*

He is pure of all name.

*The Bab*

There is only one omnipotent and omnipresent God. He is named variously and we remember him by the name which is most familiar to us.

*Gandhi*

Radiant is the Light of Lights that which the knowers of the soul know...The whole world is illuminated by its light. God truly is this immortal.

*The Mundaka Upanishad*

To know the One and Supreme, the supreme Lord, the Immense Space, the Superior Rule, that is the summit of knowledge.

*Chuang Tse*

It is impossible to use our concepts and words to describe God...It's very wise not to say anything about God.

*Thich Nhat Hanh*

Call Him what name you will; for to those who know, He is the possessor of all names.

*Baha-ullah*

Numerous are the names of the Ineffable and infinite the forms which lead towards Him. Under whatever name or in whatever form you desire to enter into relation with him, it is in that form and under that name that you will see Him.

*Ramakrishna*

It penetrates all and It does not perish. It may be regarded as the mother of the universe. For myself I know not Its name, but to give it a name I call it Tao.

*Lao Tzu*

There is no suitable name for the eternal Tao.

*Lao Tzu*

The supreme Brahman without beginning cannot be called either Being or Non-being.

*The Bhagavad Gita*

When thou art preparing to commit a sin, think not that thou will conceal it; there is a God that forbids crimes to be hidden.

*Tibullus*

From Wankan Tanka, the Great Spirit, there came a great unifying force that flowed in and through all things...

*Chief Standing Bear*

Nothing in all creation is hidden from God's sight. Everything is uncovered and laid bare before the eyes of him who we must give account.

*The Book of Hebrews*

I know the Great Spirit is looking down on me from above, and will hear what I say.
*Sitting Bull*

We are all children of the one God. God is listening to me. The sun, the darkness, the winds, are all listening to what we now say.
*Geronimo*

God has nothing hidden from Him.
*African Proverb*

God is aware of everything... He is with you wherever you are, and God sees what you do.
*Mohammed*

The deeds of man never deceive the gods.
*Ovid*

Your mind cannot possibly understand God. Your heart already knows.
*Emmanuel*

If any man hopes to do a deed without God's knowledge, he errs.
*Pindar*

He is not far but very near. He witnesses all that you do, knows all that you think.
*Swami Muktananda*

God has many names, though He is only one Being.
*Aristotle*

The Stoics also teach that God is unity, and that he is called Mind and Fate and Jupiter, and by many other names besides.
*Diogenes*

God has a million faces.
*The Bhagavad Gita*

The one Being the wise call by many names.
*The Rig Veda*

The Great Spirit sees and hears everything, and He never forgets.
*In-Mut-Too-Yah-Lat-Lat*

The Great Spirit is looking at me, and will hear me.
*Chief Joseph*

It is the heart which experiences God, not the reason.
*Blaise Pascal*

Worship God as if you see Him, and remember that even if you see him not, He still sees you.
*Hadith*

The sea receives ten thousand rivers and still the sea is never full.
*Chinese Proverb*

Tao is like the ocean. All rivers run to the ocean without filling it up. All water comes from it without ever emptying it.
*Zhun Mang*

Tao is like an empty space that can never be filled up. Yet it contains everything... Hidden, but always present.
*Lao Tzu*

All Buddhas and all ordinary beings are nothing but the one mind. This mind is beginningless and endless, unborn and indestructible... This pure mind, which is the source of all things, shines forever with the radiance of its own perfection.
*Huang-Po*

One Universe made up of all that is; and one God in it all, and one principle of Being, and one Law, the Reason, shared by all thinking creatures, and one Truth.
*Marcus Aurelius*

He is everywhere in the world and stands with all in His embrace.
*The Bhagavad Gita*

184

The Great Spirit sees and hears everything, and He never forgets.

*In-Mut-Too-Yah-Lat-Lat*

The Great Spirit is looking at me, and will hear me.

*Chief Joseph*

Your mind cannot possibly understand God. Your heart already knows.

*Emmanuel*

The complete truth is that God is always with you.

*Mohammad*

Called or not called, God is Present.

*Carl Jung*

We believe that Wankan Tanka is everywhere.

*Chased-By-Bears*

He is in and as everything.

*Sai Baba*

For the kingdom of God is within you.

*Jesus*

The Great Spirit is in all things, he is in the air we breathe. The Great Spirit is our Father...

*Big Thunder*

God is light.

*The Gospel of John*

Tao is the Being that resides in all beings.

*Tai Gong Diao*

God is the power in everything.

*Sai Baba*

# ALL is ONE

生

No man is an island, entire of itself; every man is a piece of the continent, a part of the main.

*John Donne*

Of a truth, men are mystically united; a mystic bond of brotherhood makes all men one.

*Thomas Carlyle*

To be is to live with God.

*Emerson*

All men are separated from each other by the body, but all are united by the same spiritual principle which gives life to everything.

*Tolstoy*

The kingdom of God is within you.

*Jesus*

There is one body and one spirit.

*The Apostle Paul*

A river does not resemble a pond, a pond a tun, nor a tun a bucket: but in a pond, a river, a tun and a bucket there is the same water. And so too all men are different, but the spirit that lives in them all is the same.

*Tolstoy*

May they know that they are related to all that moves upon the universe...

*Slow Buffalo*

There are two ways of looking at beings; either as distinct individuals or as all one in Tao.

*Lao Tzu*

For all is full of God.

*Hermes*

There is no need to exhaust yourselves in the search for God. He is there like butter in milk, like the chicken in the egg, in every atom of creation. He does not come from somewhere or go elsewhere. He is here, there, everywhere. From the atom to the cosmos, from the microcosm to the macrocosm, He is everywhere.

*Sai Baba*

For you and your neighbor are one and the same.

*The Kabbalah*

Everything is interwoven, and the web is holy, none of its parts are unconnected. They are composed harmoniously, and together they compose the world. One world, made up of all things. One divinity, present in them all. One substance and one law... And one truth.

*Marcus Aurelius*

With realization, all things are one unity; without realization, all things are distinct.

*Wu-Men*

Listen to Nature: she cries out to us that we are all members of one family.

*Saadi*

I am one with the Earth.

*Navajo Maxim*

All things share the same true nature.

*Bodhidharma*

The Universe is a unity.

*Philolaus*

186

Without being divided in creatures It dwells in them as if divided.
*The Bhagavad Gita*

This world is a republic, all whose citizens are made of one and the same substance.
*Epictetus*

Soul is one, Nature is one, life is one.
*Hermes*

All is only one great body of which we are the members.
*Seneca*

The universe is a single life comprising one substance and one soul.
*Marcus Aurelius*

The truth is that everything is One.
*Roshi Philip Kapleau*

Life is one indivisible whole.
*Gandhi*

Just as seeing from a distance makes things blur into one, from the enlightened perspective everything is a part of the undifferentiated primal unity.
*Chuang Tzu*

See one promontory, one mountain, one sea, one river and see all.
*Socrates*

All things are connected like the blood which unites one family.
*Chief Seattle*

Fundamentally the marksman aims at himself.
*Zen in the Art of Archery*

Everything the same; everything distinct.
*Zen Maxim*

Everything is God.
*Sai Baba*

Even the commonest sticks and stones have spiritual essence.
*LaFlesche*

Even in one leaf of a tree, or in one blade of grass, God is present.
*Shinto Maxim*

The soul of the soul is the Holy Ancient One. All is connected, this one to that one.
*The Kabbalah*

The Dakota could despise no creature, for all were of one blood, made by the same hand, and filled with the essence of the Great Mystery.
*Chief Luther Standing Bear*

The Great Spirit is in all things.
*Big Thunder*

The voice of the Great Spirit is heard in the twittering of the birds, the rippling of mighty waters, and the sweet breathing of the flowers.
*Zitkala Sa*

We are all children of one God.
*Geronimo*

We believe that the Spirit pervades all creation.
*Ohiyesa*

There is nothing in this world that is not God.
*The Upanishads*

All beings are parts of the Whole.
*Chuang Tzu*

The human soul is but a part of a burning torch which God separated from Himself at Creation.
*Kahlil Gibran*

The universe is the body of one Being.
*Lao Tzu*

We ought not to understand God and creation as two things distinct from each other, but as one and the same.
*Johannes Scotus Erigena*

The infinite variety of particular objects constitutes one sole and identical Being.
*Giordano Bruno*

The body is a unit, though it is made up of many parts; and though all its parts are many, they form one body... we were all baptized by one Spirit into one body...
*The Apostle Paul*

Peace comes within the souls of men when they realize their relationship, their oneness, with the universe and all its powers, and when they realize that at the center of the Universe dwells Wankan Tanka, and that this center is really everywhere, it is within each of us.
*Black Elk*

He who sees me everywhere and sees everything in me will not be lost to me, and I will not be lost to him.
*The Bhagavad Gita*

There is one body and one Spirit...one Lord, one faith...one God and Father of all, who is over all and through all and in all.
*The Apostle Paul*

We should understand well that all things are the work of the Great Spirit. We should know that He is within all things.
*Black Elk*

I exist in all creatures, so the disciplined man devoted to me grasps the oneness of life; whatever he is, he is in Me.
*The Bhagavad Gita*

The lovers of God have no religion but God alone.
*Rumi*

In the universe there is nothing which is not God.
*Hermes*

God is all and all is God.
*Eckhart*

When you contemplate the Creator, realize that his encampment extends beyond, infinitely beyond, and so, too, in front of you and behind you, east and west, north and south, above and below, infinitely everywhere. Be aware that God fashioned everything and is within everything.
*The Kabbalah*

God is one in all things.
*Angelus Silesius*

God is unified oneness...The entire chain is one. Down to the last link, everything is linked with everything else.
*The Kabbalah*

Know then that the visible world and the invisible are God Himself. There is only He and all that is, is He.
*Farid-uddin Attar*

It is one and the same Being who manifests in all that lives.
*Schopenhauer*

He sees rightly who beholds the Supreme Lord dwelling equally in all existences and not perishing when they perish.
*The Bhagavad Gita*

For there is one world formed of all, one God pervading all, one substance, one Law, one Reason common to all intelligent beings.
*Marcus Aurelius*

The Lord who is established in the secret place of every soul pervades the whole universe.
*The Upanishads*

Through out the ages, the scriptures of all religions have proclaimed that humanity is one great family…In fact, almost all the principles that are associated with religious thought are shared by every religion… When their inherent similarities are revealed, the collected wisdom of the world's religions shows a profound "Oneness" of the human spirit… our differences are superficial, and that our similarities are deep.

*Jeffrey Moses*

Do not attach yourself to a particular creed exclusively so that you disbelieve in all the rest; otherwise you will lose much good; nay, you will fail to recognize the real truth of the matter. God, the omnipresent and omnipotent, is not limited by any one creed.

*Ibn Arabi*

The Great Spirit does right. He knows what is best for his children… We do not worship the Great Spirit as the white men do, but we believe that forms of worship do not matter to the Great Spirit; what pleases him is the offering of a sincere heart.

*Chief Red Jacket*

The Essence of all things is one and identical.

*Ashwaghosha*

All that exists is but the transformation of one and the same Matter and is therefore one and the same thing.

*Diogenes*

For all souls are one. Each is a spark from the original soul, and this soul is wholly inherent in all souls, just as your soul is in all members of your body.

*Shmelke of Nikolsburg*

He is all things and all things are one.

*Zohar*

The humble, meek, merciful, just, pious and devout souls everywhere are of one religion, and when death has taken off the mask, they will know one another, though the diverse liveries they wore here make them strangers.

*William Penn*

Every truth without exception – and whoever may utter it – is from the Holy Spirit. The old pagan virtues were from God. Revelation has been made to many pagans.

*Saint Thomas Aquinas*

The man who does not think about religion imagines that there is only one that is true, the one in which he was born. But you have only to ask yourself what would happen if you were born in another religion, you, Christian, if you were born a Muhammadan, you Buddhist, a Christian, and you, Muhammadan, a Brahmin. Is it possible that we alone with our religion should be in the truth and that all others should be subjected to falsehood? No religion can become true merely by your persuading yourself or persuading others that it alone is true.

*Tolstoy*

A human being is a part of the whole that we call the universe, a part limited in time and space.

*Einstein*

All men of wisdom have one religion; they all have one caste; they all behold the face of the One!

*Dadu*

Matter and Spirit are one since the first beginning.

*Ashwaghosha*

There is one self in all existences which appears as if different in different creatures.

*The Amritabindu Upanishad*

189

Within man is the soul of the whole, the wise silence, the universal beauty to which every part and particle is equally related, the eternal One.

*Emerson*

All existence is God, and the stone is a thing pervaded by divinity.

*The Kabbalah*

We are the leaves of one branch, the drops of one sea, the flowers of one garden.

*Jean Baptiste Henry Lacordaire*

Whatever you see, whatever you touch, that is God.

*Lucan*

There is not a body, however small, which does not enclose a portion of the divine substance.

*Giordano Bruno*

Whatsoever is, is in God, and without God nothing can be, or be conceived.

*Benedict Spinoza*

All here is God.

*The Mandukya Upanishad*

The universe is nothing but Brahman.

*Shankara*

The whole universe is one commonwealth of which both gods and men are members.

*Cicero*

Humankind has not woven the web of life. We are but one thread within it. Whatever we do to the web, we do to ourselves. All things are bound together. All things connect.

*Chief Seattle*

As he is one, so we call Him God, the Deity, the Divine Nature, and other names of the same signification.

*John Hales*

For your incorruptible spirit is in all.

*The Wisdom of Solomon*

# GOD'S INSIGHT

生

For God shall bring every work into judgment, with every hidden thing, whether it be good or whether it be evil.
*The Book of Ecclesiastes*

God's mill grinds slow but sure.
*George Herbert*

Weigh well your words and deeds before they are weighed at the last judgment.
*Caliph Omar*

Remember that there is above an All-Seeing Eye, an All-Hearing Ear, and a record of all your actions.
*The Talmud*

He looks at our acts.
*Gandhi*

An unjust deed doesn't escape the gods' attention.
*Plato*

Man sees only what is visible, but the Lord sees into the heart.
*The Book of Proverbs*

Heaven is above us yet; there sits a judge that no king can corrupt.
*Shakespeare*

The Great Spirit will not punish us for what we do not know.
*Chief Red Jacket*

Every crime will tell its tale upon the Day of Judgment.
*Chinese Proverb*

When the One Great Scorer comes to write against your name, He marks, not that you won or lost, but how you played the game.
*Grantland Rice*

I tremble for my country when I reflect that God is just; that his justice cannot sleep forever.
*Thomas Jefferson*

We are all pencils in the hand of God.
*Mother Teresa*

God does not play dice.
*Einstein*

Sir, my concern is not whether God is on our side; my greatest concern is to be on God's side, for God is always right.
*Lincoln*

To do it no more is the truest repentance.
*Martin Luther*

191

# RELIGION

生

One man considers one day more sacred than another; another man considers every day alike. Each one should be fully convinced in his own mind.
*The Book of Romans*

The nearer the church, the further from God.
*John Heywood*

The Lord showed me, so that I did see clearly, that He did not dwell in these temples which men had commanded and set up, but in people's hearts...his people were his temple, and he dwelt in them.
*George Fox*

I like the silent church before the service begins, better than any preaching.
*Emerson*

Big churches, little saints.
*German Proverb*

A great church and little devotion.
*Italian Proverb*

Temples cannot imprison within their walls the Divine Substance.
*Euripides*

There is only one temple in the world and that is the human body.
*Novalis*

Your daily life is your temple and your religion. Whenever you enter into it take with you your all.
*Kahlil Gibran*

Religion's in the heart, not in the knees.
*Douglas Jerrold*

Religion is nothing else but love to God and man.
*William Penn*

In what does religion consist? It consists in causing as little suffering as possible and in doing good in abundance. It consists in the practice of love, of compassion, of truth, of purity in all domains of life.
*Ashoka*

Ordinary men pronounce a sack-full of discourses on religion, but do not put a grain into practice, while the sage speaks little, but his whole life is religion put into action.
*Ramakrishna*

Compassion and love, behold the true religion!
*Ashoka*

Love towards all beings is the true religion.
*Jatakamala*

So long as a man disputes and discusses about doctrines and dogmas, he has not yet tasted the nectar of the true faith. When he has tasted it, he becomes tranquil and full of peace.
*Ramakrishna*

I am for religion against religions.
*Victor Hugo*

Many have quarreled about religion that never practiced it.
*Franklin*

Religion...is a man's total reaction upon life.
*William James*

My own mind is my church.
*Thomas Paine*

192

Let us not fear to reject from our religion all that is useless, material, tangible as well as all that is vague and indefinite; the more we purify its spiritual kernel, the more we shall understand the true law of life.

*Tolstoy*

Clearly the person who accepts the Church as an infallible guide will believe whatever the Church teaches.

*Saint Thomas Aquinas*

Men never do evil so completely and cheerfully as when they do it from religious conviction.

*Blaise Pascal*

This would be the best of all possible worlds, if there were no religion in it.

*John Adams*

I believe that religion, generally speaking, has been a curse to mankind.

*H. L. Mencken*

One must make a distinction between what God himself said and what the clergy has said in His name.

*Claude Henri de Rouvroy*

We have just enough religion to make us hate, but not enough to make us love one another.

*Jonathan Swift*

As long as there are fools and rascals there will be religions.

*Voltaire*

I do not think that thanks and compliments, though repeated weekly, can discharge our real obligations to each other, and much less those to our Creator.

*Franklin*

There is nothing that is so apt to obscure the face of God as a religion.

*Martin Buber*

Most of the world's people worship the offspring, while one who is spiritually mature embraces the Source and never becomes the slave of any social or religious movement.

*Lao Tzu*

Religion is always man-made. It cannot therefore be the whole truth.

*Mabel Collins*

God never made an agreement with any religion...All religions are of fairly recent origin, but God has existed since the beginning of time. He could not have signed a contract with any religion founder saying, "You are my exclusive salesman."

*Swami Muktananda*

He whose thought is always fixed on the Eternal has no need of any devotional practice or spiritual exercise.

*Ramakrishna*

The worship of the different religions, which are like so many small streams, move together to meet God, who is like the ocean.

*Rajjab*

Decry not other sects nor depreciate them but, on the contrary, render honor to that in them which is worthy of honor.

*Ashoka*

All religions, all this singing, is one song. The differences are just illusion and vanity. The sun's light looks a little different on this wall than it does on that wall...but it still comes from the same sun.

*Rumi*

A truly religious man ought to think that the other religions are also paths leading towards the Reality. We should always maintain an attitude of respect towards other religions.

*Ramakrishna*

All philosophers of the world who had a religion have said in all ages: "There is a God; and one must be just." That then is the universal religion established in all ages and throughout mankind. The point in which they all agree is therefore true and the systems through which they differ therefore false.

*Voltaire*

In quarreling about the shadow, we often lose the substance.

*Aesop*

You and I are all children of one faith, for the diverse paths of religion are fingers of the loving hand of one Supreme Being, a hand extended to all, offering completeness of spirit to all, eager to receive all.

*Kahlil Gibran*

The Eternal Religion is the mother of all religions.

*Sai Baba*

The paths are many, but the goal is one… if you consider the goal, however, they are all in harmony and are one… they realize that what they were fighting about was the roads only, and that their goal was one.

*Rumi*

You may follow one stream. Know that it leads to the Ocean, but do not mistake the stream for the Ocean.

*Jan-Fishan*

There are as many ways to God as there are created souls.

*Hadith*

In fact, there's only One Light that appears through different windows and which reaches us through the person of each prophet. All of these lights stream from the same Sun.

*Rumi*

God has no religion.

*Gandhi*

I turn to the Great Spirit's book which is the whole of his creation. You can read a big part of that book if you study nature.

*Walking Buffalo*

Ancestors handed down our religion…it teaches us to love each other, to be united.

*Chief Red Jacket*

Our religion is an attitude of mind, not a dogma.

*Ohiyesa*

The Christian ideal has not been tried and found wanting. It has been found difficult; and left untried.

*G. K. Chesterton*

In order to see Christianity, one must forget almost all the Christians.

*Henri Frederic Amiel*

Religion is the masterpiece of the art of animal training, for it trains people as to how they shall think.

*Arthur Schopenhauer*

One who knows what virtue is but does not practice it – of what use is his religion?

*Sakya Pandit*

Say nothing of my religion. It is known to God and myself alone. Its evidence before the world is to be sought in my life: if it has been honest and dutiful to society the religion which has regulated it cannot be a bad one.

*Thomas Jefferson*

A man who should act, for one day, on the supposition that all the people about him were influenced by the religion which they professed would find himself ruined by night.

*Thomas Macaulay*

194

Trouble no one about their religion; respect others in their view, and demand that they respect yours.

*Tecumseh*

Brother, you say there is but one way to worship and serve the Great Spirit. If there is but one religion, why do you white people differ so much about it? Why not all agreed, as you can all read the Book?

*Chief Red Jacket*

The church is a sort of hospital for men's souls, and as full of quackery as the hospital for their bodies.

*Thoreau*

You must watch my life, how I live, eat, sit, talk, behave in general. The sum total of all those in me is my religion.

*Gandhi*

The religion of love's different from all other religions; for lovers, God is their religion and their faith.

*Rumi*

Truth is one; only It is called by different names.

*Ramakrishna*

All paths lead to God, for God is on them all equally for the person who knows.

*Meister Eckhart*

If your religion does nothing for your temper it has done nothing for your soul.

*Robert Clayton*

All gods are one God.

*Chinese Proverb*

Often we Christians constitute the worst obstacle for those who try to become closer to Christ; we often preach a gospel we do not live. This is the principle reason why people of the world don't believe.

*Mother Teresa*

He who has perfectly mastered himself in thought and speech and act, he is indeed a man of religion.

*Buddha*

At the day of doom men shall be judged according to their fruits. It will not be said then, did you believe? But, were you doers or talkers only?

*John Bunyan*

The first sign of your becoming religious is that you are becoming cheerful.

*Swami Vivekananda*

Lighthouses are more helpful than churches.

*Franklin*

I believe in the fundamental Truth of all the great religions of the world. I believe that they are all God-given...I came to this conclusion long ago...that all religions were true, and also that all had some error in them.

*Gandhi*

He who knows only one religion knows none.

*Max Muller*

There is only one religion, though there are a hundred versions of it.

*George Bernard Shaw*

The three religions are one.

*Chinese Proverb*

There is no religion without love, and people may talk as much as they like about their religion, but if it does not teach them to be good and kind to man and beast, it is all a sham.

*Anna Sewell*

Great evil has been done on earth by people who think they have all the answers.

*Ruby Plenty Chiefs*

# GOOD & EVIL

There are always two forces warring against each other within us.
*Paramahansa Yogananda*

The only thing necessary for the triumph of evil is for good men to do nothing.
*Edmond Burke*

There are a thousand hacking at the branches of evil to one who is striking at the root.
*Thoreau*

The world is one percent good, one percent bad, ninety-nine percent neutral. It can go one way or the other, depending on which side is pushing. This is why what individuals do is important.
*Hans Habe*

We perceive a battle between good and evil, and we also perceive good will win.
*The Iroquois Nation*

The evil of the world is made possible by nothing but the sanction you give it.
*Ayn Rand*

Unless the seed of evil is destroyed it will grow up to destroy us.
*Aesop*

Do not maintain that there is no such thing as good and evil but that there is good and evil.
*The Prakrit*

A door must either be open or shut.
*French Proverb*

There is an eternal struggle raging in man's breast between the powers of darkness and light.
*Gandhi*

Good means not merely not to do wrong, but rather not to desire to do wrong.
*Democritus*

Good can exist without evil, whereas evil cannot exist without good. Beware the man of one book.
*Saint Thomas Aquinas*

Wickedness is always easier than virtue, for it takes a short cut to everything.
*Samuel Johnson*

To every man there opens a high way and a low way, and every man decides the way his soul will go.
*John Oxenham*

There's right and there's wrong. You got to do one or the other. You do the one, and you're living. You do the other, and you may be walking around but you're dead as a beaver hat.
*John Wayne*

Moral philosophy is nothing else but the science of good and evil.
*Thomas Hobbes*

Don't be overcome by evil, but overcome evil with good.
*The Book of Romans*

He who imitates evil always goes beyond the example that is set; he who imitates what is good always falls short.
*Francesco Guicciardini*

Right is right, even if nobody does it. Wrong is wrong, even if everybody is wrong about it.
*G. K. Chesterson*

# SACREDNESS

生

When people live far from the scenes of the Great Spirit's making, it's easy for them to forget his laws.
*Walking Buffalo*

We regard all created beings as sacred and important…We should understand well that all things are the work of the Great Spirit.
*Black Elk*

Every part of the earth is sacred to my people.
*Chief Seattle*

To the soul, the ordinary is sacred and the everyday is the primary source of religion.
*Thomas Moore*

The whole inhabited earth is sacred space in which God lives, breathes, and acts.
*Carter Heyward*

We see no need for the setting apart one day in seven as a holy day, since to us all days belong to God.
*Ohiyesa*

From a grain of sand to a great mountain, all is sacred.
*Peter Blue Cloud*

The maker of all is Wankan Tanka…to honor Him, I must honor his works.
*Brave Buffalo*

One should hallow all that one does in one's natural life.
*Martin Buber*

Everything is sacred.
*Black Elk*

Remember the sacredness of things.
*Pawnee Prayer*

Things that are holy are revealed only to men who are holy.
*Hippocrates*

For everything that lives is holy.
*William Blake*

In all God's creation there is not a single object without a purpose.
*The Talmud*

Each being is sacred.
*Starhawk*

Honor the sacred. Honor the Earth – our Mother. Honor the Elders. Honor all with whom we share the Earth: Four-legged, two–legged, winged ones, swimmers, crawlers, plant and rock people. Walk in balance and beauty.
*Native American Maxim*

# KARMA

生

If you do evil, expect to suffer evil.
*Spanish Proverb*

Have I done a neighborly act? I am therefore benefited... Whoever does wrong, wrongs himself; whoever does injustice does it to himself.
*Marcus Aurelius*

We gather the consequences of our own deeds.
*Garuda Purana*

Events, circumstances, etc. have their origin in ourselves. They spring from seeds which we have sown.
*Thoreau*

A human being fashions his consequences as surely as he fashions his goods or his dwelling. Nothing that he says, thinks, or does is without consequences.
*Norman Cousins*

We create our fate every day...most of the ills we suffer from are directly traceable to our own behavior.
*Henry Miller*

When you're good to others, you are best to yourself.
*Franklin*

We choose our joys and sorrows long before we experience them.
*Kahlil Gibran*

Whoever digs a pit will fall into it.
*The Book of Proverbs*

No man is hurt but by himself.
*Diogenes*

Now, though I do no wrong, I'm punished by my past. Neither gods nor men can foresee when an evil deed will bear its fruit... When you meet with adversity don't be upset, because it makes sense... If we should be blessed by some great reward...it's the fruit of a seed planted by us in the past.
*Bodhidharma*

Everything in nature is a cause from which there flows some effect.
*Baruch Spinoza*

Individuals create karma; karma doesn't create individuals... They never escape.
*Bodhidharma*

To accommodate yourself accommodate others.
*Chinese Proverb*

Whoso has done an atom's weight of good shall see it; and whoso has done an atom's weight of evil shall see it.
*The Koran*

The evil deeds of a wicked man ensnare him; the cords of his sin hold him fast.
*The Book of Proverbs*

Do not judge, and you will not be judged. Do not condemn, and you will not be condemned. Forgive, and you will be forgiven. Give, and it will be given to you...For with the measure you use, it will be measured to you.
*Jesus*

A man reaps what he sows.
*The Apostle Paul*

Your goodwill toward others returns to yourself in the end.
*Japanese Proverb*

198

What we gave, we have; What we spent, we had; What we left, we lost.
*Inscription on the tomb of Edward the Good*

One reaps the same corn one sows.
*Finnish Proverb*

Curses come back to you.
*Japanese Proverb*

Always do your best. What you plant now, you will harvest later.
*Og Mandino*

Good deeds return to the house of their author.
*Iranian Proverb*

One's own deed returns to oneself.
*Korean Proverb*

The bad deed turns on its doer.
*Irish Proverb*

The sinner sins against himself.
*Marcus Aurelius*

The ills we inflict upon our neighbors follow us as our shadows follow our bodies.
*The Bhagavad Gita*

The good deeds you do now are the treasure of the future.
*Philippine Proverb*

Whosoever doeth iniquity, doeth it unto himself.
*Book of Mormon*

He who wishes evil to another man will suffer his own loss.
*Indian Proverb*

The grief you put on others will not take long to come back on you.
*Demophilus*

There is no act, however trivial, but has its train of consequences.
*Samuel Smiles*

I know that when you sow bitter seeds you cannot grow sweet grain.
*Sai Baba*

You cannot do wrong without suffering wrong...The thief steals from himself. The swindler swindles himself...Thou shalt be paid exactly for what thou hast done, no more, no less.
*Emerson*

All suffering recoils on the wrongdoer himself. Thus, those desiring not to suffer refrain from causing others pain.
*Tiruvalluvar*

An evil deed, like newly-drawn milk, does not turn suddenly; smoldering, like fire covered by ashes, it follows the fools.
*Buddha*

When you do a good deed you are doing it to yourself; when you do a bad turn to some person, remember you are injuring yourself.
*Sai Baba*

Even an evil-doer sees happiness so long as his evil deed does not ripen; but when his evil deed ripens, then does the evil-doer see evil. Even a good man sees evil days so long as his good deed does not ripen; but when his good deed ripens, then does the good man see good things.
*Buddha*

We should never use expressions which might hurt even an enemy. They immediately will return to us like an echo from a rock.
*Sakya Pandit*

Kindness gives birth to kindness.
*Sophocles*

199

Hidden things always come to light. Do not sow bad seed. Be sure, they'll come up… We can't know where our pain is from. We don't know all that we've done… If you cause injury to someone; you draw that same injury toward yourself.
*Rumi*

What you plant here, you will reap there.
*Ibn Arabi*

Sow good and you'll reap good; sow bad and you'll reap bad.
*Cambodian Proverb*

I stumbled over the roots of a tree I had myself planted.
*Goethe*

Do evil thoughts of retaliation injure oneself or one's enemy?
*Nagarjuna*

He harms himself who does harm to another, and the evil plan is most harmful to the planner.
*Hesiod*

Your descendants shall gather your fruits.
*Virgil*

Surely God wrongs not men, but themselves men wrong.
*The Koran*

Whatever one does, good or bad, will follow him. We reap the fruits of actions and desires.
*Sai Baba*

You bite in the form of a snake, and suffer as the person bitten.
*Swami Muktananda*

A fool does not know when he commits his evil deeds: but the wicked man burns by his own deeds, as if burnt by fire.
*Buddha*

Chance is a word void of sense; nothing can exist without a cause.
*Voltaire*

In nature, there are neither rewards nor punishments; there are consequences.
*Robert Greene Ingersoll*

The thorns which I have reaped are of the tree I planted.
*Lord Byron*

Everyone is the son of his own works.
*Cervantes*

When we show our respect for other living things, they respond with respect for us.
*Arapaho Proverb*

Take away the cause and the effect must cease.
*English Proverb*

Sow beans and reap beans.
*Chinese Proverb*

Life is a mirror: if you frown at it, it frowns back; if you smile, it returns the greeting.
*Thackeray*

For it is in giving that we receive.
*Saint Francis of Assisi*

Sow much, reap much; sow little, reap little.
*Chinese Proverb*

The more we give of anything, the more we shall get back.
*Grace Speare*

The sin you do two and two you must pay for one by one.
*Rudyard Kipling*

What is man's chief enemy? Each man is his own.
*Anacharsis*

# INTUITION

It is only with the heart that one can see rightly; what is essential is invisible to the eye.
*Antoine de Saint-Exupery*

All our reasoning ends in surrender to feeling.
*Blaise Pascal*

The truth of a thing is the feel of it, not the think of it.
*Stanley Kubrick*

Trust the instinct to the end, though you can render no reason.
*Emerson*

Examine all things well, and leave yourself always to be guided and directed by the understanding that comes from above, and that ought to hold the reins.
*Pythagoras*

It is wisdom to believe the heart.
*George Santayana*

Nothing is impossible when we follow our inner guidance, even when its direction may threaten us by reversing our usual logic.
*Gerald Jampolsky*

The heart has reasons which reason cannot understand.
*Blaise Pascal*

What mortals see are delusions. True vision is detached from seeing.
*Bodhidharma*

Trust to your heart…for it is never untrue to itself.
*Baltasar Gracian*

Don't follow the advice of others; rather, learn to listen to the voice within yourself.
*Dogen*

The monitor within my breast has taught me the will of the Great Spirit.
*Senachwine*

Nothing is so deceptive as human reasoning, - nothing so slippery and reversible as what we have decided to call "logic." The truest compass of life is spiritual instinct.
*Marie Corelli*

He who uses only the sight of his eye is acted on by what he sees; it is the intuition of the spirit that gives the assurance of certainty. That the sight of the eyes is not equal to the intuition of the spirit is a thing long acknowledged. And yet stupid people rely on what they see.
*Chuang Tzu*

Close both eyes to see with the other eye.
*Rumi*

Intuition is a spiritual faculty and does not explain, but simply points the way.
*Florence Scovel Shinn*

You are used to listening to the buzz of the world, but now is the time to develop the inner ear that listens to the inner world.
*Saint Bartholomew*

Whoever with a deep mind investigates the truth and desires to be deceived by no deviations should turn back into oneself the light of the inner sight.
*Boethius*

The heart is wiser than the intellect.
*Josiah Gilbert Holland*

# PRAYER

生

Pray to God, but keep rowing to shore.
*Russian Proverb*

Prayer is not hearing yourself talk, but being silent, staying silent and waiting until you hear God.
*Soren Kierkegaard*

By saying a blessing before you enjoy something, your soul partakes spiritually.
*The Kabbalah*

Prayer does not change God, but changes him who prays.
*Soren Kierkegaard*

A pure prayer which issues from a taintless heart is heard without fail by God.
*Swami Muktananda*

When you are praying, imagine God speaking with you teaching and conducting you.
*The Kabbalah*

If you pray to the Lord with a true and loving heart, He will heed your prayer.
*Swami Muktananda*

Prayer is a virtuous act. However, the soul and spirit of prayer are more virtuous than the form. Through them we arrive at Union with God, in a way that only God knows.
*Rumi*

Prayer – the daily recognition of the Unseen and the Eternal – is our one inevitable duty.
*Ohiyesa*

May your way be blessed with life by the unifying force of the Great Spirit.
*Cherokee Prayer*

Prayer is a threshold at the entrance to God's reality.
*Muhammad*

The meaning of prayer is that I want to invoke that divinity in me.
*Gandhi*

Cleanse your heart before praying.
*The Talmud*

The first requirement for prayer is silence. People of prayer are people of silence.
*Mother Teresa*

Prayer is the opening of the soul to God so that he can speak to us.
*Georgia Harkness*

An authentic life is the most personal form of worship. Everyday life has become my prayer.
*Sarah Ban Breathnach*

Without prayer there is no peace.
*Gandhi*

Trust in God, but tie your camel.
*Arabian Proverb*

Our prayers should be for blessings in general, for God knows best what is good for us.
*Socrates*

We, ignorant of ourselves, beg often our own harms, which the wise powers deny us for our good.
*Shakespeare*

The fewer the words the better the prayer.
*Martin Luther*

202

# MEDITATION

If during the day one feels work becoming annoying, one should sit in meditation.
*Confucius*

Still the mind; become its master. Hear nothing, speak nothing, see nothing, think nothing. Seek only the inner Witness.
*Swami Muktananda*

Tao is only known through silent contemplation. To truly understand this is the beginning of enlightenment.
*Lao Tzu*

The most profound use of intelligence is to think of nothing.
*Chuang Tzu*

Make your mind one-pointed; quiet all your mental tendencies. Always meditate on your own inner Self.
*Swami Muktananda*

Meditate…Be quiet.
*Buddha*

Retire into yourself as into an island and set yourself to the work.
*The Dhammapada*

Real action is in silent moments.
*Emerson*

Ask questions from your heart, and you will receive answers from your heart.
*Omaha Maxim*

Quieten your body. Quieten your mind.
*Buddha*

When one turns one's vision inward, the inner eye sees the reality of the bliss of Supreme Consciousness.
*Sai Baba*

True meditation consists in closing the eyes and ears of the mind to all else except the object of one's devotion.
*Gandhi*

We believe that God is nearer to us in solitude.
*Ohiyesa*

The only real rest comes when you are alone with God.
*Rumi*

To follow Tao, look within and return to the universal Self.
*Lao Tzu*

Anyone who withdraws into meditation on compassion can see God with his own eyes, talk to him face to face and consult with Him.
*Buddha*

Only in quiet waters things mirror themselves undistorted. Only in a quiet mind is adequate perception of the world.
*Margolis*

Practice meditation… meditation will enable you to unite yourself with the divine.
*Srimad Bhagavatam*

When you pray, go into your room, close the door and pray to your Father, who is unseen.
*Jesus*

Without meditation it is not possible to control and master the mind. Thus, meditation is essential – to immerse the mind in Supreme Consciousness.
*Sai Baba*

The Eternal is seen when the mind is at rest. When the sea of the mind is troubled by the winds of desire, it cannot reflect the Eternal and all divine vision is impossible.
*Ramakrishna*

As you prepare to speak with your Creator, to seek the revelation of his power, be careful to empty your mind of all mundane vanities.
*The Kabbalah*

Be still, and know that I am God.
*The Bible*

In the silence of the heart God speaks. If you face God in prayer and silence, God will speak to you.
*Mother Teresa*

Meditate on the Eternal either in an unknown nook or in the solitude of the forest or in the solitude of your own mind.
*Ramakrishna*

One is inspired only in solitude.
*Goethe*

Without discipline, he has no understanding or inner power; without inner power, he has no peace; and without peace where is joy?
*The Bhagavad Gita*

Look within...The secret is in you.
*Hui Neng*

The quieter you become the more you can hear.
*Baba Ram Dass*

What is gained from our inner nature is exact knowledge, which gives us a far-reaching outlook over the earth. The many powers of inner nature are hidden in everyone, and these are identified with Wankan Tanka.
*Blue Thunder*

Delve within; within is the foundation of good, and it is always ready to bubble up, if you always delve.
*Marcus Aurelius*

Practice meditation in the morning or in the evening or at any leisure time during the day. You will soon realize that your mental burdens are dropping away one by one, and that you are gaining an intuitive power previously undreamed of.
*Dogen*

Reading makes a full man – Meditation a profound man.
*Franklin*

Through meditation...The fire of anxiety will consume you no longer, and you will attain undying peace.
*Swami Muktananda*

Whoever meditates with awareness obtains great joy.
*The Dhammapada*

Without contemplation there is no tranquility and without tranquility how shall there be happiness?
*The Bhagavad Gita*

To attain you must be alone, so that your contemplation not be disturbed. In your mind, cultivate aloneness to the utmost. Strip the body from your soul, as if you do not feel that you are clothed in matter at all – you are entirely soul. The more you strip yourself of material being, the more powerful your comprehension.
*The Kabbalah*

It is far more useful to commune with oneself than with others.
*Demophilus*

Where there is peace and meditation, there is neither anxiety nor doubt.
*Saint Francis of Assisi*

204

Through meditation wisdom is gained; through lack of meditation wisdom is lost.
*The Dhammapada*

Assuredly, whoever wishes to discover the universal truth must sound the depths of his own heart.
*Tauler*

Seek and you will find…It is when we seek for the things which are within us that quest leads to discovery.
*Meng Tse*

Meditation is stopping, calming, and looking deeply.
*Thich Nhat Hanh*

Meditation is successfully identifying with the Lord.
*Patanjali*

When your mind is restrained, you become one with God.
*Swami Muktananda*

Look within yourself; within you is the source of all good and a source inexhaustible provided you dig in it unceasingly.
*Marcus Aurelius*

If a man could cast a firm and clear glance into the depths of his being, he would see there God.
*Tauler*

Every man who returns into himself will find there traces of the Divinity.
*Cicero*

Look into your heart and you will see there His image.
*Farid-uddin Attar*

Slowly but surely, reap the fruits of your meditation.
*Swami Muktananda*

Contemplate the mirror of your heart and you will taste little by little a pure joy and unmixed peace.
*Saadi*

Let him destroy by deep meditation the qualities that are opposed to the divine nature.
Laws of Manu

As in a house with a sound roof the rain cannot penetrate, so in a mind where meditation dwells passion cannot enter.
*The Dhammapada*

Muddy water, let stand, becomes clear.
*Lao Tzu*

When all discrimination is abandoned, when contact with things is broken, the mind is brighter than sun and moon together, cleaner than frost and snow.
*Zen Maxim*

Whoever gives oneself to distractions and does not give oneself to meditation, forgetting true purpose and grasping at pleasure, will eventually envy the one who practices meditation.
*The Dhammapada*

If the soul would give itself leisure to take breath and return into itself, it would be easy for it to draw from its own depths the seeds of the true.
*Seneca*

In inner quiet lies the salvation of the spirit.
*Baltasar Gracian*

Our true glory and true riches are within.
*Seneca*

# CHANGE

生

Everything flows, nothing stays still.
*Heraclitus*

Every movement brings change, every hour makes a difference.
*Zhuang Zi*

One cannot step twice into the same river.
*Heraclitus*

Everything changes with time.
*Leonardo da Vinci*

Have patience. All things change in due time.
*Ginaly-Li*

We must always change, renew, rejuvenate ourselves; otherwise we harden.
*Goethe*

Change yourself and your fortune will change.
*Portuguese Proverb*

You are young, my son, and, as the years go by, time will change and even reverse many of your present opinions.
*Plato*

Any path is only a path, and there is no affront to oneself or to others, in dropping it if that is what your heart tells you.
*Carlos Castaneda*

How many things are there that we regarded as articles of faith yesterday and that we tell as fables today?
*Montaigne*

That which to us appears changeless and eternal, may change.
*Chief Seattle*

You must be the change you wish to see in the world.
*Gandhi*

It is the greatest mistake to think that man is always one and the same. A man is never the same for long. He is continually changing. He seldom remains the same even for half an hour.
*George Ivanovitch Gurdjieff*

Only the supremely wise and the abysmally ignorant do not change.
*Confucius*

Any change, even a change for the better, is always accompanied by drawbacks and discomforts.
*Arnold Bennett*

Because things are the way they are, things will not stay the way they are.
*Bertolt Brecht*

He that will not apply new remedies must expect new evils; for time is the greatest innovator.
*Francis Bacon*

If we don't change, we don't grow. If we don't grow, we aren't really living.
*Gail Sheehy*

Life belongs to the living, and he who lives must be prepared for changes.
*Goethe*

All things change, nothing is extinguished.
*Ovid*

# DEATH

Old and young, we are all on our last cruise.
*Robert Louis Stevenson*

We begin to die as soon as we are born, and the end is linked to the beginning.
*Marcus Manilius*

Living is a spring dream, dying like going back home.
*Chinese Proverb*

A living body is a dying body.
*Japanese Proverb*

Death is as natural as life.
*Schopenhauer*

None dies except in appearance. In fact what is called birth is the passage from essence to substance, and what is called death is on the contrary the passage from substance to essence. Nothing is born and nothing dies in reality, but all first appears and then becomes invisible.
*Apollonius of Tyana*

What springs from the earth dissolves to earth again, and heaven born things fly to their native seat.
*Marcus Aurelius*

Nothing is born of nothing, nothing can be annihilated, each commencement of being is only a transformation.
*Thales*

The soul has not been and will not be, it always is.
*Tolstoy*

Life is immortality.
*The Upanishads*

It is as clear to me as daylight that life and death are but phases of the same thing, the reverse and obverse of the same coin.
*Gandhi*

When you are intent upon a journey, after you purchase your ticket and board the train – whether you sit quietly, lie down, read or meditate, the train will take you to the destination. So, too, at birth each living thing has received a ticket to the event of death and is now on the journey.
*Sai Baba*

Life is not independent from death – it only appears that way.
*Blackfoot Proverb*

The road uphill and the road downhill are one and the same.
*Heraclitus*

God has thrown open the door and says to you, "Go." Where? To nothing you need to fear, but back to that from which you came, to what is friendly and akin to you...
*Epictetus*

The fact of death should not sadden us.
*Mother Teresa*

Fear not death; for the sooner we die, the longer shall we be immortal.
*Franklin*

Do you not know that disease and death must overtake us, no matter what we are doing?...What do you wish to be doing when it overtakes you?...If you have anything better to be doing when you are so overtaken, get to work on that.
*Epictetus*

He that fears death does not live.
*George Herbert*

For to be afraid of death, men, is nothing other than seeming to be wise when one is not; for it is seeming to know what one does not know. For no one knows whether death happens to be the greatest good of all for a person but it is feared as if one knows well that it is the greatest of all evils.

*Socrates*

Man when he dies, knows that nothing peculiar will happen to him, only what has already happened to millions of beings, and all he does is to change his mode of journeying, but it is impossible for him not to feel an emotion when he comes to the place where he must undergo the change.

*Tolstoy*

...for a just man there is no ill in life and no ill in death.

*Socrates*

Give up fearing death; it's at all times foolish to miss life's pleasures for fear of death.

*Disticha Moralia*

It is as great a folly to fear death as to fear old age.

*Seneca*

It is not death that a man should fear, he should fear never beginning to live.

*Marcus Aurelius*

People living deeply have no fear of death.

*Anais Nin*

A good life fears not life, nor death.

*Thomas Fuller*

He who fears death cannot enjoy life.

*Spanish Proverb*

To those who fully admit the immortality of the human soul, the destruction of our world will not appear so dreadful.

*Charles Darwin*

When it comes your time to die, be not like those whose hearts are filled with fear of death, so that when their time comes they weep and pray for a little more time to live their lives over again in a different way. Sing your death song and die like a hero going home.

*Tecumseh*

Men die but live again in the real world of Wankan Tanka, where there is nothing but the spirits of all things; and this true life we may know here on earth if we purify our bodies and minds thus coming closer to Wankan Tanka who is all-purity.

*Black Elk*

The grave is the first stage of the journey into eternity.

*Muhammad*

Birthless and deathless and changeless remains the spirit, dead though the house of it seems.

*The Bhagavad Gita*

The virtuous rest in bliss in this world and in the next.

*The Dhammapada*

All distant beings are temporarily differentiated from the Whole, and their destiny is to return again to the Whole, which has always been their essential Nature.

*Chuang Tzu*

Neither life nor death brings any changes to the Self.

*Lao Tzu*

Life terminates in a sleep that is followed by a new awakening.

*Chuang Tzu*

Your real "country" is where you're heading, not where you are.

*Rumi*

Every exit is an entry somewhere else.
*Tom Stoppard*

Persevere onward to the place where the Creator dwells in peace. Let not the things of the earth hinder you.
*Iroquois Constitution*

It is the general belief of the Indians that after a man dies his spirit still lives.
*Chased-By-Bears*

Death is the great awakening, after which one says of life that it was a long dream. But few among the living understand this. Most believe themselves wide-awake!
*Chuang Tzu*

There is no death. Only a change of worlds.
*Chief Seattle*

Then death comes like dawn, and you wake up laughing at what you thought was your grief.
*Rumi*

Death is a bridge whereby the lover rejoins the Beloved.
*Rabia*

The end of life is to be like God, and the soul following God will be like Him.
*Socrates*

The truest end of life is to know the life that never ends.
*William Penn*

All beings are from all eternity.
*Ashwaghosha*

All that is has already existed, but will not remain in the form in which we see it today.
*Baha-ullah*

Death is no more than a turning of us over from time to eternity.
*William Penn*

This human soul returns to the Supreme Imperishable Soul.
*The Prashna Upanishad*

If the immortal is also indestructible, it is impossible for the soul, when death comes upon it, to perish.
*Socrates*

Then when death comes upon a person the mortal part of one, it seems, dies, and the immortal, safe and incorruptible, going away is gone, withdrawing from death.
*Socrates*

All things return to God.
*Muhammad*

A good man never dies.
*Callimachus*

One short sleep past, we wake eternally. And death shall be no more.
*John Donne*

Therefore death to us is nothing, nor concerns us in the least, since nature of mind is mortal evermore.
*Lucretius*

Is death the last sleep? No, it is the last and final awakening.
*Sir Walter Scott*

What is cannot perish.
*Apollonius of Tyana*

Death cannot kill what never dies.
*William Penn*

So live your life that the fear of death can never enter your heart.
*Tecumseh*

There is not a grain of dust, not an atom that can become nothing, yet man believes that death is the annihilation of his being.
*Schopenhauer*

There is in all this only transformations of things one into another; there is no annihilation...There is nothing else in a departure, it is only a slight change. There is nothing else in death; it is only a great change. The actual being changes, not into a non-existence, but into something it is not at present.

*Epictetus*

There where all ends, all is eternally beginning.

*Hermes*

All changes but nothing is abolished...
*Giordano Bruno*

That which is was always and always will be.

*Melissus*

All that exists in the world, has always existed.
*Antoine the Healer*

In death he sees life.
*Baha-ullah*

The wise weep not for the dead or the living: all of us were before and shall not cease to be hereafter.
*The Bhagavad Gita*

The origin of things is the Infinite: necessarily they disappear into that which put them into birth.
*Anaximander*

There is no birth of terrestrial things and there is no disappearance of them by death's destruction, but only a reunion and a separation of materials assembled together: birth is only a word habitual to the human mind.
*Empedocles*

I shall not wholly die.
*Horace*

Our bodies are known to end, but the embodied self is enduring, indestructible, and immeasurable... It is not born, it does not die; having been, it will never not be; unborn, enduring, constant, and primordial, it is not killed when the body is killed... As a man discards worn-out clothes to put on new ones, so the embodied self discards its worn-out bodies to take on other new ones.
*The Bhagavad Gita*

At the hour of death it is pleasant to have done good.
*The Dhammapada*

Nor do I regret that I have lived, since I have so lived that I think I was not born in vain, and I quit life as if it were an inn, not a home.
*Cicero*

Do not seek death. Death will find you. But seek the road which makes death a fulfillment.
*Dag Hammarskjold*

Let us endeavor so to live that when we come to die even the undertaker will be sorry.
*Mark Twain*

Just as a good day's work leads to pleasant sleep, so a life well spent leads to a pleasant death.
*Leonardo da Vinci*

Every person ought daily to reflect upon the uncertainty of life, and the consequences of sudden death.
*Charles Simmons*

The greatest gratification is embodied in the knowledge on one's deathbed that one has no regrets from his or her life, and that one has spent one's days with a sincere and harmonious attitude.
*Kok Yim Ci Yuen*

210

The sun exactly at noon is exactly beginning to go down. And a creature exactly when he is born is exactly beginning to die.

*Hu Shih*

Eternity is not something that begins after you are dead. It is going on all the time. We are in it now.

*Charlotte Perkins Gilman*

It is a poor thing for anyone to fear that which is inevitable.

*Tertullian*

Death is not a subject for mourning when it is followed by immortality.

*Cicero*

For life has no terror for the one who truly understands that there is nothing terrible in not living.

*Epicurus*

Death and decrepitude are inherent in the world. The sage who knows the nature of things, does not grieve.

*The Metta Sutta*

A good death does honor to a whole life.

*Petrarch*

Our theories of the eternal are as valuable as are those that a chick which has not broken its way through its shell might form of the outside world.

*Buddha*

Oh Tao! It makes me supremely happy to know that I was born from You and on death will return to You.

*Chuang Tzu*

One should not consider death as a tragedy. Annihilation is not total. True, the physical self ceases to exist. But the impersonal transcendent Self continues.

*Confucius*

The wise flow with Tao in life and in death they merge with the Oneness of things.

*Chuang Tzu*

No matter what road I travel, I'm going home.

*Shinso*

The spirit never perishes, only the body decays.

*Mou Zi*

Everyone who lives and believes in me will never die.

*Jesus*

Passing beyond, the wise leaving this world become immortal.

*The Upanishads*

The wise soul is not born nor does it die. This one has not come from anywhere nor has it become anyone. Unborn, eternal, constant, primal, this one is not killed when the body is killed.

*The Katha Upanishad*

The soul that dwells in the body of every man is unslayable, and therefore you should not weep for all these beings.

*The Bhagavad Gita*

To die in peace with God is the culmination of any human life.

*Mother Teresa*

I begin life over again after death even as the sun every day.

*The Book of the Dead*

The smallest drop of water united to the ocean no longer dries.

*Hindu Maxim*

Since one is alive, one will eventually die, and one must recognize that death is drawing closer day by day.

*Kok Yim Ci Yuen*

No man can be ignorant that he must die, nor be sure that he may not this very day.
*Cicero*

If you would endure life, be prepared for death.
*Sigmund Freud*

Look at the end of life.
*Solon*

Death, a necessary end, will come when it will come.
*Shakespeare*

Man lives freely only by his readiness to die.
*Gandhi*

When one follows the Way, there is no death upon the earth.
*Lao Tzu*

There is something beyond the grave; death does not end all...
*Sextus Propertius*

Be still prepared for death: and death or life shall thereby be the sweeter.
*Shakespeare*

The Tao is diffused in the universe. All existences return to It as streams and mountain rivulets return to the rivers and the seas.
*Lao Tzu*

This life is but tillage for the next, do good that you may reap there.
*Muhammad*

Those who remember that we must come to an end in this world, their quarrels cease at once.
*The Dhammapada*

Die before you die.
*Muhammad*

Let death be daily before your eyes, and you will never entertain any abject thought, nor too eagerly covet anything.
*Epictetus*

I do not die, I go forth from time.
*Lebrun*

Men fear death as children fear to go in the dark; and as that natural fear in children is increased by tales, so is the other.
*Francis Bacon*

The day which we fear as our last is but the birthday of eternity.
*Seneca*

'Tis very certain the desire of life prolongs it.
*Lord Byron*

To himself everyone is immortal; he may know that he is going to die, but he can never know that he is dead.
*Samuel Butler*

While I thought that I was learning how to live, I have been learning how to die.
*Leonardo da Vinci*

What we have done for ourselves alone dies with us; what we have done for others and the world remains and is immortal.
*Albert Pike*

Heaven means to be one with God.
*Confucius*

212

# SUCCESS
# &
# WEALTH

If you should lay up even a little upon a little, and should do this often, soon would even this become great.
*Hesiod*

Grain by grain, a loaf; stone by stone, a castle.
*Bulgarian Proverb*

Great fortunes depend on luck; small fortunes depend on diligence.
*Chinese Proverb*

Tis good to keep a nest egg.
*Cervantes*

Save money and money will save you.
*Jamaican Proverb*

When you have money, think of the time when you had none.
*Japanese Proverb*

Prosperous as his life may appear, unless a man measures well his wealth, it will disappear without a trace.
*Tiruvalluvar*

Do not rely on your present good fortune; prepare for the year when it may leave you.
*Chinese Proverb*

That crown is well spent which saves you ten.
*Italian Proverb*

Whatever your wages are, save a little.
*Andrew Carnegie*

For age and want save while you may; no morning sun last the whole day.
*Franklin*

To do two things at once is to do neither.
*Syrus*

Singleness of purpose is one of the chief essentials for success in life, no matter what may be one's aim.
*John D. Rockefeller, Jr.*

The first law of success…is concentration – to bend all the energies to one point, and to go directly to that point, looking neither to the right nor to the left.
*William Mathews*

The secret of success is constancy of purpose.
*Benjamin Disraeli*

What you do is more important than how much you make, and how you feel about it is more important than what you do.
*Jerry Gillies*

It is not enough to be industrious; so are the ants. What are you industrious about?
*Thoreau*

The biggest mistake people make in life is not trying to make a living at doing what they most enjoy.
*Malcolm S. Forbes*

I honestly think it is better to be a failure at something you love than to be a success at something you hate.
*George Burns*

There is no more fatal blunderer than he who consumes the greater part of his life getting his living.
*Thoreau*

You have not found your place until all your faculties are roused, and your whole nature consents and approves of the work you are doing…
*Orison Swett Marden*

Do what you love.
*Thoreau*

Only those who do leisurely what others do busily can do busily what others do at their leisure.
*Chinese Proverb*

The wise never undertake an enterprise that rashly risks existing capital to reach for potential profits.
*Tiruvalluvar*

He who buys what he doesn't need must often sell what he does need.
*English Proverb*

If you pay the laborer in advance, you have to gather your own harvest.
*Russian Proverb*

At a good bargain pause and ponder.
*Italian Proverb*

First health, then wealth, then pleasure, and do not owe anything to anybody.
*Catherine the Great*

A small leak will sink a great ship.
*Russian Proverb*

Don't rely on the label on the bag.
*French Proverb*

Fish see the bait but not the hook; men see the profit but not the peril.
*Chinese Proverb*

Father used to say, "Never give away your work. People don't value what they don't have to pay for."
*Nancy Hale*

Everything is worth what its purchaser will pay for it.
*Syrus*

Wealth withdraws from the man who refuses to acknowledge the informal friendliness his workers wish to share with him.
*Tiruvalluvar*

Beware of little expenses: a small leak will sink a great ship.
*Franklin*

Silver and gold will not make men better.
*Plato*

Wealth does not bring goodness, but goodness brings wealth and every other blessing, both to the individual and to the state.
*Socrates*

He that would catch fish, must venture his bait.
*Franklin*

Too many people overvalue what they are not and undervalue what they are.
*Malcolm S. Forbes*

A change in fortune hurts a wise man no more than a change of the moon.
*Franklin*

What folly it is to play a game in which you can lose incomparably more than you can win.
*Francesco Guicciardini*

To do good you need means.
*Goethe*

Do not spend now, relying on future profits, for they very often do not come or are smaller than expected. Whereas, on the contrary, expenses always multiply.
*Francesco Guicciardini*

One should work but not seek wealth alone. But, if wealth is gained, it must be shared with those in need. Beware lest wealth close the door of life. Riches are but means to doing good and should not become the goal of life.
*The Rig Veda*

It is very easy to ruin a good position, but very hard to acquire it. Therefore, if you are enjoying a good livelihood, make every effort not to let it slip through your fingers.
*Francesco Guicciardini*

Live within your means; spend more on your clothing and most on your home.
*The Talmud*

The success of very important matters often depends on doing or not doing something that seems trivial. Even in little things, therefore, you must be cautious and thoughtful.
*Francesco Guicciardini*

Lend your money and lose your friend.
*William Caxton*

Don't put your affairs into the hands of someone who has failed to manage his own.
*Maltese Proverb*

Neither a borrower nor a lender be.
*Shakespeare*

Wise economy consist not so much in avoiding spending – for that is often necessary – as in knowing how to spend well; that is, to spend a dollar, and get two dollars worth.
*Francesco Guicciardini*

Live within your harvest.
*Persian Proverb*

Better buy than borrow.
*English Proverb*

Ask too much to get enough.
*Spanish Proverb*

The shortest and best way to make your fortune is to let people see clearly that it is in their interests to promote yours.
*Jean de La Bruyere*

We do not know what is really good or bad fortune.
*Rousseau*

Asking cost little.
*Italian Proverb*

Buy cheap and sell dear.
*Petronius*

Necessity never made a good bargain.
*American Proverb*

When you go to buy, don't show your silver.
*Chinese Proverb*

It is good to buy when another wants to sell.
*Italian Proverb*

There are more foolish buyers than foolish sellers.
*French Proverb*

Make something your specialty. Life is a very uncertain affair. Knowing a little about five hundred things won't do us much good. We must be able to do something well, that our work will be needed and valuable.
*Thomas Carlyle*

If you would not be cheated, ask the price at three shops.
*Chinese Proverb*

Buying on credit is robbing next year's crop.
*African Proverb*

Let your bargain suit your purpose.
*Irish Proverb*

Be not made a beggar by banqueting upon borrowing, when you have nothing in your purse.

*Apocrypha*

Go to a man who is in a difficulty and you'll get a bargain.
*Irish Proverb*

The perfect does not lie in quality, but in quality. All that is best is always scant, and rare, for mass in anything cheapens it.
*Baltasar Gracian*

The season of failure is the best time for sowing the seeds of success.
*Paramahansa Yogananda*

Rather than be in debt for a long time go without rice for a short time.
*Japanese Proverb*

To desire riches for no other reason than their enjoyment would be a sign of a base and deformed spirit. But life in this world being as corrupt as it is, anyone who wants a reputation is forced to seek wealth. For with wealth, those virtues shine and are esteemed which in a poor man are scarcely regarded and hardly known.
*Francesco Guicciardini*

Avoid three qualities: jealousy, greed, and arrogance... do not borrow anything from anyone... If you want to live more freely, borrow less.
*Hadith*

Winning is not a sometime thing; it's an all-time thing. You don't win once in a while, you don't do things right once in a while, you do them right all the time. Winning is a habit. Unfortunately, so is losing.
*Vince Lombardi*

No one ever fails at anything. Everything you do produces a result...Failure is a judgment. It's just an opinion.
*Wayne Dyer*

Say farewell to luck when winning: it is the way of the gamblers of reputation...lock up your winnings when they are enough, or when great.
*Baltasar Gracian*

Better be proficient in one art than a smatterer in a thousand.
*Japanese Proverb*

Always think in terms of what the other person wants.
*James Van Fleet*

Wake early if you want another man's life or land. No lamb for the lazy wolf. No battle's won in bed.
*The Havamal*

If you buy what you don't need, you steal from yourself.
*Swedish Proverb*

One who proudly displays his wealth invites trouble.
*Lao Tzu*

In every enterprise consider where you would come out.
*Syrus*

Good bargains empty the purse.
*Italian Proverb*

Bargain like a gypsy, but pay like a gentleman.
*Hungarian Proverb*

In the middle of difficulty lies opportunity.
*Eisnstein*

Caveat emptor (Buyer beware).
*Latin Proverb*

216

If I should sell both my forenoons and afternoons to society, as most appear to do, I am sure, that, for me, there would be nothing left worth living for.
*Thoreau*

You never achieve real success unless you like what you are doing.
*Dale Carnegie*

How swiftly a generous man's riches dwindle and die, if he does not evaluate the limits of his means.
*Tiruvalluvar*

A little by little, collected together, become a great deal; the heap in the barn consist of single grains, and drop and drop make the inundation.
*Saadi*

If you cannot work with love but only with distaste, it is better that you should leave your work...
*Kahlil Gibran*

In strategy, secrecy is esteemed.
*Japanese Proverb*

Necessity never made a good bargain.
*Franklin*

Never permit a dichotomy to rule your life, a dichotomy in which you hate what you do so you can have pleasure in your spare time. Look for a situation in which your work will give you as much happiness as your spare time.
*Pablo Picasso*

He that is of the opinion money will do everything may well be suspected of doing everything for money.
*Franklin*

There is only one success in life – to be able to spend your life in your own way.
*Christopher Morley*

Six essential qualities that are the key to success: Sincerity, personal integrity, humility, courtesy, wisdom, charity.
*William Menniger*

If we had no winter, the spring would not be so pleasant; if we did not sometimes taste of adversity, prosperity would not be so welcome.
*Anne Bradstreet*

Action is the foundational key to all success.
*Pablo Picasso*

Always bear in mind that your own resolution to succeed is more important than any other.
*Lincoln*

Defeat is not the worst of failures. Not to have tried is the true failure.
*George Edward Woodberry*

Develop success from failures. Discouragement and failure are two of the surest stepping stones to success.
*Dale Carnegie*

Failure is success if we learn from it.
*Malcolm Forbes*

One secret of success in life is for a man to be ready for his opportunity when it comes.
*Benjamin Disraeli*

Success consists of going from failure to failure without loss of enthusiasm.
*Winston Churchill*

Success is dependent on effort.
*Sophocles*

The highest use of capital is not to make more money, but to make money do more for the betterment of life.
*Henry Ford*

# DESTINY

生

In his heart a man plans his course, but the Lord determines his steps.
*The Book of Proverbs*

Chance is a word void of sense; nothing can exist without a cause.
*Voltaire*

Your destiny is in your hand, and your important decisions are your own to make.
*Spencer K. Kimball*

Each individual is the master of his own life and death, the master of mortality and eternal life. What he does is what he is. This is the spiritual truth.
*Lao Tzu*

Every soul has a definite task, and the fulfillment of each individual purpose can alone lead man aright.
*Hazrat Inayat Khan*

Every man is the architect of his own fortune.
*Sallust*

Luck affects everything; let your hook always be cast. In the stream where you least expect it, there will be fish.
*Ovid*

We make our fortunes and we call them fate.
*Benjamin Disraeli*

I am the master of my fate; I am the captain of my soul.
*William Ernest Henley*

Fate leads those who are willing, but must push those who are not.
*Chinese Proverb*

New day, new fate.
*Bulgarian Proverb*

Do not strive for things occurring to occur as you wish, but wish the things occurring as they occur, and you will flow well.
*Epictetus*

Nothing under the sun is accidental.
*Gotthold Ephraim Lessing*

When you are born, your work is placed in your heart.
*Kahlil Gibran*

Every man's life is a plan of God.
*Horace Bushnell*

Worry never thwarted destiny.
*Chinese Proverb*

You cannot foresee the actions of God who causes all things to happen.
*The Book of Ecclesiastes*

One cannot change fate one way or the other.
*Lieh Tzu*

Every little thing is sent for something.
*Black Elk*

You have come into this world for a particular task, and that is your purpose; if you do not perform it, then you will have done nothing.
*Rumi*

For man is man and master of his fate.
*Alfred Tennyson*

What the Great Spirit made and planned, no power on earth can change it.
*Hopi Proverb*

No snowflake ever falls in the wrong place.
*Zen Saying*

When the student is ready, the master appears.
*Japanese Buddhist Proverb*

If you want what fate wants, then nothing can happen against your will.
*Chuang Tzu*

The lot assigned to every man is suited to him, and suits him to itself.
*Marcus Aurelius*

Whatever happens at all happens as it should.
*Marcus Aurelius*

Everything on earth has a purpose, every disease an herb to cure it, and every person a mission.
*Mourning Dove*

Our lives are in the hands of the Great Spirit.
*Tecumseh*

Each of us has some kind of vocation…For each one of us, there is only one thing necessary: to fulfill our own destiny, according to God's will, to be what God wants us to be.
*Thomas Merton*

It is not in the stars to hold our destiny but in ourselves.
*Shakespeare*

We are not permitted to choose the frame of our destiny. But what we put into it is ours.
*Dag Hammarskjold*

It is a mistake to look too far ahead. Only one link of the chain of destiny can be handled at a time.
*Winston Churchill*

A consistent soul believes in destiny, a capricious one in chance.
*Benjamin Disraeli*

A person often meets his destiny on the road he took to avoid it.
*Jean de La Fontaine*

Destiny grants us our wishes, but in its own way, in order to give us something beyond our wishes.
*Goethe*

Destiny is no matter of chance. It is a matter of choice. It is not a thing to be waited for, it is a thing to be achieved.
*William Jennings Bryan*

You have a definite purpose and it is a sacred responsibility.
*Joyce Sequichie Hifler*

The destiny of man is in his own soul.
*Herodotus*

# GOVERNMENT

生

You ask which form of government is the best. Whichever teaches us to govern ourselves.
*Goethe*

It is dangerous to be right when the government is wrong.
*Voltaire*

The more corrupt the state the more numerous the laws.
*Tacitus*

Liberty is meaningless where the right to utter one's thoughts and opinions has ceased to exist. That, of all rights, is the dread of tyrants. It is the right which they first of all strike down.
*Frederick Douglas*

The basis of our political systems is the right of the people to make and to alter their constitutions of government.
*George Washington*

We Americans have no commission from God to police the world.
*Benjamin Harrison*

Liberty cannot be preserved without a general knowledge among the people.
*John Adams*

Resistance to tyrants is obedience to God.
*Thomas Jefferson*

Useless laws diminish the authority of necessary ones.
*French Proverb*

The power to tax involves the power to destroy.
*John Marshall*

The people never give up their liberties but under some delusion.
*Edmond Burke*

Power must never be trusted without a check.
*John Adams*

Among a people generally corrupt, liberty cannot long exist.
*Edmond Burke*

When men are pure, laws are useless; when men are corrupt laws are broken.
*Benjamin Disraeli*

Never complain and never explain.
*Benjamin Disraeli*

Restriction of free thought and free speech is the most dangerous of all subversions. It is the one un-American act that could most easily defeat us.
*William O. Douglas*

Don't oppose forces, use them.
*R. Buckminster Fuller*

There will never be peace between nations...until there is true peace in the souls of men.
*Black Elk*

The most tyrannical governments are those which make crimes of opinions, for everyone has an inalienable right to his thoughts.
*Baruch Spinoza*

In proportion as the structure of government gives force to public opinion, it is essential that public opinion should be enlightened.
*George Washington*

Sense has ever been centered in the few...Votes should be weighed, not counted. The State must sooner or later be wrecked where the majority rules and ignorance decides.

*Friedrich Von Schiller*

Government has no rights; it is a delegation from several individuals for the purpose of securing their own.

*Percy Bysshe Shelley*

Government is essentially immoral.

*Herbert Spencer*

They that can give up essential liberty to obtain a little temporary safety deserve neither liberty nor safety.

*Franklin*

Government is an association of men who do violence to the rest of us.

*Tolstoy*

It is time for people to understand that governments not only are not necessary, but are harmful and most highly immoral institutions, in which a self-respecting, honest man cannot and must not take part...And as soon as people understand this, they will...cease to give the governments soldiers and money. And as soon as a majority of people cease to do this, the fraud which enslaves people will be abolished.

*Tolstoy*

Let the punishment of criminals be useful. A hanged man is good for nothing, and a man condemned to public works will serve the country, and is a living lesson.

*Voltaire*

I have always given it as my decided opinion that no nation has a right to intermeddle in the internal concerns of another.

*George Washington*

Five Basic reasons for the Decline of the Roman Empire:

1) The undermining of the dignity and sanctity of the home.
2) Higher and higher taxes: the spending of public money for free bread and circuses for the populace.
3) The mad craze for pleasure, with sports and plays becoming more exciting, more brutal and more immoral.
4) The building of great armaments when the real enemy was within – the decay of individual responsibility.
5) The decay of religion, whose leaders lost their touch with life, and their power to guide the people.

*Edward Gibbon*
*1788 "Decline and Fall of the Roman Empire"*

It is seldom that liberty of any kind is lost all at once.

*David Hume*

The democracy will cease to exist when you take away from those who are willing to work and give to those who would not.

*Thomas Jefferson*

It is, Sir, the people's Constitution, the people's government, made for the people, made by the people, and answerable to the people.

*Daniel Webster*

I predict future happiness for Americans if they can prevent the government from wasting the labors of the people under the pretense of taking care of them.

*Thomas Jefferson*

Find out just what people will submit to and you have found out the exact amount of injustice and wrong which will be imposed upon them.

*Frederick Douglas*

The public would rather complain incessantly about how badly it is served than take any trouble to ensure better service.

*Goethe*

No free man shall ever be debarred the use of arms.

*Thomas Jefferson*

To compel a man to subsidize with his taxes the propagation of ideas which he disbelieves and abhors is sinful and tyrannical.

*Thomas Jefferson*

Even when laws have been written down, they ought not always to remain unaltered.

*Aristotle*

Is freedom anything else than the right to live as we wish?

*Epictetus*

None are more hopelessly enslaved than those who falsely believe they are free.

*Goethe*

The people made the Constitution, and the people can unmake it. It is the creature of their own will, and lives only by their will.

*John Marshall*

One of the greatest delusions in the world is the hope that the evils in this world are to be cured by legislation.

*Thomas Brackett Reed*

There can be no 50-50 Americanism in this country. There is room here for only 100% Americanism.

*Theodore Roosevelt*

The strongest reason for the people to retain the right to keep and bear arms is, as a last resort, to protect themselves against tyranny in government.

*Thomas Jefferson*

The laws keep up their credit, not by being just, but because they are laws; 'tis the mystic foundation of their authority... They are often made by fools; still oftener by men who, out of hatred to equality, fail in equity; but always by men, vain and irresolute authors.

*Montaigne*

To be turned from one's course by men's opinions, by blame, and by mis-representation shows a man unfit to hold an office.

*Quintus Fabius Maximus*

There is danger from all men. The only maxim of a free government ought to be to trust no man living with power to endanger the public liberty.

*George Washington*

Giving money and power to government is like giving whiskey and car keys to teenage boys.

*P. J. O'Rourke*

Government is not reason; it is not eloquent; it is force. Like fire, it is a dangerous servant and a fearful master.

*George Washington*

Here is my first principle of foreign policy: good government at home.

*William E. Gladstone*

I'm tired of hearing it said that democracy doesn't work. Of course it doesn't work. We are supposed to work it.

*Alexander Woolcott*

In the absence of justice, what is sovereignty but organized robbery?

*Saint Augustine*

For in reason, all government without the consent of the governed is the very definition of slavery.

*Jonathan Swift*

If ye love wealth greater than liberty, the tranquility of servitude greater than the animating contest for freedom, go home from us in peace. We seek not your counsel, nor your arms. Crouch down and lick the hand that feeds you; and may posterity forget that ye were our countrymen.
*Samuel Adams*

In general, the art of government consists of taking as much money as possible from one class of citizens to give to another.
*Voltaire*

If you make any money, the government shoves you in the creek once a year with it in your pockets, and all that don't get wet you can keep.
*Will Rogers*

The American Republic will endure until the day Congress discovers that it can bribe the public with the public's money.
*Alexis de Tocqueville*

Educate and inform the whole mass of the people... They are the only sure reliance for the preservation of our liberty.
*Thomas Jefferson*

When the federal government spends more each year than it collects in tax revenues, it has three choices: It can raise taxes, print money, or borrow money. While these actions may benefit politicians, all three options are bad for average Americans.
*Ron Paul*

A government that is big enough to give you all you want is big enough to take it all away.
*Barry Goldwater*

A government is the most dangerous threat to man's rights: it holds a legal monopoly on the use of physical force against legally disarmed victims.
*Ayn Rand*

Let the people think they govern and they will be governed.
*William Penn*

The best argument against democracy is a five-minute conversation with the average voter.
*Winston Churchill*

The worst thing in this world, next to anarchy, is government.
*Henry Ward Beecher*

We hang the petty thieves and appoint the great ones to public office.
*Aesop*

Our major obligation is not to mistake slogans for solutions.
*Edward R. Murrow*

A nation of sheep will beget a government of wolves.
*Edward R. Murrow*

Democracy is a form of government that substitutes election by the incompetent many for appointment by the corrupt few.
*George Bernard Shaw*

You cannot build character and courage by taking away a man's initiative and independence.
*Lincoln*

Why has government been instituted at all? Because the passions of man will not conform to the dictates of reason and justice without constraint.
*Alexander Hamilton*

There is an inverse relationship between reliance on the state and self-reliance.
*William F. Buckley, Jr.*

Democracy is the art and science of running the circus from the monkey cage.
*H. L. Mencken*

# FINAL
# WORDS
# of
# WISDOM

The fruits of philosophy are the important thing, not the philosophy itself. When we ask the time, we don't want to know how watches are constructed.
*Georg Christoph Lichenberg*

All you learn, and all you can read, will be of little use, if you do not think and reason upon it yourself. One reads to know other people's thoughts; but if we take them upon trust, without examining and comparing them with our own, it is really living upon other people's scraps, or retailing other people's goods.
*Lord Chesterfield*

Prepare yourself for you must travel alone. The Master can only indicate to you the road.
*Book of the Golden Precepts*

We love to listen to the old tunes but few today can play the music.
*Yamaoka Tesshu*

No matter how many good words you read and speak of, what good will they do you if you do not put them into practice and use them?
*Buddha*

What do I know?
*Montaigne's Motto*

All truly wise thoughts have already been thought thousands of times; but to make them truly ours, we must think them over again honestly, until they take root in our personal experience.
*Goethe*

The words printed here are concepts. You must go through the experience.
*Saint Augustine*

Wisdom is not in words; it is in understanding.
*Hazrat Inayat Khan*

If you understand, things are just as they are. If you do not understand, things are just as they are.
*Zen Maxim*

I feel again a spark of that ancient flame.
*Virgil*

All my best thoughts were stolen by the ancients.
*Emerson*

The mere reading of a book or journal will not bring discrimination. That which is seen, heard, or read about, must be put into actual practice.
*Sai Baba*

Words are used to express meaning; when you understand the meaning, you can forget about the words.
*Chuang Tzu*

It is you who must make the effort; the sages can only teach.
*The Dhammapada*

26238384R00130

Made in the USA
Lexington, KY
24 September 2013